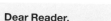

GAPtravel
READER SURVEY 2007

N! ODIES WORTH £1,500

Dear Reader,

We'd really like you to fill in this questionnaire and we promise that it'll help make a difference to your magazine. Send us the completed survey and you could win gap goodies worth over £1,500! What's more, it won't even cost you the price of a stamp as you can return the form to us via Freepost. Your answers will help us to shape this magazine according to your needs and interests, helping us to give you just what you want with every issue.

Good luck with the competition!

LISA DOERR
Publisher, Merricks Media

SECTION A YOU AND GAP TRAVEL

1. Why did you buy Gap Travel Guide?
(PLEASE TICK ALL THAT APPLY)
☐ A friend recommended it
☐ The cover appealed to me
☐ I'm interested in a specific article mentioned on the cover
☐ I flicked through it at the newsstand
☐ I buy all magazines on travel

2. Compared with other magazines, do you think Gap Travel Guide is good value for money?   ☐ Yes   ☐ No

3. Which of the following best describe your feeling about Gap Travel Guide?
☐ The best gap travel magazine I've seen
☐ The second-best gap travel magazine I've seen
☐ I don't feel strongly
☐ I'm not keen on the magazine

4. How often do you think you'll refer back to Gap Travel Guide?
☐ Very often   ☐ Occasionally   ☐ Not very often

5. How long do you plan to keep your copy of Gap Travel Guide for?
☐ A week   ☐ A month   ☐ 2-6 months
☐ 6-12 months   ☐ Longer than 12 months

6. How many other people have looked at your copy of Gap Travel Guide?
☐ No one   ☐ 1 person   ☐ 2-3 people
☐ 4-5 people   ☐ More than 5 people

7. What do you like about Gap Travel Guide?
_____
_____
_____

8. What do you dislike about Gap Travel Guide?
_____

_____
_____
_____

9. Would you buy this guide twice a year?
☐ Yes   ☐ No

10. Would the advertising in Gap Travel Guide help you decide:
Where to go on your gap year?   ☐ Yes   ☐ No
What to do on your gap year?   ☐ Yes   ☐ No
Who to plan your gap year with?   ☐ Yes   ☐ No

SECTION B ABOUT YOU

11. Are you: ☐ Male   ☐ Female

12. Are you: ☐ Under 25   ☐ 25-34   ☐ 35-44
☐ 45-54   ☐ 55-64   ☐ 65 or older

13. Are you:
☐ Single   ☐ Living with partner
☐ Married   ☐ Divorced/widowed/separated

14. Where do you live?
☐ South east   ☐ South west   ☐ South
☐ Midlands   ☐ Wales   ☐ East Anglia
☐ North east   ☐ North west   ☐ Scotland
☐ N Ireland   ☐ Greater London

15. Do you work?
☐ Full time (30+ hours per week)
☐ Part time (up to 29 hours per week))
☐ Housewife/househusband   ☐ Student
☐ Self-employed   ☐ Unemployed
☐ Semi-retired   ☐ Retired

16. What is your occupation?
_____

17. What is your approximate household annual income before tax?
☐ Under £25,000   ☐ £25-49,000

Competition details

We've arranged a goodie bag of prizes worth over £1,500, which will kit you out and prepare you for your gap year, whatever you choose to do!

1st Prize
A week for two people at the charity base of Madina Salaam in the Gambia with Tilly's Tours. Prize includes three meals a day and airport transfers. Flights not included. See www.tillystours.com or ring 0208 873 3148 for more details.

2nd Prize
A video iPod worth £160 and a three-day Savvy Traveller course that will prepare you for the trials and tribulations you'll be faced with when planning and enjoying your gap year.

3rd Prize
Savvy Traveller course for one worth £235.

4th & 5th Prize
Two vouchers worth £120 courtesy of online travel gear store Ready to Leave.

No cash alternative is available in place of prizes. Employees of VentureCo Worldwide, readytoleave. com and Merricks Media Ltd may not enter. Only completed survey forms will be entered into the draw. Closing date is Monday 11th June 2007, after which the winner will be chosen at random and notified within 21 days. The Savvy Traveller course is available on the following dates: Friday July 6th or Friday 16th November 2007.

Ready to Leave www.readytoleave.com
VentureCo Worldwide 01926 411122
www.ventureco-worldwide.com

IPOD IMAGE COURTESY OF APPLE

GW00717064

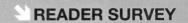
☐ £50-74,999   ☐ £75-99,000
☐ £100,000+

18. How many children do you have?
☐ None   ☐ 1   ☐ 2   ☐ 3   ☐ Other:
_____

19. How many children under 18 do you have living at home?
_____

SECTION C OTHER MEDIA

20 Which of these newspapers do you read?
☐ Financial Times   ☐ Daily Mail   ☐ Daily Mirror
☐ Daily Express   ☐ Guardian   ☐ Independent
☐ Daily Telegraph   ☐ Times   ☐ Sun
☐ Other:
_____

21 Have you used the internet to research gap year travel?   ☐ Yes   ☐ No

22. Which online sites have you referred to?
_____
_____
_____

23. Which other travel/gap year magazines do you buy on a regular basis?
☐ Sunday Times Travel magazine
☐ Wanderlust   ☐ Conde Nast Traveller
☐ Real Travel   ☐ Other:
_____

24. Which other brand of travel books do you/would you buy
☐ Rough Guides   ☐ Lonely Planet   ☐ Time Out
☐ Bradt Guides   ☐ Other:
_____

SECTION D YOUR TRIP

25. Are you going to be taking:
☐ A student gap year   ☐ A career breaker
☐ A retirement gap year   ☐ Other:
_____

What is your reason for taking your trip?
_____

26. What are you planning to do on your gap year? (YOU MAY TICK MORE THAN ONE)
☐ Volunteer   ☐ Conservation work
☐ TEFL/teaching   ☐ Sports/activity gap year
☐ Pure travel   ☐ Work
☐ Organised tour   ☐ Study or take a course

27. How long are you planning to go on your gap year for?
☐ 1-2 months   ☐ 2-4 months

☐ 6 months   ☐ 6 months to one year
☐ One year or more

28. When are you planning to go?

	Spring	Summer	Autumn	Winter
2007	☐	☐	☐	☐
2008	☐	☐	☐	☐
2009	☐	☐	☐	☐
2010	☐	☐	☐	☐

29. Who are you planning to go with?
_____

30. What is your budget?
☐ Under £1,000   ☐ £1,000 to £2,000
☐ £2,000 to £3,000   ☐ £3,000 to £4,000
☐ £4,000 to £5,000   ☐ £5,000+

31. Where are you looking to go on your trip?
(YOU MAY TICK MORE THAN ONE)
☐ Europe   ☐ Africa
☐ Australasia   ☐ North-east Asia
☐ South-east Asia   ☐ Indian subcontinent
☐ Russia   ☐ South America
☐ North America and the Caribbean
☐ The Middle East

32. How will you book your trip?
☐ On the internet   ☐ By phone
☐ Face to face   ☐ Other:

33. How long do you expect the research/planning for your trip to take?
☐ 3 months   ☐ 3-6 months
☐ up to a year   ☐ One year or more

34. Which sources were most helpful in planning your trip?
Please grade in order of importance from 1-5
☐ Reading newspapers   ☐ Magazines
☐ Guide/book information   ☐ Online research
☐ Other:

35. What's your style of travel? Will you...
☐ Join a group   ☐ Travel independently
☐ Bit of both

36. If you plan to join a group, what group size would you prefer?
☐ Small (<16 people)   ☐ Medium (16 to 25 people)
☐ Large (25+ people)

37. What natural habitats would you like to explore?
☐ Deserts   ☐ Mountains   ☐ Jungles
☐ Ice caps and glaciers   ☐ Islands
☐ Savannah and grasslands   ☐ Urban jungles

38. Which of the following activities do you

plan to experience?
☐ Trekking (low altitude)   ☐ Trekking (mountains)
☐ Mountain biking   ☐ White-water rafting
☐ Canoeing   ☐ Others:

39. How will you prepare for your travels overseas?
☐ Read-up on the country/ies you'll visit
☐ Take a Savvy Traveller course
☐ Talk to friends who've been there
☐ Other

40. Will you do a first aid course before you go?   ☐ Yes   ☐ No

41. Do you plan to learn the language of your host country?
☐ Yes – before you go   ☐ No!
☐ Yes – I'll join a language school in the country

42. How important is responsible travel to you?
☐ Crucial   ☐ Fairly
☐ Not really   ☐ Don't care

43. How would you describe 'responsible travel' in your own words?
_____
_____
_____
_____

44. Would you like to know more about VentureCo's projects?
☐ Yes   ☐ No

45. Would you like to know more about VentureCo's Savvy Traveller course?
☐ Yes   ☐ No

SECTION D YOUR DETAILS

NAME _____

ADDRESS _____
_____
_____
_____

HOME TEL _____

WORK TEL _____

MOBILE _____

EMAIL _____

Post your entry in an envelope to
Gap Travel Guide Reader Survey, FREEPOST SWB 10668, Bath, BA1 2ZZ

GAP travel
THE ULTIMATE GUIDE TO TIME OUT

Compiled, edited and designed by
Merricks Media Ltd
3 & 4 Riverside Court
Lower Bristol Road
Bath, BA2 3DZ
Tel: 01225 786800
redguides@merricksmedia.co.uk
www.gaptravelguides.co.uk

EDITORIAL
Managing Editor Leaonne Hall
Deputy Editor Mark Wheatley
Designers Mark Bishop, Naomi Knight,
Sarah Nichol, Lisa Singleton
Contributors Kate Collyns, Anna Scrivenger

ADVERTISING
Advertising Manager Debbie Blackman
Account Manager Matt Hobbs

PRODUCTION
Production Manager Cee Pike
Advertisement Design Becky Hamblin

SENIOR MANAGEMENT
Publishing Director Lisa Doerr
Financial Controller Richard Hurd
Circulation Manager Richard Drake

is a trademark of Merricks Media Ltd

Cover image © Tasmania Tourist Board

All rights reserved. First edition 2007.
Printed and bound by Polestar Wheatons.
Copyright © 2007 Merricks Media Ltd.
ISBN 1-905049-27-7. British Library Cataloguing in Publication Data. A catalogue record for this magazine is available from the British Library.

Tom Griffiths

Recognised as the authority on gap years in the UK and around the world, the 'Gap Year Guru' has dedicated his life to persuading people of all ages to grab a little bit of adventure. He was first published at 22, awarded Young Travel Writer of the Year in 1997, and in 1998, he set up gapyear.com. Over a million people from around the world use the website each year. Tom also regularly appears in the media and consults the government on any issues related to gap years.

Welcome!

First invented in the 60s and 70s by hippies heading out to India, the gap year and the concept of gap travel has now come full circle. Not only are there over 200,000 people aged between 18 to 24 taking gaps from the UK every year, but there are also 200,000 people over the age of 55, and another 100,000 in between. The hippies are now grandparents: 'SAGA louts', busy breaking all the rules again, growing old disgracefully and changing the face of travel.

We're all at it. "Gappers do it with a backpack on!" will be my new fridge magnet. Put simply, you have one life and loads of opportunities that you either take or you don't. So what are you going to do in 2007 that ticks a box on your '100 things to do before I die' wishlist? Travel on the Trans-Siberian Express? Visit the Great Barrier Reef? Hike the Inca Trail? Help to conserve wild orang-utans? Whatever it is, 2007 should be the year that you achieve it. Let's face it – if you don't do it now, you probably never will.

Don't spend your life looking at other people's photos and thinking, "I'd love to have done that." This Gap Travel Guide is packed with ideas and advice, so to tick something off that wishlist, all you need to do is pluck up the courage.

Go on, I dare you. Live a little…

Tom Griffiths
Founder of gapyear.com

How to use this guide

It's easy to find and plan your perfect gap year, career break or retirement tour with our 10 detailed regional guides and fact-packed Essentials section, so what are you waiting for?

⬇ Introduction

Discover the best gap options available, and use our world map to find where you want to go…

⚑ The Essentials

Our comprehensive guide reveals how to fund and organise your gap year, as well as how to deal with the culture shock of arriving in a new country and the best ways to readjust on your return home to the UK

⬇ Where to go and what to do

Our inspirational, at-a-glance regional overviews make it easy for you to find your ideal gap year, and to help you quickly find your perfect break, we've divided the options as follows…

⬇ GET ACTIVE

Ideal for the adventurous adrenaline junkie
- Expeditions • Watersports • Winter sports
- Climbing • Hiking • Cycling • Extreme sports

⬇ GET EDUCATED

Your guide to everything from serious study to language and sports instructor courses
- Teach English as a foreign language • Learn a foreign language • Serious study • Courses, from art history to sports and instructor training

⬇ GET UP & GO

This section focuses on pure travel packages and looks at a number of typical itineraries
- Organised tours • Off the beaten track
- Classic routes • Country or region hotspots

⬇ GET EXPERIENCED

On these exciting breaks, you can try something completely different, and learn new skills too
- Retreats and pilgrimages • Work experience, exchanges and placements • Conservation

⬇ Pricing

We've graded our gap years by cost to make it easy for you to see if they fall into your budget

💰 BUDGET
£1,500 and under

💰💰 AFFORDABLE
£2,500 and under

💰💰💰 LUXURY
£2,500+

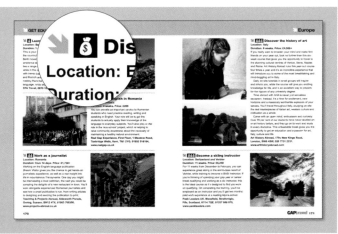

Contents

222

272

16

20

↘ **WHERE TO GO**

A round-the-world look at the best gap options open to you, from conservation and volunteering to adrenaline-fuelled extreme sport breaks and awe-inspiring sight-seeing tours

WIN GOODIES WORTH OVER £1,500!
See our reader survey

237

278

NEXT 96 km

284

�’ THE ESSENTIALS

All the information you need on everything from visas and passports to advice on staying safe, keeping in touch and readjusting to work or university on your return home…

61

➘ CASE STUDIES

Get inspired to don your backpack and boots by our real-life stories from people who've taken a break…

298

288

In association with
gapadvice.org
Independent advice on gap years, for people of all ages

GAP travel   **9**

A.	ANDORRA	C.A.R.	CENTRAL
AL.	ALBANIA		AFRICAN REPUBLIC
ARM.	ARMENIA	C.D'I.	CÔTE D'IVOIRE
AUS.	AUSTRIA	CR.	CROATIA
AZ.	AZERBAIJAN	CYP.	CYPRUS
B.	BURUNDI	CZ.R.	CZECH REPUBLIC
BE.	BENIN	DEN.	DENMARK
BEL.	BELGIUM	EQ.G.	EQUATORIAL GUINEA
B.H.	BOSNIA-	FR.G.	FRENCH GUIANA
	HERZEGOVINA	GEOR.	GEORGIA
BN.	BAHRAIN	GER.	GERMANY
BUR.	BURKINA	GH.	GHANA
CAM.	CAMEROON	GUY.	GUYANA

Winkel Tripel Projection

Collins bring the world to life with user-friendly atlases for the whole family.
For more information visit **www.collins.co.uk**

HUN.	HUNGARY	Q.	QATAR
ISR.	ISRAEL	R.	RWANDA
JOR.	JORDAN	S.	SERBIA
K.	KUWAIT	SL.A.	SLOVAKIA
KYR.	KYRGYZSTAN	SL.	SLOVENIA
LEB.	LEBANON	SUR.	SURINAME
LITH.	LITHUANIA	SW.	SWITZERLAND
LUX.	LUXEMBOURG	T.	TOGO
M.	MONTENEGRO	TAJIK.	TAJIKISTAN
MA.	MACEDONIA	TURKM.	TURKMENISTAN
MO.	MOLDOVA	U.A.E.	UNITED ARAB
NETH.	NETHERLANDS		EMIRATES
NI.	NIGERIA	UZBEK.	UZBEKISTAN

© Collins Bartholomew Ltd 2006

1 Europe

♂♂♂ Study art history in Italy

If you really want to broaden your mind and make firm friends on your year out, look no further than this fantastic six-week tour of Italy with Art History Abroad. www.arthistory abroad.com

You'll travel to Venice, Siena, Naples, Rome and other incredible cities on an unforgettable journey that will introduce you to some of the most breathtaking art in Italy, while giving you plenty of time to enjoy the food, wine and culture of this amazing country.

As well as viewing some of the world's best works of art, there are daily on-site tutorials that you'll find inspirational and informative, making this the perfect way to prepare for the rigours of any university degree. It's also a great way to experience a different culture and learn about art in a friendly and supportive group.

Art History Abroad is always looking to improve this intoxicating recipe of education, exhilaration and life-changing moments, and one recent addition to the programme is an unmissable private visit to Michelangelo's Sistine Chapel.

Price: £4,950+

For more information, turn to page 171 now!

2 Central Asia

♂♂ Live with Mongolian nomads

Fancy getting away from it all? Forget exotic beaches or desert islands: Mongolia is the place for you! On this project, you'll camp in the Gobi Desert, where you can look for dinosaur fossils with a local expert.

Living in a tent, your daily life may include everything from riding horses and caring for livestock to helping produce dairy products and teaching English to the local people. This is a great way for you to learn more about this ancient way of life and how it's being affected by modern-day Mongolia.

In exchange for your help, the family you'll be staying with will involve you fully in their way of living, letting you discover a lifestyle that few westerners are likely to have experienced. **£1,495-£2,045 for one to three months.** www.teaching-abroad.co.uk

3 North-east Asia

👣👣👣 **Learn martial arts in China**

The Shaolin Kung Fu Academy offers one of the best environments in the world to learn kung fu. Based at the foot of the Kunyu Mountains, you'll be able to study with some of the best Shaolin masters in China.

Typical training plan
- Theory and history
- Flexibility training
- Introduction to tai chi, Qi Gong, Sanda (kickboxing) and Shaolin fist forms
- Basic punching and kicking techniques
- Low-level weapons training, such as with a staff, sword or whip
- Mandarin lessons

Students at the Academy even have the opportunity to learn hard Qi Gong. This means that at the end of three months of study, you should be able to cut through a brick using your bare hands! **Price: From £799 for five weeks, up to £2,899 for 24 weeks**

4 Australasia

👣👣👣 **Work on a cattle ranch**

This is a fantastic chance to combine working on a traditional cattle station in northern Australia with helping on the toad-busting conservation project in Kimberley. **Price: £3,914+ for six weeks**

You'll help with the livestock, arrange bush picnics and participate in activities such as fishing, mud crabbing and camping out. The other part of your time will be spent on the toad-busting conservation project. www.theleap.co.uk

5 South America

👣👣 **Help endangered animals in Bolivia**

The Bolivian Amazon rainforest is known for its vast biodiversity, with over 2,000 species of plants, more than 80 species of mammals and around 650 types of birds. Among these species are many endangered animals that are at risk because of illegal trade: the sale of rare animals is the third biggest smuggling operation in the world, surpassed only by the arms and drugs trade. Your help is urgently needed to improve the lives of these creatures, and on this placement, you'll have the opportunity to make a real difference.

You'll be working at an animal sanctuary, looking after monkeys, jaguars, pumas and other animals, while also helping to improve their living conditions and environment. **Duration: 2-6 weeks Price: £1,665+ www.quest overseas.com**

Where to go

From conservation to cookery courses, this is your complete guide to the best gap options

Africa

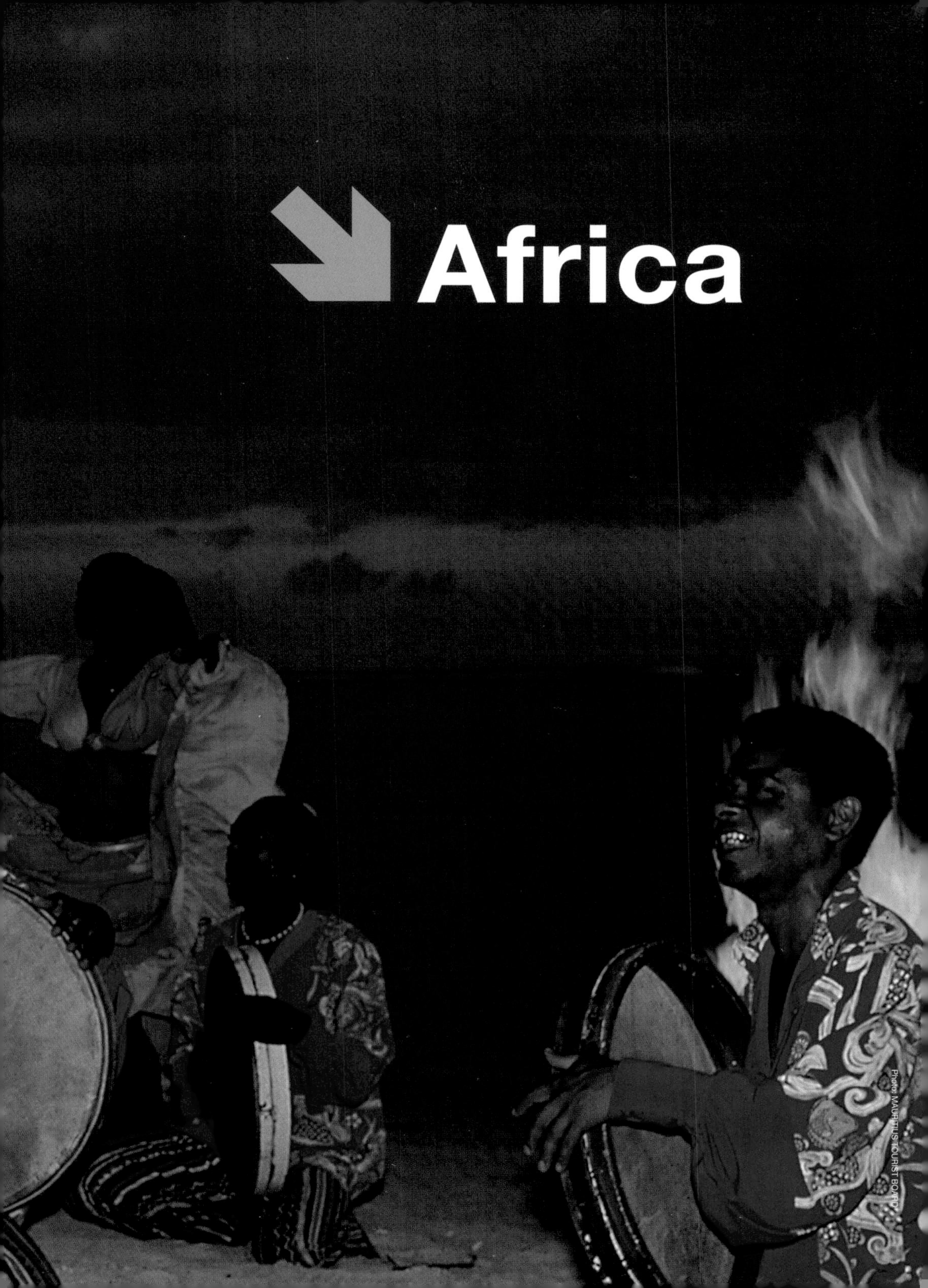

Photo: MAURITIUS TOURIST BOARD

Africa radiates a kind
of honesty and realism
that's unknown to many
Westerners, and it's sure
to captivate and enthral
anyone who visits

↘Africa

The birthplace of mankind is a magical place that's guaranteed to provide an unforgettable gap year

Africa is a mind-blowing mix, from the Moorish mystery in the northern tips to Egypt's awesome pyramids and the exotic Arab trails of the Sahara. There are undiscovered jungles and up-close wildlife encounters, ancient nomadic tribes, powder-white beaches and vibrant coral reefs. Meanwhile, the cities are a breathtaking combination of opulence and desperate hunger. Africa radiates a kind of honesty and realism unknown to many Westerners, and it's sure to captivate and enthral anyone who visits.

Border disputes, civil wars and corrupt governments mean that many countries, such as Sierra Leone, Uganda and Sudan, are volatile hotbeds of political instability, and home to many poverty-stricken civilians. Many gap travellers volunteer for charities such as Medecins Sans Frontiers, the Red Cross and Oxfam in order to improve medical facilities, dig wells or aid food distribution in these countries.

There are also plenty of opportunities for teaching, while conservation projects abound, especially flora and fauna programmes, with new species being discovered every week in the islands off the coast. The top draw for many is still Africa's wildlife, though. Big game hunting now takes the form of safari tours, with eager visitors hoping to catch glimpses of lions, giraffes, elephants and even the odd endangered rhino.

⬊CAPE TOWN

💰 **WANDER** the streets of Bo-Kaap, Cape Town's oldest residential district, watch the sun set over Camps Bay, take the cable car to the top of Table Mountain and enjoy the unparalled views, then relax on Houts Bay beach.

💰💰 **SWIM** with penguins on Boulders Beach, party the night away in Cape Town, take a tour of Robben Island, drive to Cape Point in Table Mountain National Park, and then visit the Cape of Good Hope Nature Reserve.

💰💰💰 **EXPLORE** the Stellenbosch wine routes, swim with sharks off Cape Point, go shopping on the V&A waterfront, drive the Garden Route and see Chapman's Peak, then take a helicopter tour of the peninsula.

2

⬆MOROCCO

₫ **VISIT** the stunning 14th-century city of Fes, stop off at the Kasbah de Oudïas in Rabat, enjoy the nightlife of Marrakesh – but remember, no alcohol! – and then sample a Berber night party, dining on steamed snails.

₫₫ **SPEND** time in Marrakesh and take a day trip to the High Atlas mountains, take a camel excursion into the Sahara desert and watch the stars come out, visit Essaouira and the Rif Mountains, and explore the souks.

₫₫₫ **CHARTER** an Imperial City tour of Morocco, enjoy a round of golf at one of the many courses, ski in the High Atlas mountains between January and March, and explore the long, sandy beaches on horseback.

3

↗MADAGASCAR

💰 **TREK** the Park National de l'Isalo and see the wildlife, wander the Digue Market, and visit the UNESCO World Heritage sites of Tsingy de Bemaraha Strict Nature Reserve and the sacred Royal Hill of Ambohimanga.

💰💰 **TAKE** a river expedition or wildlife tour with www.madagascar-travel.net, explore the seas and see manta rays, whale sharks and humpback whales, trek the rainforests and soak up the sun in Nosy Iranja or Tsarabanjina.

💰💰💰 **ENJOY** a safari by helicopter or private plane, indulge in an island-wide tour of the reefs and rainforests, tour the Spiny and Gallery forests to see the lemurs, and head to north Madagascar to search for the rare aye-aye.

4

↗TANZANIA AND ZANZIBAR

💰 **VISIT** one of the many superb national or marine parks, visit the Sukuma Museum in Bujora for the weekly performance of traditional dance, take a boat trip on Lake Victoria or go canoeing along the Tanzanian coastline.

💰💰 **CLIMB** 5,895 metres to the top of Mount Kilimanjaro, go scuba diving and snorkelling around the islands of Mafia and Zanzibar, enjoy a dhow trip and then luxuriate on the beaches of Kunduchi, Mbwa Maji and Mjimwena.

💰💰💰 **TAKE** a dolphin safari, discover Zanzibar's plantations and sample the intoxicating spice, fruit and herbs on offer, take a hot air balloon trip and, for a truly unforgettable experience, visit the Serengeti National Park.

5

↘KENYA

💰 **VISIT** the Kenya Marineland and Snake Park, Bamburi Quarry Nature Trail, the Mamba Crocodile Village in Freretown, the Great Rift Valley, and the Ngomongo Villages Cultural Park to learn about the local Kenyan tribes.

💰💰 **SAIL** in a dhow from Mombassa, go scuba diving, snorkelling, water-skiing, swimming and surfing on Kenya's Coral Coast, climb Mount Kenya, take a sunset cruise across Lake Victoria and abseil the Great Rift Valley.

💰💰💰 **ENJOY** a safari at the Shimba Hills National Reserve or Mwalu-Ganje Elephant Sanctuary, take a flight over the awesome Masai Mara National Reserve, meet the region's tribespeople and enjoy a camel safari.

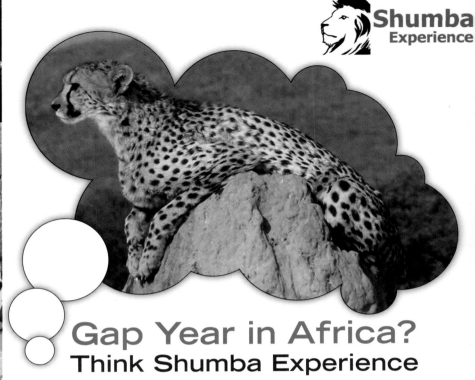

1 Madagascar
♂♂ Conservation

This is a great opportunity to enjoy a diving holiday while partaking in a highly regarded environmental conservation project based at one of the most remote and beautiful locations in the world.

There's the chance to go snorkelling and play football against the local fisherman's team, while there's a beach bar for the less energetic! Meals consist of fish, rice and vegetables, and you'll stay in a beautiful beachside eco-cabin.

Volunteers from all walks of life and all ages are welcome to join these six-week expeditions. Novice divers are trained to PADI certification level (Advanced Open Water or higher) and you'll be trained by marine science staff with knowledge and skills specific to the region. Teams of volunteers from all over the world work side by side with international scientists, Madagascar's national marine institute, NGOs, and community members whose livelihoods depend on the coral reef ecosystems. Together, they carry out essential research and conservation programs in the region.
Cost: £1,880 for six weeks. See www.blueventures.org

2 Tanzania
♂♂ Community work

Camp Tanzania operates from the Moshi area of Northern Tanzania, in the foothills of Kilimanjaro. There's a strong focus on community and wildlife in all of the projects that are undertaken in this region.

Tanzania is home to over a quarter of Africa's wildlife and you'll find an incredible safari route included as part of your stay. If you're feeling adventurous, you can use your third week to climb Kilimanjaro or Mount Meru, and to finish things off, you'll have 10 days on Zanzibar Island at the end of your trip.

You can work with the local children and learn about the community, snorkel with dolphins, take a spice tour and relax on the beaches in this stunning location.
**Visit www.camps international.com.
Price: £1,950+**

KENYA

- **Area:** 580,370 sq. km
- **Population:** 34.5 million
- **Capital:** Nairobi
- **People:** Kikuyu, Luhya, Luo, Kalenjin, Kamba, Kisii, Meru, and Maasai/Samburu

- **Languages:** Mainly English and Kiswahili
- **Currency:** Kenyan shilling
- **Exchange rate:** £1 = KSh138
- **Government:** Democratic republic
- **Religion:** 50% are Protestant, 31% are Roman Catholic and 8% are Muslim

3 South Africa

♦♦♦ With Ticket to Ride, you'll travel around the coast of the diverse country of South Africa and over a three-month period, you'll learn to surf on some of the best waves in the world, taking your skills to the next level.

You'll spend your final five days in Durban, where you can unwind and enjoy the nightlife. There's also the chance for you to upgrade your equipment, and to secure your Surf Rescue qualification too.
Price: £4,850

South Africa is a country with incredible diversity and you'll be able to experience true African culture first-hand by engaging with charitable organisations around the country. Helping with community projects means you can put something back into the areas that you'll be living in while you learn to surf. Your intinerary includes two weeks in Cape Town to help with the Salesians Society and the Valley Development Project Day Centre for local kids. You'll also assist with training in the nearby township, as well as working on beach conservation projects.
www.tickettoride.co.uk

4 Mombasa

♦ **Community work with AIDS orphans**
This project presents the perfect opportunity to help those whose lives have been affected by the AIDS epidemic in Kenya. Working at a home for orphaned children, you can help with a number of essential tasks.

Help is needed with everything from cooking food to assisting with lessons. You may also find yourself getting involved with counselling sessions. Whatever you do, you can make a real difference here by helping to promote community development in Kenya.
Price: £595+ for 6-12 weeks.
www.i-to-i.co.uk

5 Malawi

♦ **Help conserve the environment**
Your help is needed on a wide range of conservation projects that aim to protect the environment and wildlife of Malawi, and to improve conditions for the local communities. Your tasks will include everything from path building to fencing and tree planting, combined with some educational work in local schools. Malawi offers wonderful opportunities for resourceful and self-motivated volunteers. All the placements require absolute commitment and they're all very demanding, but you'll also find that they're incredibly satisfying.

Placements cost a flat fee of £1,200, with your food and accommodation provided. Note that flights and insurance are not included in this cost. For further information on this rewarding project, see page 36, or visit the GAP Activity Projects website.
www.gap.org.uk

SOUTH AFRICA

- **Area:** 1.23 million sq km
- **Population:** 42.6 million
- **Capital:** Pretoria/Tshwane
- **People:** African, Indian and Asian

- **Languages:** Mainly English and Afrikaans
- **Currency:** Rand
- **Exchange rate:** £1 = ZAR13.79
- **Government:** Constitutional democracy
- **Religion:** 85% are Christian

💰💰💰 Become a surf instructor

Location: South Africa
Duration: 3 months. Price: £4,850

With Ticket to Ride, you'll travel around the coast of South Africa and during this time you'll learn to surf on some of the best waves in the world. As well as endless surfing possibilities, South Africa is a country with incredible diversity and you'll be able to experience true African culture first-hand by engaging with charitable organisations and community projects. This will enable you to give something back to the areas that you'll temporarily be calling home.

Your adventure will start in Cape Town where for two weeks you'll help with the Salesians Society and the Valley Development Project, as well as lending a hand at the day centre for local kids. You'll also assist with training in the nearby township, in addition to helping on a number of beach conservation projects.

You'll then head out along the Garden Route where you can watch humpback whales and dolphins. At Jeffreys Bay, you'll continue to combine surfing and charity work, experiencing the best waves in the world. A stay at a sugar shack will allow you to enjoy some additional adventure activities, including a horseback safari, before you move onto Ballito for your surf instructors' course. Your adventure ends with five full days of unwinding and partying in the thriving and exciting city of Durban.

Ticket to Ride, 263 Putney Bridge Road, London, SW15 2PU, 0208 7888 668, www.ttride.co.uk

💰💰💰 Discover southern Africa

Location: Swaziland, Mozambique, Botswana and South Africa
Duration: 12 weeks. Price: £4,240+

Working with the Lubombo Conservancy in Swaziland, this expedition gives you the chance to undertake conservation and community development work alongside rangers and wildlife in spectacular reserves. You'll be helping to create wildlife corridors and develop environmental education schemes, making this a great way to see the highlights of this beautiful country.

Quest Overseas, The North-West Stables, Borde Hill Estate, Balcombe Road, Haywards Heath, West Sussex, RH16 1XP, 01444 474744, www.questoverseas.com

↘ 💰💰 Explore southern Africa

Location: Swaziland, Mozambique, South Africa, Botswana and Zambia
Duration: 6 weeks. Price: £2,495

Combine adventure and community work on this break! You'll be working in Marangu village to improve the community's education facilities. The project is followed by six weeks of activities through five countries, from trekking in Swaziland to scuba diving in Mozambique and bungee jumping off Victoria Falls in Zambia.
Quest Overseas, The North-West Stables, Borde Hill Estate, Balcombe Road, Haywards Heath, West Sussex, RH16 1XP, 01444 474744, www.questoverseas.com

↘ 💰💰💰 Trek Uganda

Location: Uganda
Duration: 14 days. Price: £2,720

Enjoy the unique experience of trekking the world heritage site of the Rwenzori Mountains and rainforests. For those who want to attempt a climb, several peaks provide challenges that match those in the Alps, with six peaks carrying permanent snow and three with glaciers. However, the main attractions of this area are the luxuriant vegetation and wildlife, and you'll have the chance to spot hyraxes, blue monkeys, chimpanzees and giant forest hogs.
Footprint Adventures, 5 Malham Drive, Lincoln, LN6 0XD, 01522 804929, www.footprint-adventures.co.uk

↘ 💰💰💰 See southern Africa

Location: Botswana, Mozambique and South Africa
Duration: 12 weeks. Price: £4,240

Work alongside local rangers to manage and develop Swaziland's stunning reserves, before going on an expedition that includes trekking in the mountains of Swaziland, a week of diving off the coast of Mozambique, plus river tubing, canyoning, bridge swinging and caving in South Africa. You'll also experience a dug-out canoe safari in the Okavango Delta, Big Five spotting in the world-famous national parks of Botswana, and either bungee jump or micro-light over the immense Victoria Falls in Zambia. This is a unique chance to experience the real Africa close up.
Responsible Travel, www.responsibletravel.com

💰💰 Explore Malawi and Zambia

Location: Malawi and Zambia
Duration: 3 weeks. Price: £1,980+

This Explorer Expedition is the perfect way to experience the sights, sounds and adventures of Africa in a little more comfort than most other overland expeditions offer!

The itinerary includes spending two days meeting Quest Overseas' project partners and the communities they work with in Blantyre, followed by guided walks on Mount Mulanje and the chance to sample the famous tea at the plantations at Satemwa, explore the wetlands of Liwonde National Park, walk on the highlands of the Viphya Plateau, and visit welcoming coastal villages on the shores of Lake Malawi.

You'll finish this expedition in style with a five-day Big Five safari in South Luangwa National Park in Zambia, a game park that's famous for its frequent sightings of the elusive leopard.

Throughout the journey, you'll stay at specially selected lodges and you'll be accompanied by Quest Overseas' Africa Operations Manager, who will give you a fascinating insight into this amazing country. The cost of this expedition includes all food, activities and accommodation, as well as a $50 donation to the Joshua Orphan Care Centre.

Quest Overseas, The North-West Stables, Borde Hill Estate, Balcombe Road, Haywards Heath, West Sussex, RH16 1XP, 01444 474744, www.questoverseas.com

💰💰 Go on an African adventure

Location: Swaziland, Mozambique, South Africa, Botswana and Zambia
Duration: 6 weeks. Price: £2,495

Discover Southern Africa's hidden highlights! Trek in the mountains of Swaziland, learn to scuba dive alongside whale sharks and manta rays in the blue waters off Mozambique's coast, enjoy river tubing, canyoning and bridge swinging in South Africa, canoe into the depths of the Okavango Delta, and head off on a safari in Botswana's world-famous game parks.

Quest Overseas, The North-West Stables, Borde Hill Estate, Balcombe Road, Haywards Heath, West Sussex, RH16 1XP, 01444 474744, www.questoverseas.com

⬇ 💰 Discover Malawi

Location: Malawi
Duration: 3 weeks. Price: £1,165

Few have seen the beauty and variety of Malawi, but you can be one of those few. This three-week tour includes trekking across the peaks of Mount Mulanje, boat cruises through the wetlands of Liwonde National Park, getting up close to elephants, hippos and lions, kayaking at Cape MacClear, walking in the highlands of the Viphya Plateau and relaxing on Kande Beach.

Quest Overseas, The North-West Stables, Borde Hill Estate, Balcombe Road, Haywards Heath, West Sussex, RH16 1XP, 01444 474744, www.questoverseas.com

⬇ 💰💰 Take a family safari

Location: Nairobi, Mount Kenya, Lake Nakuru, Masai Mara and Mombasa
Duration: 11 days. Price: on application

Career breakers with kids will find this 11-day Tembo safari tour ideal. It takes in Kenya, Nairobi and Mombasa, and is great for young children. Accommodation is comfortable and there's the chance to see some of Africa's most exciting wildlife. The safari includes a visit to the Nairobi Giraffe Centre and Karen Blixen Museum, plus a visit to a school in Nyeri.

Tour Africa Safaris, Palacina Court, Kitale Lane, Off Dennis Prit Road, PO Box 34187, Nairobi, Kenya, 00254 20 2729333, www.tourafrica-safaris.com

⬇ 💰💰💰 Explore East Africa

Location: East Africa
Duration: 14 days. Price: on application

This is the ultimate east African safari, designed to showcase the best of Kenya and Tanzania, with the emphasis on first-class travel, international cuisine and high-standard accommodation. The adventure begins in Nairobi, followed by the Mount Kenya region where you'll overnight at a tree hotel. Then it's on to the slopes of the magical Mount Kenya before flying to the famous Masai Mara. Other highlights include Tanzania, Lake Manyara and the Ngorongoro Crater.

Tour Africa Safaris, Palacina Court, Kitale Lane, Off Dennis Prit Road, PO Box 34187, Nairobi, Kenya, 00254 20 2729333, www.tourafrica-safaris.com

💰💰💰 Work with orphans

Location: Malawi
Duration: 12 weeks. Price: £4,240+

Provide food and shelter to orphans by helping to build community centres that will act as health clinics, canteens and classrooms for the village children. The beauty of this project is that you'll experience the warmth of the Malawian people directly. It's followed by a six-week tour of Malawi, Swaziland, Mozambique, South Africa, Botswana and Zambia.

Quest Overseas, The North-West Stables, Borde Hill Estate, Balcombe Road, Haywards Heath, West Sussex, RH16 1XP, 01444 474744, www.questoverseas.com

💰💰 Help wildlife and people

Location: Tanzania and Zanzibar
Duration: 6 weeks. Price: £1,950+

The Camp Tanzania programmes operate from the Moshi area of Northern Tanzania, in the foothills of Kilimanjaro. Tanzania is home to over a quarter of Africa's wildlife and you'll experience a great safari here. The really adventurous can climb Kilimanjaro or Mount Meru, and to finish things off, you can spend 10 days relaxing on the beautiful Zanzibar Island.

Camps International Limited, Unit 1, Kingfisher Park, Headlands Business Park, Blashford, Ringwood, BH24 3NX, 0870 2401 843, www.campsinternational.com

💰💰 Teach in the Wild Coast

Location: South Africa
Duration: 4-12 weeks. Price: £1,099-£2,449

This South Africa volunteer programme provides an excellent opportunity for gappers to work with African children and to contribute to the local communities in a positive way. The project is based in the Wild Coast region of South Africa, which remains largely undeveloped and rural. The communities here have a large number of underprivileged children whose access to education, resources and equal opportunities are limited. Choose this project and help make a difference.

Real Gap Experience, First Floor, 1 Meadow Road, Tunbridge Wells, Kent, TN1 2YG, 01892 516164, www.realgap.co.uk

Originally, Richard was only supposed to spend two months in Madagascar to "get away from it all". Now over two years later, he's made a career change and is working for Blue Venture in their London office.

Richard got the chance to discover new cultures and new friends.

For over 10 years, Richard had been working in London in sales and marketing for television and radio stations. "I needed a break from the hectic and pressurised work life. I also had a strong desire to take some time off and go out there, see the world and work in a new environment. I wanted to challenge myself, as well as making a positive contribution through a conservation project."

Richard's friends, family and partner were all hugely supportive of his idea and plans. "This helped me make the decision to take a three-month break and join Blue Ventures' conservation expedition in Madagascar."

The break was supposed to be for two months, but it turned into 16 months. Richard volunteered on Blue Ventures' Marine Conservation programme for six weeks from March 2004, and then spent a month travelling in Madagascar. "My experiences as a volunteer in Andavadoaka with Blue Ventures and my travels in the rest of Madagascar were extraordinary." Richard then decided that Madagascar was a place where he wanted to spend more time.

On returning to the UK in late May, Richard applied for the position of Expedition Leader in Madagascar and was back working there in July,

staying until June 2005. "Since then, I've been General Manager and now Managing Director of Blue Ventures in London," says Richard.

The high point of Richard's experience was living and working in a remote community with volunteers from many countries, as well as the local people. "It gave me a huge sense of achievement, as we all contributed to a successful and award-winning marine project."

Living in Madagascar was a wonderful experience that has given me a huge sense of achievement and a new focus and impetus to work in a new sector

"Working and living in Madagascar was a wonderful experience that has given me a new focus and an impetus to work in a new sector. Seeing and travelling in another culture is always interesting but to live in a different culture and work there gives you a deeper insight and understanding."

Explore the beautiful coastal waters by sailing or surfing during your gap.

You can make a massive contribution to local communities by working here.

Madagascar's amazing flora and fauna will take your breath away.

➘ 💰 Study journalism in Ghana

Location: Accra, Ghana
Duration: from 1 month. Price: £1,445+

Accra, the capital of Ghana, is an incredible place to either start or broaden your journalism career. As the centre of politics in a key democratic west African state, there's always something going on. While here you can choose from radio or print journalism, and working for a newspaper will give you experience of a busy newsroom and the skills to cope with deadlines, as well as giving you the chance to build a unique portfolio.
Teaching & Projects Abroad, Aldsworth Parade, Goring, Sussex, BN12 4TX, 01903 708300, www.projects-abroad.co.uk

➘ 💰 Teach sports in South Africa

Location: South Africa
Duration: from 1 month. Price: £1,395+

Situated on a private beach with access to a lagoon and its own swimming pool, this children's camp in KwaZulu Natal is well equipped for children of all ages. Fun and learning are the aims, and volunteers are needed to help achieve this. If you want to be actively involved in water-sports, including surfing, windsurfing, swimming, boogie boarding, kayaking and snorkelling, this is definitely the placement for you!
Teaching & Projects Abroad, Aldsworth Parade, Goring, Sussex, BN12 4TX, 01903 708300, www.projects-abroad.co.uk

➘ 💰 Practise veterinary medicine

Location: Ghana
Duration: from 1 month. Price: £1,345+

In Ghana, Teaching & Projects Abroad works in city clinics. In the mornings this involves dealing with pets such as dogs and cats, but many of the patients are small back-garden livestock such as goats and chickens. In the afternoon there are sometimes great opportunities to go out into the field to visit farms or even Accra Zoo. You'll be involved in administering vaccinations, as well as observing and assisting in operations, laboratory work and post mortems.
Teaching & Projects Abroad, Aldsworth Parade, Goring, Sussex, BN12 4TX, 01903 708300, www.projects-abroad.co.uk

⬇ 💰 Help protect Malawi

Location: Malawi
Duration: from 1 month. Price: £900+

This project offers gappers the opportunity to carry out essential conservation work in the fascinating country of Malawi. Volunteers are needed to help out with conservation projects that will involve path building, fencing and tree planting, combined with some educational work in local schools. This is a once in a lifetime opportunity to meet the wonderful people of Malawi and to make a real difference, while enjoying and experiencing a new culture.
GAP Activity Projects, 44 Queen's Road, Reading, Berkshire, RG1 4BB, 0118 9594914, www.gap.org.uk

⬇ 💰 Work with AIDS orphans

Location: Mombasa
Duration: 6-12 weeks. Price: £595+

This project gives you the opportunity to help those whose lives have been affected by the AIDS epidemic in Kenya. Working at a home for children who have lost their parents to AIDS or HIV-related diseases, you can help with all manner of tasks, from cooking and serving food to the children to assisting with their basic education, sports and English lessons. You may also have the chance to get involved with counselling sessions. The project comes with full TEFL training included in the price.
i-to-i, 0870 333 2332, www.i-to-i.com

⬇ 💰💰 Work at a safari lodge

Location: Mozambique
Duration: 6-10 weeks. Price: £1,857+

Mozambique is a wonderful country and it offers some of the most spectacular beaches and reefs in the world. This project is based on the shores of Lake Malawi at the award-winning Nkwichi Safari Lodge. This lodge is situated on a 1,000-acre private concession hugging some of Lake Malawi's wildest coast and most pristine beaches. You can help run this exclusive safari lodge while carrying out rewarding community and conservation projects, such as teaching English and removing animal snares from the bush.
The Leap, 121 High Street, Marlborough, Wiltshire, SN8 1LZ, 01672 519922, www.theleap.co.uk

↘ 💰💰 Help the marine environment

Location: Andavadoaka, Madagascar
Duration: 6 weeks. Price: £1,880

This is a great chance to travel with an award-winning charity to work in south-western Madagascar. You'll be able to enjoy a diving holiday while partaking in a highly regarded environmental conservation project based at one of the most remote and beautiful locations in the world. Volunteers from all walks of life and all ages are welcome, novice divers are trained to PADI certification level and all volunteers are trained by marine science staff with specific knowledge of the region.

Teams of volunteers from all over the world work side by side with international scientists, Madagascar's national marine institute, NGOs and community members whose livelihoods depend on the coral reef ecosystems. Together, these teams carry out research and conservation projects in the region.

Madagascar's marine environments remain relatively unknown and unexplored, yet the coral reefs provide a vital resource for the island's rapidly expanding coastal population. You'll play a crucial role in collecting data and relaying results in seminars and workshops for local fishermen, schools and villagers.

Aside from project work, you can go offshore snorkelling, play football against the local fisherman's team and relax at the fantastic beach bar.

Blue Ventures Expeditions, 52 Avenue Road, London, N6 5DR, 0208 341 9819, www.blueventures.org

↘ 💰 Monitor wild lions

Location: South Africa
Duration: 2-12 weeks. Price: £995+

This is an unmissable chance for any lion lover to learn and practise tracking and research techniques in this amazing reserve, based between the small towns of Gravelotte and Mica in the Limpopo Province. It covers over 30,000 hectares of African wilderness and is home to elusive elephants, white rhino and various antelope species. You'll be in the midst of some of the world's most fascinating wildlife on a daily basis, and your assistance in monitoring a lion pride will be vital for the future development and overall success of this incredibly important project.

i-to-i, 0870 333 2332, www.i-to-i.com

⬎ 💰 Work on a game reserve

Location: Near Cape Town, South Africa
Duration: 2-12 weeks Price: £795+

This is a great opportunity to work at a 385-hectare reserve located just 45 minutes from central Cape Town. The reserve is currently in the process of reintroducing natural vegetation to the Roodeburg Mountain, and it has already reintroduced many antelope species, a buffalo herd and a black rhino. By supporting this amazing reserve in South Africa, you'll be playing a vital role in regenerating the country's landscape and helping to reintroduce a wealth of plant and animal species back into this area.

i-to-i, 0870 333 2332, www.i-to-i.com

⬎ 💰 Camp Kenya

Location: Kenya
Duration: 2-4 months. Price: £1,400+

On this break, you'll be involved with a wide range of initiatives, from Makongeni Primary School where your work may cover classroom refurbishment and teaching, to re-plantation projects and our wildlife project based at the Mwaluganje Elephant Sanctuary. Here you'll camp and work alongside the park rangers, local people and, of course, the elephants.

Camps International Limited, Unit 1, Kingfisher Park, Headlands Business Park, Blashford, Ringwood, BH24 3NX, 0870 2401 843, www.campsinternational.com

⬎ 💰💰 Water relief project

Location: Kenya
Duration: 4-5 weeks. Price: £1,585+

Drought has left over 42 per cent of the population in sub-saharan Africa with no access to safe water. Every day, a large number of children miss school due to diseases like diarrhoea or simply because they have to spend hours collecting water. This is where you can help, with support, funds and safe water sources in the form of sand dams. You'll also get to help and interact with the friendly, local Akamba people.

Quest Overseas, The North-West Stables, Borde Hill Estate, Balcombe Road, Haywards Heath, West Sussex, RH16 1XP, 01444 474744, www.questoverseas.com

↘ CASE STUDY

Who: Gavin Lester
Location: Kenya

Like most twenty-somethings, Gavin felt he had fulfilled the goals of college, university and securing a decent job. Next up was to buy a house, settle down and live happily ever after, but he had some other goals to pursue first…

Gavin and other volunteers working on the Water Relief project in Kenya.

Following his time volunteering Gavin travelled down Africa's east coast.

The local people Gavin meet were extremely friendly and welcoming.

"For the last few years I hadn't quite been able to shake the niggling feeling in the back of my head that reminded me of all those personal goals – such as that of independent travel – I had yet to achieve. I hadn't really pushed the boundaries of my own safety net and it wasn't until I fell and broke my arm in an accident that I finally decided to change my destiny and start chasing my ambitions."

The idea of voluntary work really appealed to Gavin. His wish list was to work somewhere that he wouldn't normally go, for it to be physically and mentally demanding, and to really be of benefit to the people he worked with. "As soon as I saw the Water Relief project in Kenya, I knew it was for me as it would place me way out of my comfort zone and it was going to provide sustainable benefits for a local community."

Upon being accepted, Gavin embarked on a series of fundraising events that saw him jumping out of an aeroplane and running a marathon – both things he'd wanted to do but had never got round to. He also decided to quit his job. "This was the start for a whole new beginning for me.

"Going to Kenya was a fantastic experience. I met a bunch of like-minded volunteers from different backgrounds, learnt about how different cultures live, and found out a lot about myself. It was a thoroughly worthwhile experience."

Upon finishing the project, Gavin decided not to rush back to the UK, but instead continued to travel down the east African coast, into Tanzania and the wonderful island of Zanzibar. Then, on a whim, he jumped on a plane to India and spent a month travelling along the train lines from Mumbai to the Himalayas. "It felt so good to be in control of my own destiny."

> **It felt so good to be in control of my own destiny. The risk I took in giving everything up to follow my heart has paid off and I've never felt better!**

After returning home, Gavin immediately embarked on realising his dream career. "I now work as a visual effects artist for film and television. The risk I took in giving everything up to follow my heart has paid off. I've never felt better!"

Volunteers hard at work on the Water Relief project!

Australasia

'South Island is where you'll find the snow-capped peaks of Tolkien's imagination, punctuated by mile-high waterfalls, rivers of springwater and nature at its wildest

Photo: NEW ZEALAND TOURIST BOARD

↘ Australasia

A favourite gap year destination, the land Down Under is an adventurer's dream

Sun, sea, sand and socialising – these are just four of the attractions that make Australasia the ultimate location for thrill-seekers. High value is also placed on conservation, so it's great for eco-minded volunteers, while work permits enable young people to easily find casual work.

Top of the pops is Australia, the gapping mecca. The tropical north boasts rainforests, deserts and warm, shallow seas alive with coral reefs. Meanwhile, the cooler southern regions have bustling cities, crashing surf, vineyards and eucalyptus-cloaked hills, making this the ideal place for adventurers.

Next is New Zealand. Roughly the size of the UK, it only has four million inhabitants, and so vast tracts of the country remain pristine. It's divided into two islands: the North Island is a centre of Maori culture and home to the largest city, Auckland. This is a buzzing metropolis, dotted with extinct volcanoes and surrounded by water and idyllic islands. South Island is where you'll find the snow-capped peaks of Tolkien's imagination, punctuated by mile-high waterfalls, lakes, rivers of springwater, forests and nature at its wildest.

Finally, you can find sun-drenched paradise in the Polynesian, Micronesian and Melanesian islands. Each has its own distinctive culture, as well as offering a paradise of coral reefs and white-sand beaches.

➥SYDNEY

💰 **ADMIRE** the Sydney Opera House, wander the Circular Quay and the historic district of The Rocks, enjoy lunch in The Domain, browse the glamorous boutiques of Market Road and visit the New South Wales Art Gallery.

💰💰 **TAKE** surf lessons on Bondi Beach, climb the Harbour Bridge, visit Sydney Aquarium, explore the harbour on a cruise boat, discover the Botanic and Chinese Gardens, and be amazed by the Powerhouse Museum.

💰💰💰 **FLY** over Sydney Harbour and Bondi Beach, take a high-speed jet-boat ride across the harbour, sample the cuisine of the city's best restaurants, take a trip to Hunter Valley's wineries and invest in some Aboriginal art.

2

↘THE FIORDLANDS

💰 **CRUISE** the fiord from Milford Sound, cycle through the mountains around Te Anau, visit Te Anau Wildlife Centre, enjoy the Lake Henry walk, sample the bars and restaurants of Te Anau and trek to Lady Bowen Falls.

💰💰 **DIVE** in the fiord off Milford Sound, take a kayak out into the Fiordlands National Park, visit the Te Anau Glow Worm Caves, walk the Kepler Track, see the Milford Sound Underwater Observatory and visit Manapouri.

💰💰💰 **WALK** the celebrated Milford Track – all 54 kilometres of it! Take a flight over Milford Sound and see the fiord from the air, tour the southern fiords and view the coral structures of Milford with a submarine adventure.

3

➦AYERS ROCK / ULURU

💰 **VIEW** the unspoilt night sky at the Ayers Rock Observatory, walk one of the two great hiking trails at the Olgas, travel three hours into the desert and visit Kings Canyon, then enjoy the visitor's centre and tour the base of Uluru.

💰💰 **CLIMB** Ayers Rock and enjoy the views, tour the rock and caves with an Aboriginal guide who will tell you all about the history of Uluru, and then relax with a glass of champagne and watch the sun set over the rock.

💰💰💰 **TAKE** a four-day safari around Ayers Rock, view the national park from the air, enjoy a gourmet dinner under the stars and take a dawn camel tour around Uluru. You can then enjoy a two-day tour of the outback.

4

↘THE GREAT BARRIER REEF

💰 **SWIM** with the fishes off the Great Barrier Reef, especially around Orpheus Island. Also, visit the uninhabited Whitsunday Island and the stunning Fraser Island, or laze the days away on the many picture-postcard beaches.

💰💰 **LEARN** to dive off the Barrier Reef, go dolphin and seal watching, tour the Barrier Reef islands in a glass-bottomed boat or cruise to the outer-islands. Finally, enjoy the nightlife on the islands surrounding the reef.

💰💰💰 **RENT** a yacht and tour the Barrier Reef at your leisure, be pampered at Azure Spa on Lizard Island, spend the night at sea on a luxury yacht and hire a seaplane to get breathtaking views of the reef from the air.

5

↘ FIJI

💰 SUNBATHE on the glorious beaches, hike across the island of Savusavu, meet the real Fijians on Ovalau, tour the highlands of Viti Levu with its tropical rivers, and then partake in a traditional *yaqona* (*Kava*) ceremony.

💰💰 FISH the teeming ocean, go diving and view Fiji's underwater world, trek through the tropical rainforests, go white-water rafting on the Luva River and get active by trying some of the various watersports on offer.

💰💰💰 ENJOY an adventure cruise around Fiji's lesser-known islands, charter a luxury yacht to explore the Pacific in style, sample some of Fiji's delicious gourmet food and go shopping on Suva for some unique gifts.

NEW ZEALAND TRAVEL SPECIALISTS

For friendly and expert advice on:

Tailor made self-drive holidays
Escorted coach tours
Motorhome holidays
Accommodation
Sightseeing

For copies of our 2007/08 Holiday Planner
and Coach brochures, please call:

0800 856 5494 or 0208 944 5423

nztravelspecialists@kirratours.com   www.kirratours.com

ABTA

1 New Zealand

The ultimate Kiwi experience!
Spend 12 months in New Zealand on a 23-month working visa. Handily, all the paperwork is done for you! Ideal for the adventurous student or backpacker.

12 months in the adventure capital!
New Zealand offers a huge array of sporting and adventure activities, and you can indulge in everything from bungee jumping to white-water rafting and surfing.

Live in the heart of Auckland
Immerse yourself in Kiwi life
The Real Gap hostel and office are located right in the heart of the city. This great location means that restaurants, bars, shopping, movies, art galleries, post offices, theatres and the Sky Tower are all just minutes away. So not only is it in the best place to explore this incredible city, but it's also a fun place to meet fellow travellers! Even better, the friendly staff will assist you with all your work, play and travel requirements. The trip costs £599. Visit **www.realgap.co.uk** for more information.

2 Australia

Cattle station
Combine working on a traditional cattle station in northern Australia with helping out the station rangers on the 'toad-busting' conservation project in Kimberley. For more details, see www.theleap.co.uk

Eco-tourism
Your tasks will include arranging bush picnics and dinners, assisting the fishing guides and helping with boat and vehicle maintenance.

Be a toad-buster
Help the rangers prevent the invading toads spreading.

Have an adventure!
Muster cattle, ride the horses, fish the rivers, visit Aboriginal art sites and ride in helicopters!

Cost
6 weeks: £3,914
10 weeks: £5,334

See page 67 for details.

AUSTRALIA

- **Area:** 3.28 million sq km
- **Population:** 20.2 million
- **Capital:** Canberra
- **People:** 92% are of European or Asian descent
- **Languages:** Mainly English, with some European, indigenous and Asian languages
- **Currency:** Australian dollar
- **Exchange rate:** £1 = A$2.5
- **Government:** Constitutional monarchy, a federation and a parliamentary democracy
- **Religion:** Predominantly Christian with Buddhist, Jewish and Muslim
- **Head of state:** Her Majesty, Queen Elizabeth II

3 Australia
🔥 Community work

Formed in 1986, the group you'll be assisting is committed to aiding people who are poor and underprivileged, through the dedication of young and enthusiastic volunteers such as yourself.

Placements
The cost is a flat fee of £900, with food and accommodation provided. Flights and insurance are not included in this price.

Make a difference
This project enables you to make a real difference in the lives of some of the people who most need help. You'll see people living in absolute poverty, with no money, food or clothes, but by visiting these families and helping out with the project's organisation, you'll be able to make their lives better. This is an incredible opportunity to make a selfless contribution, and it's a really worthwhile way in which you can spend your gap year.

Visit www.gap.org.uk for more information.

4 Australia
🔥 Conservation

Experience the real Australia by visiting the Outback and helping to preserve this incredibly rich and diverse landscape. This will be an unforgettable experience and it's ideal for those who love the outdoors.

The work involves:
Volunteers will be planting trees in the desert, cleaning up after bush fires and building bush tracks through one of the National Parks.

Visit **www.gap.org.uk** for more information, or turn to page 66.

5 Pacific
🔥 Teach in Vanuatu
Placements in the South Pacific

Get away from it all and teach in some of the beautiful and remote locations in Vanuatu. Volunteers will be assisting in secondary boarding schools and their duties will include helping to teach English, maths, science and basic computing. This is a great opportunity for anyone who's looking to improve their French language skills. It's worth noting that many of these placements have limited facilities and that some of them also have a limited electricity supply.
This is a real alternative teaching experience!

A unique experience
Placements cost a flat fee of £900 with food and accommodation provided.

Flights and insurance are not included.

www.gap.org.uk
Tel: 0118 9594914

See page 68 for details.

NEW ZEALAND

- **Area:** 268,680 sq km
- **Population:** 4.4 million
- **Capital:** Wellington
- **People:** New Zealand European, Maori, European, Pacific Islander and Asian
- **Languages:** English and Maori
- **Currency:** New Zealand dollar
- **Exchange rate:** £1 = NZ$2.9
- **Government:** Parliament
- **Religion:** Anglican, Presbyterian, Roman Catholic, Methodist and Baptist

↘💰💰 Take an adventure cruise

Location: Kimberley coastline, Australia
Duration: 11 days. Price: £2,402+

Explore the 3,000 islands sprinkled across the 2,500 kilometres of the Kimberley coastline and you'll enter a landscape little changed over the past billion years. Whether exploring the shoreline, swimming in lily-fringed rock pools fed by cascading waterfalls, or visiting ancient rock art sites, your days will be filled with exploration and adventure.

Aurora Expeditions, 182 Cumberland Street, The Rocks, NSW 2000, Australia, 0061 2 9252 1033, www.auroraexpeditions.com.au

↘💰 Swim with sharks

Location: Port Lincoln, Australia
Duration: 2-8 days. Price: £603+

The focus of the expedition is to have as much time as possible observing and photographing great white sharks from a dive cage. However, this is also a unique opportunity to visit a rookery of New Zealand fur seals and to see the rare Australian sea lion. You'll be able to witness thousands of seals and sea lions eating, sleeping, mating and fighting for territory, and you can also enjoy an excursion to Hopkins Island, where you can dive with Australian sea lions.

Rodney Fox Shark Experience, 0061 8 8363 1788, www.rodneyfox.com.au

↘💰 Join a desert expedition

Location: Central Australia
Duration: 5 days. Price: £549

Australia is a vast country and although there are major cities such as Sydney and Melbourne, much of the country's interior is essentially uninhabited desert. On an expedition into this incredible landscape, you can explore the 'red desert' centre, which is a barren but beautiful place. You'll also be able to see some unique wildlife in its natural surroundings, including kangaroos and, if you're lucky, creatures such as frill-necked lizards and thorny devils.

Real Gap Experience, First Floor, 1 Meadow Road, Tunbridge Wells, Kent, TN1 2YG, 01892 516164, www.realgap.co.uk

Take an Uluru safari

Location: Ayers Rock, Australia
Duration: 5 days. Price: £249

Ayers Rock rises 1,150 feet above the ground and has a circumference of five miles. Not surprisingly, it's considered to be one of the greatest natural wonders of the world. This once-in-a-lifetime opportunity allows you to view the spectacular Ayers Rock, plus Olgas – which many people find more impressive than Uluru – and Kings Canyon. You can even take an optional camel ride to the top of Ayers Rock for the spectacular views.
Outer Edge Expeditions, 4830 Mason Rd, Howell, MI 48843 9697 USA, 001 800 322 5235, www.outer-edge.com

Enjoy a surf holiday

Location: Queensland, Australia
Duration: 5 days. Price: varies

Pure Vacations offers an amazing Australian surfing holiday experience aimed at all levels of surfer. It gives you the chance to experience Australia to the full while staying in good-quality accommodation. The surf programme is based along the lovely coastline of Queensland. The warm, clear, crystal blue water of this area is fantastic and is understandably the best sun and surf destination in Australia.
Pure Vacations Ltd, Suite 8, John Wilson House, 119-120 John Wilson Park, Whitstable, Kent, CT5 3QY, 01227 264 264, www.purevacations.com

Hike the Larapinta Trail

Location: West MacDonnell Ranges, Australia
Duration: 8 days. Price: £760

The Larapinta Trail is one of the finest walks in Australia. Walking the high ridgelines of the West MacDonnell Ranges enables you to gain a rare perspective of the vast flood plains, razorback rocky outcrops and sheer scale of this ancient land. You'll be following an itinerary that will appeal to the active walker, and so you must be prepared to cover between eight and 16 kilometres each day. In the evenings, you can enjoy a delicious bush tucker meal.
World Expeditions, 3 Northfields Prospect, Putney Bridge Road, London, SW18 1PE, 020 8870 2600, www.worldexpeditions.co.uk

↘ 💰 Enjoy Aussie sports

Location: Queensland, Australia
Duration: from 14 days. Price: £888

An action-filled adventure featuring virtually every outdoor sport possible in the land Down Under! You'll mountain bike on lush rainforest tracks, canoe through the jungle, hike into the wilderness on secret Aboriginal trails, kayak remote ocean islands and dive in colourful reef environments. This is an incredibly active and exciting way to explore the lush wilderness that can be found in Australia's Queensland.

An outdoor playground, this area has untouched tropical rainforests, remote mountains, rivers, small, pristine islands and, of course, the amazing Great Barrier Reef. Some of the explorations will take you into parts of Queensland that have been seen by very few people, and all of the adventures enable you to truly experience Australia.

As well as the kayaking, mountain biking, diving, backpacking and canoeing on offer, you'll also enjoy exploring wild Australia. You'll see paddemelons, brushtail possums, sugargliders and other wildlife as you hike on ancient Aboriginal trails. You also take to the Mulgrave River by canoe and you'll spend time on the Atherton Tablalands and in Bartle Frere Rainforest, before diving off the Great Barrier Reef, making this a truly unique experience.

Outer Edge Expeditions, 4830 Mason Rd, Howell, MI 48843- 9697 USA, 001 800 322 5235, www.outer-edge.com

↘ 💰 Tour New Zealand

Location: New Zealand
Duration: from 38 days. Price: £705

Experience a unique tour of New Zealand, taking in both the North and South islands, with stopovers and activities included along the way. Explore some of New Zealand's lesser-known areas with a local guide, indulge in a spot of wine tasting, go white-water rafting and try sandboarding. Then you can trek to the top of Mount Maunganui, go boogie boarding, take a dip in the sea and relax in the natural hotpools. For the ultimate thrill, try an awesome bungee jump.

Kiwi Experience, 195-197 Parnell Road, Auckland, New Zealand, 0064 9 366 9830, www.kiwiexperience.com

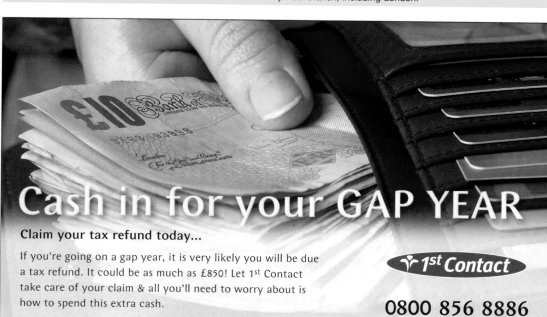

➧ 💰 Take an outback safari

Location: Australian outback
Duration: 11 days. Price: £570

Take in the majestic top end of Australia. Travel through to Alice Springs and take in Uluru, the Olgas and Kings Canyon. You'll see all the sights on the guided trip and you'll be able to experience life as it should be lived in the Outback. Smaller, more manoeuvrable vehicles are used, varying in size from 18- to 36-seater mini- or midi-coaches, and accommodation includes quality resorts, motels and lodge accommodation.

Your Outback journey begins in Alice Springs as you cross some of the oldest river systems in the world on your way to Uluru-Kata Tjuta National Park, home of mighty Uluru (Ayers Rock). In the days that follow, you'll take in Kings Canyon and Kata Tjuta, as well as the Olgas. From there it's back to Alice Springs for a hot air balloon ride, and to venture out among the West MacDonnell Ranges. The tour then explores Simpsons Gap and Standley Chasm before heading back to Alice Springs for a tour and dinner.

Other stop-offs include Banka Banka Station, Katherine, Darwin and Kakadu National Park, where you'll stay for two nights. Partake in some special extras such as a four-wheel drive full-day excursion to Jim and Twin Falls, an Aboriginal cultural cruise on the East Alligator River, or a scenic flight over the park. This is a once in a lifetime opportunity to explore the real Australia and it's an unforgettable experience.
STA Travel, 08701 630 026, www.statravel.co.uk

➧ 💰 Go white-water rafting

Location: Landsborough Valley, New Zealand
Duration: 3 days. Price: £410

The Landsborough Valley is one of New Zealand's most isolated and protected areas. The river trip begins in the very heart of this wilderness country. Your small group will glide past glaciers, 10,000-foot mountains and dense rainforests. As you camp and paddle your way down the Landsborough River, you'll have plenty of time to experience outdoor activities such as bush walking, hiking and canoeing through ancient beech forests, which are the habitat for numerous native birds.
Queenstown Rafting, 35 Shotover Street, Queenstown, New Zealand, 0064 3 442 9792, www.rafting.co.nz

⬇ $ Have fun down under!

Location: Australia
Duration: 7 days. Price: £479

This programme is specifically designed to provide a truly 'Australian' experience during your first week in this exciting country. You'll arrive in a group and spend the next seven days together taking part in loads of fun activities. This is a great Australia gap year package to join, especially if you're planning to travel alone. You can make friends on the flight over and who knows –, you may even end up travelling around Oz with them!
Real Gap Experience, First Floor, 1 Meadow Road, Tunbridge Wells, Kent, TN1 2YG, 01892 516164, www.realgap.co.uk

⬇ $ Take the Fiji bus

Location: Fiji
Duration: 1 year. Price: £139

The Feejee Experience gives you the chance to get off the beaten track and meet like-minded people who you can travel around the islands with at your leisure. There are different itineraries to choose from, depending on where you want to go. The hop-on, hop-off bus service is ideal for backpackers and it's the perfect way to explore Fiji on a gap year. Tickets are valid for a year, and with unlimited stops, you can go at your own pace.
Real Gap Experience, First Floor, 1 Meadow Road, Tunbridge Wells, Kent, TN1 2YG, 01892 516164, www.realgap.co.uk

⬇ $ Take the Kiwi bus

Location: New Zealand
Duration: 6 months. Price: £175

Travelling with Kiwi Experience is an excellent way to meet like-minded travellers. The drivers make the difference between a regular tour and a true experience. Passionate about their country, they provide full commentary and lots of advice along the way. They'll also reserve beds at hostels and make regular supermarket stops, while leading the way for those keen to party! Passes are valid for six months, giving you the freedom to fully explore New Zealand.
Real Gap Experience, First Floor, 1 Meadow Road, Tunbridge Wells, Kent, TN1 2YG, 01892 516164, www.realgap.co.uk

👜👜👜 Work in Australia and NZ
Location: Australia and New Zealand
Duration: Up to 12 months. Price: £3,199

This is an ideal complete gap year to Australia and New Zealand, providing a perfect combination of work and travel. The package gives you access to a number of jobs in Australia and New Zealand, allowing you to work abroad during your year out. It also includes other gap year experiences, such as a surf school trip and a 12-month bus pass, enabling you to really explore the lands Down Under.

Real Gap Experience, First Floor, 1 Meadow Road, Tunbridge Wells, Kent, TN1 2YG, 01892 516164, www.realgap.co.uk

👜👜👜 See New Zealand by train
Location: New Zealand
Duration: 14 days. Price: £3,020+

Combining both the North and South islands to include the major highlights of New Zealand, from Auckland to Dunedin, you'll be travelling aboard a beautifully restored steam locomotive. There's plenty to appeal to all travellers and the train travels at a leisurely pace so there's plenty of time to explore the local attractions. This is a brilliant way to discover the unspoilt beauty of New Zealand in a wonderfully relaxed fashion.

Discover the World, 29 Nork Way, Banstead, Surrey, SM7 1PB, 01737 218804, www.discover-new-zealand.co.uk

👜 Go sea kayaking
Location: New Zealand
Duration: 3 days. Price: £186+

Anyone who has already discovered the delights of sea kayaking will know just how relaxing and enjoyable this gentle mode of travel can be. Don't worry if you've never paddled before because you'll soon become one with your kayak. The trip is based in the peace and quiet of the outer Marlborough Sounds. This is a spectacular location, where the only sounds are those of nature, with the songs of forest birds and the splashes of diving gannets or surfacing dolphins.

Discover the World, 29 Nork Way, Banstead, Surrey, SM7 1PB, 01737 218804, www.discover-new-zealand.co.uk

◥ 💰💰 Discover nature Down Under
Location: New Zealand
Duration: 9-14 days. Price: £2,388+

From the sub-tropical Coromandel Peninsula and thermal wonders of Rotorua to the alpine high country of Arthurs Pass, you'll experience the myriad contrasts of these wild and exciting islands. With time to enjoy the cities of Christchurch and Queenstown, as well as the Maori cultural sites of Rotorua, you'll see another side to this land and its people, while enjoying the rainforests, glaciers and beaches of the west coast.
Discover the World, 29 Nork Way, Banstead, Surrey, SM7 1PB, 01737 218804, www.discover-new-zealand.co.uk

◥ 💰 Tour reefs and rainforests
Location: Australia
Duration: 15 days. Price: £830+

On this unforgettable expedition, you'll be able to take in the highlights of Queensland's islands, beaches and the incomparable Great Barrier Reef, along with a guided four-wheel drive excursion to the World Heritage listed Daintree National Park. You'll travel from Sydney to Byron Bay, along the Gold Coast and on to Fraser Island, before the tour ends in Cairns. For the adventurous, white-water rafting on the Tully River is a must, while you can also experience a breathtaking trip to the Great Barrier Reef.
STA Travel, 08701 630 026, www.statravel.co.uk

◥ 💰 Discover the Pacific Islands
Location: South Pacific
Duration: 14 days. Price: £1,315+

Take a tour of the remote Pacific, starting at Pitcairn Island, where you'll stay onshore with local families. After three or four days on Pitcairn, you'll travel overnight to the World Heritage site of Henderson Island. Many scientists consider Henderson to be the most pristine tropical island anywhere in the world. After enjoying diving, snorkelling and wildlife watching, you'll then travel on to the Gambier Islands, where you'll anchor at Rikitea. Here, you'll be able to relax and explore the island's picturesque village.
Pacific Expeditions Limited, www.pacific-expeditions.com, info@pacific-expeditions.com

CASE STUDY

Who: Rachel Morgan-Trimmer

Location: World tour

Rachel's career break took her to Australia and Fiji, and as well as providing her with an unforgettable experience, it was also a trip that would change her whole life…

No trip to Australia is complete without a few days on the beach.

Rachel was 29 when she decided to take her career break. "I'd been working for a gap year company, but I'd never taken a gap year myself and I realised that I might not have another chance."

Rachel spent her career break travelling all around the world, going through south-east Asia before spending a considerable amount of time in Australia and New Zealand. She then moved on to Fiji and the USA.

Her experiences included learning how to cook in Vietnam, and how to dive in Thailand. "I walked through jungles and up mountains, swam in lakes, rivers and the sea, and rode bicycles along dusty tracks. I saw giant centipedes in Malaysia, kangaroos in Australia and eels in Fiji. I visited tons of museums and art galleries, palaces and temples.

"I also met a huge number of lovely people and learnt more about foreign culture than I ever thought was possible."

When Rachel returned home, she set up a website advising other people about taking a career break. "A lot of the information on the site is stuff that I wished I'd known before going on my own trip. For example, I had no idea what to take and so I ditched some of my belongings after the first couple of days. I also found it difficult to keep track of all the things I had to think about, such as visas, final bills and all the things I needed to cancel."

Rachel believes that the best thing about taking this career break was that it gave her the confidence to start her own business.

"I remember staying in one of the dirtiest hostels I'd ever seen, where I had to spend an hour chasing mice out of my belongings, and thinking, 'If I can cope with this, I can cope with anything!'"

If I have one piece of advice for any potential gapper, it's to go for it. You may never get another chance to travel and one thing's for sure – you won't regret it!

Rachel has talked to many other career breakers about their gap years and has discovered that they all have the same advice for other people who might be thinking of doing the same thing. "Go for it! You may never get another chance, and one thing's for sure – you certainly won't regret it."

The iconic kookaburra is a must-see bird on any trip Down Under!

The oceans offer activities such as surfing, kayaking, sailing and more.

A gap year gives you the chance to see and help protect unique wildlife.

Australia and New Zealand boast amazing natural landscapes.

💰💰💰 Learn to surf

Location: Manly Beach, Sydney, Australia
Duration: 6 weeks. Price: £3,590

Combining professional training in Sydney with a surf adventure along the coast of New South Wales, this course leads to qualifications in surf rescue and instruction. The traineeship is physically demanding as it's geared to getting you through the SLSA Surf Rescue swimming test, where you must run 100m, swim 200m, then run 100m again. By the end of the programme, you'll have good coaching and communication skills, and a practical understanding of the safety issues.

Flying Fish, 25 Union Road, Cowes, Isle of Wight, PO31 7TW, 0871 250 2500, www.flyingfishonline.com

💰💰 Improve your cricket

Location: Wellington, New Zealand
Duration: 12-20 weeks. Price: £1,999-£2,699

Whether you want to be the next Freddie Flintoff or you just want to take your game to the next level, Real Gap's Cricket Academy Programme is for you. Designed for players of all abilities, the academy develops a personalised training programme and it specialises in providing the perfect environment for overseas cricketers. You can train for 12 or 20 weeks, which even includes two days watching the Ashes!

Real Gap Experience, First Floor, 1 Meadow Road, Tunbridge Wells, Kent, TN1 2YG, 01892 516164, www.realgap.co.uk

💰💰💰 Become a diving instructor

Location: Great Barrier Reef, Australia
Duration: 13 weeks. Price: £7,390

This comprehensive package of professional training at Sydney's Pro Dive Academy leads to qualification as a PADI Open Water Scuba Instructor. It starts with the Advanced Open Water Diver course, and includes a list of speciality courses to ensure that you're competent in all areas. Your first six weeks are spent at Sydney's Pro Dive Academy. Once qualified, you'll fly to Queensland for a week, staying in Cairns and diving on the Great Barrier Reef. Before you start, you'll need a PADI Open Water Diver or equivalent, plus 30 logged dives.

Flying Fish, 25 Union Road, Cowes, Isle of Wight, PO31 7TW, 0871 250 2500, www.flyingfishonline.com

Improve your rugby

Location: New Zealand
Duration: 4-16 weeks. Price: £2,999

The Rugby Academy provides all aspiring players with the opportunity to travel and develop their game, with unrivalled facilities and training from some of the best coaches available, as well as visits from world-class mentors. The only school of its kind, programmes last for between one and six months, allowing everyone the opportunity to improve. Past students have gone on to play at club, county and international level.
Real Gap Experience, First Floor, 1 Meadow Road, Tunbridge Wells, Kent, TN1 2YG, 01892 516164, www.realgap.co.uk

Improve your tennis

Location: Gold Coast, Australia
Duration: 2-8 weeks. Price: £949-£1,799

The RGS Tennis Academy provides the perfect environment to help you develop and excel as a tennis player. With a proven programme, you'll have every opportunity to become the player you want to be. The course isn't restricted to elite sportsmen, as players of all levels and ability are welcome. You'll work directly with your coach to develop a customised programme to perfect your strengths and develop your weaker areas.
Real Gap Experience, First Floor, No.1 Meadow Road, Tunbridge Wells, Kent, TN1 2YG, 01892 516164, www.realgap.co.uk

Improve your golf

Location: Gold Coast, Australia
Duration: 4-8 weeks. Price: £1,999-£3,499

The Real Gap Sports Golf Academy in Australia provides keen golfers with the opportunity to enjoy full-time professional instruction during their gap year or career break. Designed for golfers of all abilities, the programme helps each player to maximise their existing golfing ability and to develop new areas of their game. This enables them to lower their handicap and achieve new levels of competitiveness while enjoying life Down Under at the same time.
Real Gap Experience, First Floor, 1 Meadow Road, Tunbridge Wells, Kent, TN1 2YG, 01892 516164, www.realgap.co.uk

⬇ 💰💰💰 Become a yachtmaster
Location: Bay of Islands, New Zealand
Duration: 16 weeks. Price: £11,240

This is a popular skipper-training programme, offering a reliable route to the RYA/MCA Yachtmaster Offshore certificate, or Yachting Australia's equivalent qualification. These certificates are benchmark qualifications for professional yacht skippers. The course is suitable for experienced sailors and newcomers alike. Experienced candidates will find that they're fully stretched, while the flexible schedule allows beginners to progress at their own rate.
Flying Fish, 25 Union Road, Cowes, Isle of Wight, PO31 7TW, 0871 250 2500, www.flyingfishonline.com

⬇ 💰💰💰 Train as a ski instructor
Location: Queenstown, New Zealand
Duration: 8 weeks. Price: £5,850

Get into the ski industry or just improve your skills with this course. You take the NZSIA Certificate in Snowsport Instruction (CSI), followed by the NZSIA Stage One Instructor course. Technical training is at Coronet Peak, with a trip to The Remarkables. Also included are courses in everything from first aid to avalanche awareness, risk assessment, plus ski and board maintenance. Après-ski means winter in Queenstown, the adventure capital of the world!
Peak Leaders, Mansfield, Strathmiglo, Fife, Scotland, K14 7QE, 01337 860 079, www.peakleaders.com

⬇ 💰💰💰 Teach sailing or windsurfing
Location: Sydney, Australia
Duration: 12 weeks. Price: £6,590

This course is designed to allow you maximum time on the water. If you work hard, you can go from beginner to dual-qualified instructor in a short time. Training takes place at Middle Harbour Yacht Club and Balmoral Windsurfing in Sydney, while accommodation is at Manly. To gain instructor qualifications, you must demonstrate RYA Intermediate Non-Planing windsurfing skills (level 2-3), RYA Advanced Dinghy Sailing ability, plus skills such as communication, theory knowledge and an effective coaching style.
Flying Fish, 25 Union Road, Cowes, Isle of Wight, PO31 7TW, 0871 250 2500, www.flyingfishonline.com

💰💰 Coach sports

Location: New Zealand
Duration: 4-8 weeks. Price: £2,000

Volunteers will work in secondary boarding schools and are expected to help out around the boarding house. Duties may also involve supervising the younger pupils on some evenings and weekends. New Zealand schools have a great tradition in sport and many are also justly proud of their music and drama, and help with these is always required. The placements offer a variety of jobs and the overall opinion of gappers is that their year was "awesome"!

GAP Activity Projects, 44 Queen's Road, Reading, Berkshire, RG1 4BB, 0118 9594914, www.gap.org.uk

💰 Protect the outback

Location: Australian outback
Duration: varies. Price: £900

This is your opportunity to make a contribution to this beautiful and dramatic landscape by volunteering to help conserve it for future generations. You'll be involved in planting trees in the desert, cleaning up after bush fires and building bush tracks through the national parks. This is the real Australian outback experience and it's the perfect gap year for those who love the outdoors. Sleeping out under the stars is an optional extra.

GAP Activity Projects, 44 Queen's Road, Reading, Berkshire, RG1 4BB, 0118 9594914, www.gap.org.uk

💰 Help the community

Location: Australia
Duration: varies. Price: £900

You'll be helping a group that's committed to aiding people who are poor and underprivileged. Every day, you're likely to witness poverty that can seem unreal, with families sleeping on cold floors without beds, money, food or clothing. You'll have the chance to simply try to make a difference to their lives. Duties will include visiting refugee families with other volunteers and organisational work to help the project. This programme is an invitation to young people to really live out a selfless commitment to others.

GAP Activity Projects, 44 Queen's Road, Reading, Berkshire, RG1 4BB, 0118 9594914, www.gap.org.uk

➘ 💰💰💰 Work on a cattle ranch

Location: Northern Territory, Australia
Duration: 6-10 weeks. Price: £3,914-£5,334

This experience combines working on a traditional cattle station in northern Australia with helping on the 'toad-busting' conservation project in Kimberley. You'll spend part of your time helping out at the station with the livestock, arranging bush picnics for clients and participating in activities such as fishing, mud crabbing and camping out. The rest of your time will be spent helping on the toad-busting conservation project.
The Leap, 121 High Street, Marlborough, Wiltshire, SN8 1LZ, 01672 519922, www.theleap.co.uk

➘ 💰 Look after wildlife

Location: Northern Territory, Australia
Duration: 2-6 weeks. Price: from £680

Follow in Rolf Harris's footsteps and work at an animal hospital caring for injured, sick and orphaned wildlife. Home to kangaroos, possums and other small marsupials, as well as an array of birds of prey, help is needed with all manner of tasks. You could find yourself building new enclosures clearing grounds and even tending to the centre's veggie garden. It's tough, physical work and you could be outdoors in all conditions, but what better way to enjoy life Down Under and do some good at the same time?
i-to-i, 0870 333 2332, www.i-to-i.com

➘ 💰💰 Work on an Outback ranch

Location: Australia
Duration: 4-8 weeks. Price: £1,999-£3,499

Become a real Jackaroo or Jillaroo in the Outback! This programme is ideal for anyone who's looking to work in Australia on a gap year, or someone who just wants to experience working abroad. If you love horses, have any agricultural experience or just want a change of scenery, then this programme is perfect. Jobs range from cattle mustering to tractor driving, as well as working with eventers, shows jumpers and race horses.
Real Gap Experience, First Floor, 1 Meadow Road, Tunbridge Wells, Kent, TN1 2YG, 01892 516164, www.realgap.co.uk

Teach kids in Vanuatu

Location: Vanuatu, South Pacific
Duration: varies. Price: £900

Those seeking a truly alternative teaching experience will find this programme ideal. You'll head out to a remote location in Vanuatu, where you'll be helping the teachers in a secondary boarding school. You'll be working with the children on their English, maths, science and basic computer skills, often in areas where there are very limited facilities — some even have a limited electricity supply, making this a unique and challenging experience.

GAP Activity Projects, 44 Queen's Road, Reading, Berkshire, RG1 4BB, 0118 9594914, www.gap.org.uk

Conserve coral reefs

Location: Kadavu, Fiji
Duration: 4-16 weeks. Price: £1,400-£4,300

Kadavu Island is approximately 100 kilometres south of Suva, the capital of Fiji, and is well away from the usual tourist areas. The main aim of CCC's work here is the collection, collation and reporting on the coral reef resources of the area, and volunteers help out by undertaking daily dives to collect data. Innovative methods of displaying this data have been developed to pass information on to local communities.

Coral Cay Conservation, Ground Floor, 40-42 Osnaburgh Street, London, NW1 3ND, 0870 750 0668, www.coralcay.org

Pick grapes

Location: New Zealand.
Duration: varies. Price: varies

We've all heard of the lovely kiwi fruit that comes from New Zealand, but the country is also home to many more fruits and vegetables, and this is where you come in as a soon-to-be fruit-picking pro! This is the most renowned job for travellers and backpackers to undertake so you're guaranteed to meet lots of like-minded people. Workers are usually paid by the box or container, so the faster the work, the more you can earn. Make no mistake, it's hard work, but you get to hang around with a good group of people, experience life in New Zealand, and get a tan along the way!

www.seasonalwork.co.nz / www.picknz.com

▼ CASE STUDY

Who: Claire Smith
Location: Australia

Claire spent six months in Australia – five living and working in Tasmania and north Queensland – with Conservation Volunteers, a charity that aims to attract and manage volunteers in practical conservation projects for the benefit of the Australian environment.

Claire was brave enough to try the famous sport of bungee jumping!

There are numerous conservation projects in the Australian Outback.

Claire readies herself for another day of hard core volunteering!

Painting, weeding and planting were just some of Claire's daily tasks.

Want to get away from it all? There's no better place than Down Under!

After three years of studying and exams, Claire Smith was ready to hit the road. She decided to take a gap year and see the world, and quickly settled for conservation work in Australia. The scheme was run by GAP Activity Projects, and while the company organised all of Claire's placements, flights and insurance, she funded her time out through fundraising events, such as an Aussie barbie at her sailing club.

On 1st September, Claire said goodbye to her family, wished them a happy Christmas and boarded her flight. "It was a very surreal feeling as I was leaving home to go to the other side of the world, but there was no turning back!"

Her first 10-week placement took place in Tasmania. "After a week of being in Tassie, I had totally fallen in love with it – the Tasmanians are absolutely fantastic."

Claire worked with a mix of gappers and locals, and armed with secateurs and herbicide, her main job involved lots of weeding. In her third week, she was given the challenge of planting 800 trees!

"Our most interesting project was the rehabilitation of an environment for native frogs, staying in the bush with no TV or radio. Working in a remote location meant we saw lots of wildlife – I even heard a Tasmanian devil!"

Claire loved Queensland from her first moment there. "It was the complete opposite to Tassie and it was such a good contrast to work in two totally different environments."

Taking a gap year was the best decision I could have made. Travelling and seeing the world has made me realise that everyone is different and has their own story to tell

In Queensland, Claire worked in Townsville, weeding, collecting and potting seeds. After two weeks, she started a three-week project in Eungalla National Park, remodelling the car park area. "We stayed right in the heart of the rainforest and regularly saw the resident four-foot Goanna, as well as a bandicoot!"

Before long, Claire was spending her last week in the rain and mud, planting trees. "I had highs and lows, but the highs outweighed the lows. I didn't want to go home as I had fun, but all good things have to come to an end."

North-east Asia

> The richness of the culture and the unique nature of its customs and people make this a compelling year out

↘ North-east Asia

Mixing the ancient with the modern, this region offers a truly unique and unforgettable experience

Photo: CHINESE TOURIST BOARD

Westerners have always had a certain fascination with the Far East, mainly thanks to its unique and somewhat alien culture. Comprising Japan, China, Hong Kong, Korea, Mongolia, Taiwan and Tibet, the region of north-east Asia is a spiritual centre. However, it's also an area of contrasts and so spending your gap year here can be quite a culture shock. Ancient traditions and religions sit alongside overt modernity; rural poverty clashes with the lavish and hi-tech; while westernism and communism enjoy a turbulent relationship.

China is a mix of deserts, mountains, nomadic tribes, temples and shrines, contrasting with the skyscrapers of Shanghai and Beijing. This vast country is impossible to view in one outing and most gappers tend to stick to the south-west. While China remains a backpacking haven, Japan, with its sushi bars and zen gardens, is popular among those teaching English or pursuing a working holiday. Meanwhile, Tibet is a real eye-opener. Sitting 3,700 metres above sea level in the Himalayas, the country is overflowing with temples, shrines and monasteries, and makes for a fascinating pilgrimage. While travelling through this region has it pitfalls, such as tons of red tape and a strong military presence, the richness of the culture and the unique nature of its customs and people make this a compelling year out.

↘TOKYO

WANDER the streets of Shinjuku district, Tokyo's rowdiest entertainment centre. After the raucous crowds, relax at the peaceful Meiji-jingu shrine, stop off at the Imperial Palace gardens and visit the Senso-ji temple district.

VISIT Tokyo National Museum, along with the many other fine galleries of Ueno, and catch a kabuki show at Kabuki-za theatre. You can then enjoy a sushi lunch before partying the night away in riotous Roppongi.

SHOP till you drop in the ultra-chic district of Ginza, view the cityscape from the top of the Sunshine City building, book a romantic stay at one of the Love Hotels in Dogen-zaka hill and then visit an Open Air Theatre.

2

↪BEIJING

💰 **VISIT** the awesome Forbidden City (shown above), the Imperial Summer Palace, the infamous Tiananmen Square, the Gate of Heavenly Peace, General Mao's Mausoleum and enjoy the delights of the Night Market.

💰💰 **SPEND** time wandering the numerous museums, including the National Museum of Chinese History. Also, stop off at the China Art Gallery, watch the stars at the unique Ancient Observatory and explore the Lama Temple.

💰💰💰 **ENJOY** the opera, have a cheeky drink on 'Bar Street', try a different style of Chinese cuisine every night in Beijing's fine restaurants, and then take a day trip to the 13 Tombs, Eastern Qing Tombs and Tánzhè Sì temple.

3

↘SHANGHAI

💰 **SAMPLE** some delicious snacks in the Yu Gardens Bazaar, lose your way – and your sense of time – in Frenchtown, meander the muddy waterfront of the Bund and brave the maze of streets that is Old Shanghai.

💰💰 **VISIT** the incredible active Buddhist temple of Yufo Si and enjoy lunch in its vegetarian restaurant. You can then stop off at the former residence of Sun Tasen and enjoy a trip down the Huangpu Jiang river.

💰💰💰 **ENJOY** the shopping extravaganza that is Nanjing Lu, take a trip to the opera, visit Shanghai Museum, savour the views from the top of the Oriental Pearl Tower, watch the Shanghai Circus and visit the zoo.

4

↘GREAT WALL OF CHINA

💰 **TOUR** the Great Wall at Huanghua, 60 kilometres from Beijing. You can get great views of it from a cable car, and discover its history at the Great Wall Circle Vision Theatre and the China Great Wall Museum at Badaling.

💰💰 **TAKE** a round trip on a cable car at Mutianyu and get a look at the Guard Towers, plus some awesome panoramic views. Alternatively, visit the Jinshanling stretch of the Wall and hike from there back to Simatai.

💰💰💰 **WALK** along the Juyong Pass, ride the toboggan or cable car at Simatai and tour this exhilarating stretch. Alternatively, sign up to trek the Wall – you'll need at least £2,600 in sponsorship. See www.ndcschallenges.org.uk.

5

↘HONG KONG

💰 **EXPLORE** the Ladies' Market (above) to find some real bargains, then pull on your walking boots and tour the numerous hiking trails. Meanwhile, adrenaline junkies can take a ride on the Peak Tram to Victoria Peak.

💰💰 **ENJOY** a quiet drink in the evening, overlooking the bright lights of the city, go ferry hopping between the various islands of Hong Kong and for something a little bit different, take a sampan ride in the harbour.

💰💰💰 **SAMPLE** the delicacy that is dim sum in a top restaurant, brave the 700 shops on Canton Road, and visit Ocean Park theme park, which houses the world's largest aquarium. For a night on the tiles, head for Wan Chai.

1 Japan

🛄 Work in Japan
Experience the fast pace and high-tech cities of Japan. With the opportunity to both work and travel, this is ideal for those seeking to work abroad in a different and dynamic environment.
www.realgap.co.uk

Some of the jobs you might land include:
- Teaching English as an assistant
- Hospitality
- Interpreting
- Translating
- Web design
- Researching
- Acting

See page 90 for details

The main focus of this package is to help you settle in, find paid jobs in Japan, and help find you a good language school so you can master a bit of Japanese. You'll be provided with a full orientation, as well as assistance in finding work, and a place to live in after you move out of your hotel.

While you work, you can save money to fund your travels through the country. You'll be doing casual work so you won't be tied down to a job – you can work as and when you please, and spend the rest of your time exploring this fascinating country.
Duration: up to 12 months. Price: £599

2 China

🛄🛄 The Shaolin Kung Fu Academy offers one of the best environments to learn about kung fu. Based at the foot of the Kunyu Mountains, you'll study with some of the best Shaolin masters in China.

Typical training plan
- Theory and history
- Flexibility training
- Introduction to tai chi, Qi Gong, Sanda (kickboxing) and Shaolin fist forms
- Basic punching and kicking
- Low-level weapons training, with a staff, sword or whip
- Mandarin lessons

You'll also have the chance to learn hard Qi Gong. After just three months, you should be able to cut a brick using your bare hands!
Price: From £799 for five weeks, up to £2,899 for 24 weeks
www.realgap.co.uk

CHINA

- **Area:** 9.96 million sq km
- **Population:** 1.2 billion
- **Capital:** Beijing
- **People:** 92% are Han Chinese
- **Languages:** Mandarin (Putonghua)

- **Currency:** Yuan or Renminbi
- **Exchange rate:** £1 = RMB15
- **Government:** Communist
- **Religion:** Officially atheistic, but there are five state-registered religions: Daoism, Buddhism and Islam, plus Catholic and Protestant Christianity

3 Japan

💰💰 Work as a carer

GAP's caring projects in Japan are in Cheshire Homes and centres for the elderly, and much work is done on a one-to-one basis. There are different caring opportunities available, looking after a variety of residents of different ages with different needs.

These placements are a great way to help the ill or infirm, while giving you the chance to work in a different environment, learn new skills, and experience life in an exciting new culture and country. **See page 92 for further details**

Placements are scattered across the country, and you'll have help in learning Japanese in all of the projects, although it would be beneficial to start learning some of the language before you go, so you'll know a few basic phrases when you arrive.

All of the hospitals offer a variety of duties and provide excellent experience for anyone hoping to work as a doctor or nurse. Anyone interested in caring work of all kinds will be warmly welcomed. **www.gap.org.uk**

4 China

👤 Teach English

This is a unique opportunity to get paid work in China as an English teacher. During your working holiday, you'll study the Chinese language, learn all about the culture and have the chance to travel around the country.

You'll take part in Mandarin lessons and have a full orientation. This will include information on living and working, culture, customs and travelling around, helping you to settle into Chinese life. For further details, see page 86. **www.realgap.co.uk** **Price: 6 weeks from £899**

5 China

👤 Help save the giant panda

The giant panda is on the brink of extinction, with a total worldwide population of just 1,000 individuals. Of these, 270 are in the Shaanxi reserves. This is a rare opportunity for you to get up close and personal to these incredible creatures. Based at the foot of the Qingling mountains, you'll also have the chance to work with other fascinating species indigenous to China, such as the golden monkey, crested ibis and the sheep-like takin. Your work will involve highlighting the plight of all these creatures through the development of literature, programmes, teaching resources and internet facilities.

The duration of this project varies from between two and four weeks, and it costs from £995. This price includes your accommodation, meals, full TEFL training, airport pick-up and travel insurance. For further details on this amazing project, see page 92. **www.i-to-i.com**

JAPAN

- **Area:** 377,780 sq km
- **Population:** 127 million
- **Capital:** Tokyo
- **People:** 98.7% are Japanese
- **Languages:** Japanese
- **Currency:** Yen
- **Exchange rate:** £1 = ¥222
- **Government:** Representative democracy
- **Religion:** Mainly Shintoism, Buddhism and Christianity, plus several others

↘💰 Walk the Great Wall

Location: China
Duration: 2 weeks. Price: £599+

Stepping out across a peaceful, semi-ruined section of the Great Wall is like walking into the past. Far from the madding tourist crowds, you can get a great sense of the scale and the majesty of this remarkable piece of engineering, without rushing through in a big group. As you trek along contrasting sections of the wall, you'll get closer to the day-to-day life of rural China. Your journey ends in Beijing, a city steeped in history yet plunging headlong into modernisation.

Exodus, Grange Mills, Weir Road, London, SW12 0NE, 0870 950 0039, www.exodus.co.uk

↘💰 Cycle through China

Location: China
Duration: 18 days. Price: £1,450+

Visit the many must-see icons, as well as exploring a face of China experienced by few. Whether jostling with the crowds or spending long periods in complete serenity, the cycling pace is relaxed, with time to stop at sites of interest. Following your cycle ride, there's ample time to appreciate the rich culture of Xi'an and Beijing, and you'll be able to view an incomparable panorama of rural, ancient and modern China.

World Expeditions, 3 Northfields Prospect, Putney Bridge Road, London, SW18 1PE, 020 8870 2600, www.worldexpeditions.co.uk

↘💰 Climb Mount Fuji

Location: Japan
Duration: 7 days. Price: £1,225

Those who haven't conquered it dream about it; those who have are forever inspired by it. Mount Fuji, Japan's highest mountain, measures over 12,000 feet and is situated at the border of south-eastern Yamanashi and Shizuoka. This adventure begins at the 5th Station. Divided into three phases, you'll embark on a six-hour ascent to the 8th station. After a short rest in a rustic mountain hut, you'll advance in darkness on an overnight trek to the summit, where you'll witness the most spectacular sunrise you're ever likely to see.

Explorient, 75 Maiden Lane, Suite 805, New York, NY 10038, 001 800 785 1233, www.explorient.com

↘ 💰 Study martial arts

Location: Shaolin Kung Fu Academy, China
Duration: from 5 weeks. Price: £999+

Real Sport Experience's Shaolin Kung Fu Academy offers one of the best environments in the world to learn more about this historic martial art. Based at the foot of the Kunyu Mountains, East China, you'll be taught by some of the best Shaolin masters in the country.

Living with Shaolin monks, students of all abilities can learn different forms of Wushu (the Chinese term for kung fu). The serenity of the Shaolin temple and the national park surrounding it provide you with the perfect state of mind to develop a true understanding of Chinese kung fu. Highlights include learning directly from Shaolin kung fu masters; a stopover in Beijing, including trips to the Great Wall, kung fu shows, temples and palaces; and a stay in a real temple.

The Shaolin temple where the academy is based was founded in 495AD in the Northern Wei Dynasty. Today, this fantastic piece of Shaolin history is used to teach the art of kung fu. At the academy, you can specify which form of kung fu you'd like to learn, or you can improve on your existing skills. The programme includes the theory and history of Shaolin kung fu, flexibility training, an introduction to tai chi, Qi Gong, Sanda, one to six of the Shaolin fist forms, low-level weapons training and Manadarin lessons.

Real Gap Experience, First Floor, 1 Meadow Road, Tunbridge Wells, Kent, TN1 2YG, 01892 516164, www.realgap.co.uk

↘ 💰 Ski and snowboard in Japan

Location: Japan
Duration: varies. Price: £58+ a day

Escape the crowded slopes and experience the freedom of the mountains! You'll learn the basics of safe backcountry riding from our professional guides, and you can take in spectacular mountain views while hiking and riding through the Minakami mountains, home to some of Japan's best powder snow. Alternatively, trek the Kagura Peak, which is a classic backcountry. A 60- to 90-minute hike to the peak at 2,000 metres provides amazing views before you descend one of the many powder bowls.

Responsible Travel, 0870 0052 836, www.responsibletravel.com

↘📔 Journey through Japan

Location: Japan
Duration: 14 days. Price: £1,110

Japan is an intricate blend of east and west. This is a society of deep traditions and customs, but also a nation that leads the world in innovation. On this extraordinary journey, you'll visit Tokyo, the town of Takayama and the artistic and cultural centre of Kyoto. From there, you'll travel to the medieval Himeji Castle, the port city of Nagasaki, Hiroshima and the peace park, and, finally, Fuji City.
Gap Adventures, Matrix Studios, 91 Peterborough Road, Fulham, London, SW6 3BU, 0870 999 0144, www.gapadventures.com

↘📔 Explore Japan

Location: Japan
Duration: 14 days. Price: £1,100

Ever welcoming and always fascinating, Japan is a world of beauty and intrigue just waiting to be discovered. A land of ancient gods, austere traditions and groundbreaking technology, it combines new with old, innovation with tradition, and frenetic energy with soothing calm. On this break, you can experience the best this diverse country has to offer, from a sublime soak in an outdoor onsen to the excitement of Tokyo.
Gap Adventures, Matrix Studios, 91 Peterborough Road, Fulham, London, SW6 3BU, 0870 999 0144, www.gapadventures.com

↘📔 Discover the wonders of Yunnan

Location: China
Duration: 10 days. Price: £295

Yunnan is a province of unmatched complexity and diversity. Nowhere else on earth will you find such a mix of landscapes and people in such a small area. You'll travel from Kunming to Lijiang, where you can catch a traditional music performance. You'll then trek the Tiger Leaping Gorge, a spectacular trail that follows the Yangtze. Next stop is Dali, a wonderful lakeside town surrounded by snow-capped mountains. You can explore the town and catch the early morning markets.
Gap Adventures, Matrix Studios, 91 Peterborough Road, Fulham, London, SW6 3BU, 0870 999 0144, www.gapadventures.com

↘ 💰 Get a taste of China

Location: Hong Kong to Beijing, China
Duration: 15 days. Price: £1,110+

Feast your way through the highlights of China. You can explore the distinctive regional cuisine, from delicate dim sum in Hong Kong to the succulent roast duck of Beijing, and all the highlights in between.

Your first stop will be Hong Kong. This is the perfect place to enjoy a mouthwatering yum cha brunch while sipping fragrant jasmine tea. You can visit Victoria Peak for the amazing views and take time to explore this energetic city. Next comes the remote southern township of Yangshuo. Get a taste for village life as you wander the fresh produce markets, while cooking classes reveal the delicious secrets of the local cuisine.

Pulsating Shanghai is your next port of call. Here, you'll sample the fine cuisine of the restaurants and enjoy sensational shopping. Don't miss a performance from the famous Shanghai Acrobats, either.

One of the greatest stops is Xi'an and the start of the Silk Road. This city of ancient treasures is home to the Terracotta Warriors, while the bustling Muslim Quarter is the place to try kebabs and the local spicy hot pot.

The last stop is Beijing. You'll have plenty of time to explore this majestic capital, starting with Tiananmen Square and the Forbidden City, followed by a walk along the mighty Great Wall. You'll finish the trip with a feast of Beijing duck and Chinese dumplings!
Responsible Travel, 0870 0052 836,
www.responsibletravel.com

↘ 💰 Travel the Silk Road

Location: China
Duration: 19 days. Price: £1,490+

The Silk Road conjures up images of caravans carrying jewels and spices across deserts and mountains. This remarkable journey takes you along the Chinese part of this ancient route. In Beijing, you'll visit the Great Wall, in Xi'an you'll see the Terracotta Warriors, and you'll be amazed by the enormous Buddhist monastery at Xiahe. In Dunhuang, you can appreciate the Buddhist grottos before visiting the Gobi Desert, the oasis town of Turpan and the market of Kashgar.
World Expeditions, 3 Northfields Prospect,
Putney Bridge Road, London, SW18 1PE,
020 8870 2600, www.worldexpeditions.co.uk

⬎ 💰 Teach English in China

Location: China
Duration: from 6 weeks. Price: £899+

This is a rare opportunity to get paid work in China as an English teacher. During your working holiday, you'll study the Chinese language, learn all about the culture and have the chance to travel the country. During your training, you'll take Mandarin lessons and have a full orientation. This will include information on living and working, culture, customs and travelling, helping you to settle into Chinese life.
Real Gap Experience, First Floor, 1 Meadow Road, Tunbridge Wells, Kent, TN1 2YG, 01892 516164, www.realgap.co.uk

⬎ 💰💰💰 Teach English, learn Chinese

Location: China
Duration: 6 weeks. Price: £3,600

This is a fantastic opportunity to study business in China and gain TEFL qualifications at the same time. Native English speakers are required but no prior Chinese language skills are necessary. You'll receive daily Chinese lessons that are tailored to suit your particular needs and you'll undergo a six- to eight-week business internship at a local company or manufacturing plant. You can also choose to spend four weeks seeing the sights of this incredible country.
The Boland School, 0086 512 6741 3422, info@boland-china.com, http://boland-china.com

⬎ 💰 Learn Japanese

Location: Fukuoka, Japan
Duration: 4 weeks. Price: £1,210

With a population of over 1.25 million, Fukuoka is the largest city on Japan's southernmost island of Kyushu, and it's the ideal place to learn Japanese. Situated closer to Seoul than Tokyo, this city is subject to Korean influence and is currently experiencing dynamic growth and development. Fukuoka is a city rich in natural beauty, with a surprising amount of greenery and parkland. Its post-war development has been tasteful and the modern cityscape is characterised by avant-garde architecture. Meanwhile, sandy beaches offer great surfing and sunbathing opportunities in summer.
STA Travel, 0871 2300 040, www.statravel.co.uk

⬇ 💲 Teach and travel in China
Location: China
Duration: from 4 weeks Price: £1,495+

The People's Republic of China covers a fifteenth of the world's landmass and is the third largest country on Earth. It occupies almost the whole of east Asia and boasts a startling array of landscapes, from vast plateaux, deserts and mountains to river basins and bustling cities with exploding populations. Its attractions are equally as impressive, from the Great Wall and the Yangtze River to the Terracotta Warriors, the Silk Road and the Forbidden City. There's too much to see in one lifetime, but you can make a start with some unforgettable volunteer work.

You'll be based in the capital of Beijing, Yanqing County to the north, or Xi'an. You'll receive full TEFL training before you leave, giving you the practical skills you'll need. Graduates of our online and weekend TEFL courses have the opportunity to work abroad and contribute to the development of the minds and futures of the people they teach.

Meeting new people is beneficial to everyone involved, creating cultural awareness and tolerance of new ideas and people. Through teaching abroad you'll benefit from experiencing this fantastic country as a local, with many opportunities to get involved in school and community activities, and you'll also make many new friends along the way.
Responsible Travel, 0870 0052 836,
www.responsibletravel.com

⬇ 💲 Learn Chinese
Location: Beijing or Shanghai, China
Duration: from 14 days. Price: £627+

Today's China is a far cry from the days of Mao revolutionaries in buttoned-down tunics. Beijing, the cultural and political capital, is leading the way towards western modernity and it doesn't want to look back. This is an amazing city of striking contrasts, and any stay here wouldn't be complete without visiting as many of its incredible cultural highlights as possible. Steeped in history, the city offers a huge amount for visitors, making it the perfect place to live as you learn about the Chinese people and their society, while also mastering the language.
STA Travel, 0871 2300 040, www.statravel.co.uk

💰 Teach and travel in China

Location: China
Duration: from 11 weeks. Price: £1,120+

Acquire teaching skills and gain first-hand experience of life in China on this new and original way to spend a gap year. This is the perfect chance to gain English language teacher training and teaching experience in a local school for 11 weeks over the summer, six months or a full year. If you're interested in pursuing a teaching career or looking to gain new skills while spending time overseas, enjoying this incredible country, this is the ideal gap break for you. You'll have the chance to see the amazing sights of the Great Wall, the Terracotta Army and the Forbidden City, all while learning basic Mandarin Chinese and experiencing authentic Chinese culture as part of an Asian adventure.

Teach and Travel China is one of only a few programmes to offer an in-country residential English language teaching course (TEFL) that's run by native speakers. The arrival orientation and training sessions normally take place in Beijing and include comprehensive theory and teaching practice, along with practical experience and an introduction to Chinese life, culture and customs.

On completion of the training, you'll be placed in a kindergarten, primary school or secondary school, where you'll work as a teaching assistant. You're likely to be based in the south of China, which is a beautiful and awe-inspiring region that you'll never forget.
BUNAC, 0202 7251 3472, www.bunac.org

💰💰💰 Learn Chinese and local crafts

Location: Suzhou, China
Duration: from 12 weeks. Price: £3,600+

Learn to speak Chinese while studying the culture with the Cross-Cultural Studies Elective. The course focuses on Chinese fine arts, offering an introduction to drama in China, Kun Ju theatre and Beijing opera, plus an introduction to classic Chinese literature. Instruction will also be offered on Chinese paper cutting and reed weaving, as well as traditional Chinese cooking and calligraphy. Finally, martial arts or tai chi lessons will be tailored to suit your needs and full tuition will be provided, along with two weeks of sightseeing.
The Boland School, 0086 512 6741 3422,
info@boland-china.com, http://boland-china.com

⬇ CASE STUDY

Who: Lorna Davidson
Location: China

Despite having no previous experience of martial arts, Lorna spent a year out in the Shaolin Martial Arts Academy in China, where she learnt the language, along with a host of self defence skills...

Everyone at the Academy was really friendly and accommodating.

Lorna was inspired to join the Shaolin programme as it taught traditional Chinese martial arts, and it also offered Chinese lessons, which she found useful. On arrival, she found the training was as she'd expected. "I hadn't done much exercise before arriving and after hearing about the extensive training, I was worried I wouldn't be able to cope. I found it hard, but it's fulfilling and really enjoyable once you get through the first few lessons! Most of the information provided before the course was really useful, although I still wasn't fully prepared."

Following her flight, Lorna was met by a translator and shown around the town. "She was so friendly and introduced me to everyone. The transport was also good. I was shown around two main towns and shown the places that I may need, such as the bank and post office."

Lorna recalls one real surprise on her arrival at the academy. "I wasn't prepared for Fridays, running up and down the mountain! I really enjoyed training every day, although I did look forward to a massage at weekends! Everyone at the academy was amazingly friendly, and the translators and masters have great relationships with the students."

So what about the accommodation and meals? "They weren't quite

what I'd expected, but I quickly got used to them and found them fine. I don't think I realised before I came here just how basic the facilities were going to be! That's not to say I wasn't pleased with the experience: it was definitely worthwhile and I'd do it again in a heartbeat!

"Before I arrived in China, everyone was really helpful and made me feel at ease, and I knew that when I arrived, everything would be well planned. Most importantly, everyone at the academy was really friendly. In short, I loved it!"

> **I wasn't prepared for Fridays, running up and down the mountain! I really enjoyed the training every day though, and everyone was amazingly friendly**

Lorna would recommend the martial arts school to anyone. "However, you only get out what you put in, so if you do hard work, the rewards are endless. I had no experience before I arrived and I progressed further in the first month than people who learn martial arts once a week back home could in several months."

You'll discover new skills, flexibility, fitness and confidence on this break.

The Academy is located in a serene and breathtakingly beautiful region.

Shaolin monks are famous worldwide for their incredible martial arts skills.

➘ 💰💰 Teach sports in schools

Location: China
Duration: 3 months. Price: £1,599+

With the Olympics being held in Beijing in 2008, China is preparing for its largest influx of foreign visitors ever. Sport is now being given a greater emphasis in schools and China wants to compete with the rest of the world in a wider range of western sports.

This is your chance to join a sports volunteer programme and work for three months in a Chinese school as a sports coaching assistant. With Mandarin lessons and orientations to Chinese culture, this is a great opportunity to experience the real China.

Your main role is to help teach a variety of different sports during allocated Physical Education lessons. The average school has around 2,000 students of all ages, so you'll be able to teach a wide variety of age groups and abilities. The children love to meet people from the west, so you'll be warmly received and will be working with really enthusiastic pupils!

Most Chinese students learn mainstream sports like football, basketball, swimming and gymnastics. Other students also have lessons for sports, such as martial arts, table tennis and badminton. As part of a drive to develop new sports in China, some schools are now teaching other sports, such as cricket and rugby, which you can help to develop.

Real Gap Experience, First Floor, 1 Meadow Road, Tunbridge Wells, Kent, TN1 2YG, 01892 516164, www.realgap.co.uk

➘ 💰 Work in Japan

Location: Japan
Duration: 12 months. Price: £599+

Experience the fast pace and high-tech cities of Japan with the opportunity to both work and travel, while learning the language. This is ideal for those seeking to work abroad in a very different environment. You could be involved with teaching, hospitality, interpreting, translating, web design, research or acting. You'll be given a full orientation and assistance in finding work in Japan, along with a place to live while you earn enough money to fund your travels.

Real Gap Experience, First Floor, 1 Meadow Road, Tunbridge Wells, Kent, TN1 2YG, 01892 516164, www.realgap.co.uk

↘ 💰 **Help the community**

Location: China

Duration: 1-12 weeks. Price: £927+

As a volunteer in China, you'll get a rare inside view of one of the world's largest and most ancient cultures. China has a vivid and distinct history, artistic tradition, cuisine and social structure. You can volunteer or work on an intern programme in Xi'an, the crossroads of west and east China, and the starting point of the Silk Road. It's also home to the famous Terracotta Warriors, and was once the imperial capital of the country.

Your placement will be arranged by in-country staff, who match your personal skills and interests to the needs of the local community. In Xi'an, you can choose to work with infants and children, teenagers, adults, the elderly, or people with special needs, such as the mentally or physically disabled. There's also a Home-Base Structure, providing you with a safe, comfortable place to call home while you stay in China.

This volunteer experience is most effective and rewarding when coupled with the chance to learn about the local culture, customs and community development. Your cultural and learning activities will include Mandarin lessons, a detailed orientation, plus guest speakers who are chosen for their leadership in a variety of fields, such as traditional Chinese medicine, Chinese history or Chinese painting. Special events may include cooking classes or tai chi lessons.

Responsible Travel, 0870 0052 836, www.responsibletravel.com

↘ 💰 **Volunteer in China**

Location: China

Duration: 2 weeks. Price: £920+

This project is an experience-based trip, rather than just a volunteer placement. Time is split into 40 per cent volunteering, 30 per cent lectures and 30 per cent tourist activities. You'll visit community development projects in Xi'an, and you'll work on the unique giant panda conservation project, helping to protect some of the most endangered animals in the world. Finally, you'll undergo skills development work at the museum of the Terracotta Warriors and the Tomb of Qin Shihuang. You'll also receive lectures on Chinese culture and visit the amazing sites in and around Xi'an.

i-to-i, 0870 333 2332, www.i-to-i.com

South-east Asia

'As a spiritual epicentre, the hectic bustle of this colourful region co-exists alongside an air of grace and calm that's genuinely hard to resist'

Photo: THAILAND TOURIST BOARD

↘South-east Asia

The wealth of gap year options available have long made this area a backpacker's paradise

Regarded as a backpacking mecca, south-east Asia is the ultimate in gap year experiences. As a spiritual epicentre, the hectic bustle of this colourful region co-exists alongside an air of grace and calm that's genuinely hard to resist. The hedonistic nights are balanced by the tranquil days of lazing on a sugar-white beach; jam-packed nightclubs sit next door to Buddhist temples; and the golden arches of McDonalds exist as a backdrop to the traditionally-cooked food of the street vendors.

Despite the picturesque scenery and friendly people, potential gappers should bear in mind that some areas of south-east Asia are currently in turmoil, and they should check the situation of the countries they intend to visit before travelling. Thailand and Indonesia are still recovering from the Boxing Day tsunami of 2004, but rebuilding is well underway and tourism is welcomed as it's central to the economy of these regions.

In terms of gap options, this continent is bursting at the seams with ideas and opportunities. For those seeking a less strenuous year abroad, this is the perfect destination for relaxed, sun-soaked days and gentle travel. Meanwhile, the more adventurous spirits among you can do everything from trekking the jungles to indulging in a spot of spelunking in Malaysia or diving the seas off Thailand's coast.

1

↘THAILAND

💰 **MARVEL** at the Grand Palace in the historic Rattanakosin area of Bangkok, barter at the Floating Market, visit Wat Pho, Wat Arun and Wat Traimit, take a stroll through Chinatown and luxuriate on the golden, sandy beaches.

💰💰 **SHOP** till you drop at the Chatuchak Weekend Market, enjoy a night in Bangkok, eat out and sample some Pad Thai on Khao San Road, climb the Golden Mount for the views and listen to a concert at Lumpini Park.

💰💰💰 **INDULGE** yourself and have a Thai massage, take a day tour of Thailand's islands, pamper yourself in a spa on Koh Samui, learn to cook in Chiang Mai, stay overnight on a river barge and cruise the Mekong river.

2

↘THE PHILIPPINES

💰 **TOUR** Olango Wildlife Sanctuary, pay a visit to one of Davao's ethnic villages, sunbathe on one of the many luxurious beaches and relax after a day's diving by soaking in one of the natural springs.

💰💰 **VISIT** the coral island of Mactan, go climbing in Manila, the capital, try swimming, snorkelling and diving in Honda Bay and visit the breathtaking Kawasan Falls before taking time out to tour the Celestial gardens.

💰💰💰 **CHARTER** a luxury yacht and tour the islands, get a bird's-eye view by hiring an airplane, have a massage in Boracay and cap it all with a round of golf at the Alta Vista Golf and Country Club.

3

↘**BALI**

👤 **STOP** at the Goa Gajah cave temple, visit Goa Lawah with its bats and stay at Sangeh, the sacred monkey forest. Take in the waters of Tampak Siring, then see Uluwatu temple, Lake Batur and the ancient village of Trunya.

👤👤 **PARTY** the night away at Kuta, visit Klungkung, the oldest Javanese Hindu kingdom in Bali, see the temple of Pura Besakih, enjoy the theatre at Batubulan, visit Ubud, Bali's art centre, and climb Gunung Batur volcano.

👤👤👤 **VISIT** Celuk, famous for its silver and gold jewellery works, book into one of Nusa Dua's luxurious hotels, spend time in the mountain resort of Bedugul, tour the Water Palace and take an elephant ride through Taro forest.

4

↘VIETNAM

💰 **WALK** the streets of Ho Chi Minh city and peruse the Old Quarter, stopping off at the mausoleum. Then you can enjoy the beaches of Nha Trang, try a spot of tai chi by the Red River and visit Hoi An, a World Heritage site.

💰💰 **ENJOY** an authentic Vietnamese meal – food is an art form here – visit the city of Hanoi and its Old Quarter, tour the Mekong Delta, see Halong Bay and the illuminated caves, and then explore the temples of Hue.

💰💰💰 **WATCH** the legendary water puppet theatre, take a boat tour of Nha Trang island, enjoy a performance at Hanoi Opera, visit Hanoi Zoo and embark on memorable trip to Ha Long Bay on a private wooden boat.

5

↗CAMBODIA

💰 **WATCH** a traditional dance at Siem Reap, be part of the Water Festival, watch the sun rise over Angkor Wat and set over Bakheng Hill, visit the temple of Banteay Srei and stop off at Cambodia's capital, Phnom Penh.

💰💰 **TAKE** a cruise down the Mekong to Tonle Sap, watching the dolphins on the way, and then go for an elephant ride in Ratanakiri and Mondulkir. Don't miss the temples of Bayon and Angkor Thom at Angkor Wat.

💰💰💰 **ATTEND** the famous national ballet, shop at the Russian market and Siem Reap's traditional Asian market, and enjoy a night out – drink Angkor beer, eat a Khmer dinner and watch an Apsara dance performance.

1 Cambodia

Tonle Sap lake
This is a great chance to spend up to ten weeks helping the children at Tonle Sap Floating School, Tonle Sap township and families in the Kev Por commune.
Visit www.theleap.co.uk and see page 121

Community: educate families about the dangers of AIDS and build a well to provide clean drinking water. **Conservation:** teach the villagers about the benefits of keeping the lake clean. **Adventure:** live in a floating house and trek in the jungle.

Combine a diverse and exciting mix of conservation and community projects at two vibrant and contrasting locations found north of the capital, Phnom Penh. The first is at Cambodia's largest lake, Tonle Sap, situated near Siem Reap, where you will be living among a community famous for its floating houses. The second is at Battamberg Province, close to the border of Thailand, where you'll work with the Kev Por commune. This is a particularly beautiful part of the country and rural life here has remained unchanged for centuries.
It costs £2,352 for six weeks and £3,464 for 10 weeks

2 Sri Lanka

Work with the local community
At orphanages and community centres around Colombo and Kandy, you can make a real difference to young people's lives by providing homework support and English lessons.

You'll also help to generate creative play through games, sports, singing, dancing and drama. There are even opportunities to participate in health awareness programmes and to improve the quality of life for local communities by planting trees and helping to conserve the area's environment.

You'll either stay with a local family or in shared rooms. You can stay for between two and 12 weeks and it costs from £795. This includes accommodation, meals, TEFL training, airport pick-up and insurance.
See www.i-to-i.com

THAILAND

- **Area:** 513,115 sq km
- **Population:** 62 million
- **Capital:** Bangkok
- **People:** The population consists of Thai, Chinese and Malay
- **Languages:** Thai
- **Currency:** Baht
- **Exchange rate:** £1 = Bt73.13
- **Government:** Constitutional monarchy
- **Religion:** 94% are Buddhist and 5% are Muslim, with others Christian and Hindu

↘ 🛍 Travel the road to Angkor

Location: Cambodia, Thailand and Vietnam
Duration: 9 days. Price: £376

Combine the history and diversity of Cambodia with the excitement of travelling through Bangkok and Ho Chi Minh City. With magnificent ruins to explore, a rich history to contemplate and two of Asia's most energetic cities to dive into, this is an exciting overland journey from Thailand into southern Vietnam. Stop-offs include Bangkok, Siem Reap, the temples of Angkor, Phnom Penh, the Mekong Delta and, finally, Ho Chi Minh City.
Gap Adventures, Matrix Studios, 91 Peterborough Road, Fulham, London, SW6 3BU, 0870 999 0144 www.gapadventures.com

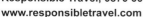

↘ 🛍🛍 Follow the Indochina loop

Location: Vietnam, Thailand, Laos and Cambodia
Duration: 29 days. Price: £1,615

Journey through the heart, the soul and the many diverse delights of Indochina. The treasures of Thailand, the locals of Laos, the vibrancy of Vietnam and the charisma of Cambodia – you'll discover it all on this awesome adventure around Asia. Visit the Mekong River, Halong Bay, Siem Reap and the temples of Angkor before experiencing the delights of Bangkok, Chiang Mai and Ho Chi Minh City.
Gap Adventures, Matrix Studios, 91 Peterborough Road, Fulham, London, SW6 3BU, 0870 999 0144 www.gapadventures.com

↘ 🛍 Backpack through Asia

Location: Malaysia, Singapore and Thailand
Duration: 8 weeks. Price: £995

Enjoy an in-depth exploration of Thailand and Malaysia. This budget alternative to backpacking allows you to make the most of your time, without any hassle and expense. Visit sedate Ayutthaya and the tourist mecca of Pattaya, with a chance to enjoy its wild nightlife and perfect beaches. Enjoy Koh Chang (Elephant Island) before sampling the wonders of Khao Yai national park. If that's not enough, you can take snorkelling trips, climbing lessons or even go on a canoeing safari! You'll end your journey at the ultimate destination, Singapore.
Responsible Travel, 0870 0052 836, www.responsibletravel.com

Teach English in Vietnam

Location: Vietnam
Duration: 5 months. Price: £1,360

Vietnam and its people are a delight, and their appetite to learn and their hospitality are infectious. Rest assured that although there's work to be done on this gap placement, it will also be a lot of fun!

These placements change regularly as this is a dynamic country, but in the south, most of the TEFL placements are in Ho Chi Minh City. However, gappers may also be sent to the university of Can Tho, in the heart of the Mekong Delta. In the north, most of the placements are in the capital, but there are also three in the neighbourhood of Thai Nguyen, which is two hours to the north of Hanoi. Gappers may also get to visit Hung Yen, Hai Duong and Hai Phong in the east.

Wherever your placement, accommodation will be provided free. Note that a bicycle is indispensable and costs $100 (around £50). All placements are for teaching English for four to five months, starting in early September or January. You'll be working as language-teaching assistants in secondary schools, primary schools and universities. You'll work for 20 hours a week in the classroom, giving you plenty of time to explore, and at the end of the placement – by which time you'll have made contacts and become acquainted with the language and some of the country – you'll have a whole month free to experience Vietnam.

GAP Activity Projects, 44 Queen's Road, Reading, Berkshire, RG1 4BB, 0118 9594914, www.gap.org.uk

Teach English in Thailand

Location: Thailand
Duration: from 4 months. Price: £1,310

This is an exciting project as the Thai people are traditional, gentle and hospitable, and their country is a wonderful place to explore. Placements are in both urban and rural areas for language-teaching assistants in primary schools. You'll teach for 15 hours per week, but may also help with extra-curricular activities too. The children are keen to learn, making this a fun challenge. On arrival, you'll spend your first week at an Orientation and Teaching Skills course in Bangkok so you'll be fully equipped to start your placement.

GAP Activity Projects, 44 Queen's Road, Reading, Berkshire, RG1 4BB, 0118 9594914, www.gap.org.uk

↰ 💰 Teach in Malaysia

Location: Malaysia

Duration: 6 months. Price: £1,385

Help teach English as a second language and lend a hand with associated co-curricular activities such as debating and drama. The schools, which are mostly for ethnic Malays, are predominantly Islamic, and most of the teaching is done in Bahasa Malay, so you should learn the basics of the language. A Teaching Skills course is essential and you should be a competent computer user so you can help the staff and pupils to improve their skills.

GAP Activity Projects, 44 Queen's Road, Reading, Berkshire, RG1 4BB, 0118 9594914, www.gap.org.uk

↰ 💰 Teach English to city guides

Location: Ho Chi Minh City, Vietnam

Duration: 4-12 weeks. Price: £918

Working in Vietnam's largest city, you'll be teaching English to the Volunteer Tourist Security Force. This group offers free tourist information on accommodation, restaurants and entertainment, while also looking after the safety and wellbeing of foreign tourists. Your role will be to teach the volunteers the English skills they need to do their jobs properly, and to give them the confidence they'll need to deal with western visitors. This is a great opportunity to live and work in Ho Chi Minh City and discover this incredible city.

i-to-i, 0870 333 2332, www.i-to-i.com

↰ 💰 Discover diving and Thai culture

Location: Thailand

Duration: 4 weeks. Price: £1,399+

This is your chance to experience Thai culture and learn to dive on this excellent Thailand sports programme. From the jungles to the beaches, you'll have many different experiences in this amazing country. Thailand is renowned for having some of the best dive-sites in the world and it offers everything a beginner diver could want. If you want to learn to dive and experience all that Thailand has to offer in one trip, this is an unmissable opportunity.

Real Gap Experience, First Floor, 1 Meadow Road, Tunbridge Wells, Kent, TN1 2YG, 01892 516164, www.realgap.co.uk

⬇ 💰 Teach in Sri Lanka

Location: Sri Lanka
Duration: 1-6 months. Price: £750+

Following the tragic tsunami of 26th December 2004, there's no better time to make a meaningful contribution to this wonderful country. In the beautiful hill region of Kandy, Mondo Challenge is working in various rural Buddhist temples, which provide not only a place to worship but also a community centre. In Manikhinna, Digana, Sarasavigama and Ranawane, you'll have the opportunity to work in pre-schools and primary education, while in Pilimathalawa, volunteers provide primary school and adult education classes involving many of the monks.

Volunteers can also help out at Bowalawatte school and at a Buddhist orphanage at Sarana Savena. On the south coast, you'll be able to help students regain some normality in their lives after the devastating effects of the tsunami.

A flexible, open mind and a sensitivity towards local cultural values are essential for this project, and by working alongside monks and local staff in the village temples, you'll quickly feel part of their community. Supporting these schools helps the local teachers by encouraging the children to use their imagination and creativity, and will give them the chance to experience English speakers and people from different cultures.

Mondo Challenge, Malsor House, Gayton Road, Milton Malsor, Northampton, NN7 3AB, 01604 858 225, www.mondochallenge.org

⬇ 💰 Teach sports to children

Location: Sri Lanka
Duration: 4 weeks. Price: £699+

Although Sri Lanka is one of the world's leading cricketing countries, it still has many regions where access to sport is limited and sports instruction doesn't exist – it's mainly confined to the larger cities and top-end schools, leaving a large proportion of the country's children with no real physical education. This project has been developed to provide sports coaching clinics in deprived areas. Based in a local school, you'll help to teach sport to a wide range of enthusiastic children.

Real Gap Experience, First Floor, 1 Meadow Road, Tunbridge Wells, Kent, TN1 2YG, 01892 516164, www.realgap.co.uk

↘ CASE STUDY

Who: Deborah Greenaway

Location: Thailand

For Deborah, her gap year was a life-changing experience – a time when she made friendships that will last a lifetime and when she learnt about life outside the UK.

Deborah found teaching in Thailand to be a really rewarding experience.

A gap year not only gives you a break from education but it also teaches you to learn in a whole new way. It provides the chance to get away but gives you new responsibilities. You'll miss home but you'll discover a different one. You have to work to make it work, but in return you'll experience a whole new world.

So says Deborah, whose first weekend of overwhelming, intensive cultural explosions – in the form of handheld fireworks atop Nan Province's biggest mountain – left her feeling both warmed and welcomed by Thai culture and the Land of Smiles.

"When a place so easily becomes home, it's the people that make it like that. The friendships I made will stay with me forever: the kindness of the Jai family, Canadian Jesse who I lived with, the fantastic children who kept me smiling, and the locals who spoke Thai to us, even though we didn't understand. Thailand and its people taught me all the things that changed me in my gap year."

Over four months, Deborah learnt how to teach and entertain a school of non-English-speaking kids. "The learning was mutual. As they taught us of their culture, their relaxed approach, original language, delicious cuisine and Buddhist

religion, it became apparent that there are different ways of learning that stretch beyond the confines of any textbook. This is life learning."

Deborah recently attended a training event on giving gap year talks in schools and she found it inspiring to listen to the stories and challenges. "I could see that each person beamed with the positivity and benefits of their experiences."

Gap years change the way we think; they widen our horizons and make them infinite. A gap year is not just a year: it's a big seed of inspiration

Deborah feels that volunteering gives energy, motivation and confidence to both the volunteer and the community in which they've worked. "Gappers are gaining life experiences, and a view of the world beyond Britain. Gap years change the way we think; they widen our horizons and make them infinite. A gap year is not just a year: it's a big seed of inspiration."

Deborah witnessed some of the many colourful festivals and traditions.

Thailand is home to many fascinating – and sadly endangered – species.

Watching Buddhist monks canoeing is a surreal and moving experience.

💰💰 Conserve coral reefs

Location: Philippines
Duration: 4-16 weeks. Price: £1,100-£3,300

CCC has been working closely with the Southern Leyte Department of Education to promote the inclusion of marine conservation in the science curriculum. You'll be helping to develop sustainable partnerships between CCC and local schools, providing assistance to increase the awareness of marine conservation issues so that ultimately, CCC can develop a school-wide, environmentally friendly ethos.

Coral Cay Conservation, Ground Floor, 40-42 Osnaburgh Street, London, NW1 3ND, 0870 750 0668, www.coralcay.org

💰💰 Protect the rainforest

Location: Philippines
Duration: 4-16 weeks. Price: £800-£2,400

This project is run by Coral Cay Conservation and it helps to ensure the protection of this biodiversity hotspot in the Philippines, and the critically endangered species that live within it. Current work includes everything from exploring and mapping the Imbag-Caliban watershed to investigating the ecotourism opportunities that have been opened by the raised status of the park.

Coral Cay Conservation, Ground Floor, 40-42 Osnaburgh Street, London, NW1 3ND, 0870 750 0668, www.coralcay.org

💰 Feed the poor

Location: Ho Chi Minh City, Vietnam
Duration: 2-12 weeks. Price: £795+

The Cooking House Project, based in Ho Chi Minh City, is funded by local donations and relies almost entirely on volunteer support. It's run by a charity in the city that provides food to poor hospital patients who can't afford their own. On this gap break, you'll be working with local volunteers in all aspects of food preparation and delivery, from chopping vegetables to handing out the meals. If you're looking for a fulfilling project that lets you use your initiative while working alongside Vietnamese volunteers and gaining a TEFL qualification, this will be perfect for you.

i-to-i, 0870 333 2332, www.i-to-i.com

↘ 💲 Help the local community

Location: Sri Lanka

Duration: 2-12 weeks. Price: £795

At orphanages and community centres around Colombo and Kandy, you can make a real difference to young people's lives by providing support with homework and English language lessons. You can also generate creative play through games, sports, singing, dancing and drama. There are even opportunities to participate in health awareness programmes, and to improve the quality of life for local communities by planting trees. Full TEFL training will be given to you before you depart on this fantastic project.

i-to-i, 0870 333 2332, www.i-to-i.com

↘ 💲 Save the orang-utan

Location: Malaysia

Duration: 4-8 weeks. Price: £1,349+

This programme is hugely rewarding and it offers the opportunity to work in one of the world's most extreme environments – Borneo. The project also includes the privilege of working to conserve orang-utans, the only great ape found outside Africa. You'll be involved in orang-utan conservation by working with the Iban tribespeople to track, record and count the orang-utans as part of their long-term conservation.

Real Gap Experience, First Floor, 1 Meadow Road, Tunbridge Wells, Kent, TN1 2YG, 01892 516164, www.realgap.co.uk

↘ 💲 Build homes in Sri Lanka

Location: Sri Lanka

Duration: from 14 days. Price: £1,299+

Are you are looking to volunteer on a worthwhile project? There are few people in more desperate need of your help than the tsunami survivors. This house-building project in Sri Lanka is fairly demanding, so be prepared for physical labour. However, the reward is worth it. A typical day will see you have breakfast at the hotel before starting work. After a picnic lunch, you'll finish at 6pm. In the evening, you can swim in the ocean, walk along the beach or relax with friends.

Real Gap Experience, First Floor, 1 Meadow Road, Tunbridge Wells, Kent, TN1 2YG, 01892 516164, www.realgap.co.uk

↘ 💰💰 Help Cambodian communities

Location: Cambodia

Duration: 6-10 weeks. Price: £2,352-£3,464

Combine a diverse and exciting mix of conservation and community projects at two vibrant and contrasting locations north of the capital, Phnom Penh. The first is at Cambodia's largest lake, Tonle Sap, situated near Siem Reap, where you'll be living among a community famous for their floating houses. The second is at Battamberg Province, close to the border of Thailand, where you'll be working with the Kev Por commune. This is a particularly beautiful part of the country and rural life has remained unchanged here for centuries.

You'll be helping the children and residents of Tonle Sap and families in the Kev Por Commune by helping to construct a well to provide clean drinking water, educating families about the dangers of AIDS and teaching primary school children English, games, computer training and sports. Conservation work includes educating the villagers about the benefits of keeping the lake clean and protecting its endangered species, setting up systems to collect lake rubbish and monitoring the impact of introducing new species of flora and fauna into the lake's natural biosystem.

Your time in Cambodia will also combine volunteering with adventure, including living in a floating house, seeing the temples of Angkor, enjoying the beaches on the Gulf of Thailand, and trekking.

The Leap, 121 High Street, Marlborough, Wiltshire, SN8 1LZ, 01672 519922, www.theleap.co.uk

↘ 💰 Care for the needy

Location: Malaysia

Duration: from 6 months. Price: £1,385

This placement involves work with either disadvantaged children or people with disabilities. A strong and proven interest in caring is essential, since befriending the residents of the homes will be your main task. Volunteers must be prepared for the work to be fairly mundane, particularly until your host gets to know you. However, you'll find it incredibly rewarding. Many placements involve teaching and speaking English, and many caring institutions have computerised records that volunteers could be asked to help with.

GAP Activity Projects, 44 Queen's Road, Reading, Berkshire, RG1 4BB, 0118 9594914, www.gap.org.uk

⬐ 💲 Build homes in Vietnam

Location: Near Ho Chi Minh City, Vietnam
Duration: 2-12 weeks. Price: £596+

Feel the warmth of the local people and experience rural Vietnam by helping local communities solve a very real problem. Monsoon rains often cause vast destruction to homes that are ill prepared to withstand the elements, and that's where you come in. Based 70 kilometres from Ho Chin Minh, you'll take on a variety of tasks. Previous experience isn't necessary but you will need to be reasonably fit. This project is part of wider poverty reduction efforts and it also offers the opportunity to teach English to the local people.
i-to-i, 0870 333 2332, www.i-to-i.com

⬐ 💲💲 Become a zookeeper

Location: Malaysia
Duration: 4-8 weeks. Price: £1,159-£1,899

This is a great chance to do hands-on work with animals you wouldn't normally get close to. Working as a zookeeper in one of Malaysia's best zoos, you'll be looking after animals and their daily maintenance. You'll learn about the animals' behaviour and act as a zoo guide for school children. This is a rewarding and fun project that's ideal for animal lovers and those keen to learn about animals in an exotic location.
Real Gap Experience, First Floor, 1 Meadow Road, Tunbridge Wells, Kent, TN1 2YG, 01892 516164, www.realgap.co.uk

⬐ 💲 Teach Thai orphans

Location: Thailand
Duration: 2-4 weeks. Price: £399-£699

If you have a passion to brighten the lives of orphans and poor children in Thailand and would love to see your efforts make a real difference, this is the perfect project for you. You can help teach English in the orphanage, play games, prepare food and help the local community by teaching English and computer skills. The children's smiling faces, the laughs and the feeling you'll get from this rewarding gap year will make this challenging project feel more than worthwhile.
Real Gap Experience, First Floor, 1 Meadow Road, Tunbridge Wells, Kent, TN1 2YG, 01892 516164, www.realgap.co.uk

↘ CASE STUDY

Who: Angus Hicks
Location: Malaysia

Angus decided to use his passion for conservation to help preserve sea turtles in Malaysia. While it was hard work, he believes it was an unforgettable and truly life-changing experience…

As well as spectacular scenery, there are thriving cities to explore and enjoy.

A keen conservationist, Angus decided to spend his gap year as a turtle and dive volunteer in Malaysia. "My time in the country was fantastic and I came back with so much to tell. On my first diving trip I managed to dive with a Hawksbill turtle and got about a foot away while she was munching on some cuttlefish eggs. I also learnt that banana pancakes are brilliant as breakfast! When I arrived in Malaysia, my first experience was of the food and the amazing views of Kuala Lumpur."

The next day, Angus travelled to the island of Kota Bharu to begin his conservation work. "The beach was amazing – I'm not joking when I say it was like film *The Beach* – paradise with rainforest vegetation, white sand and clear blue water. It had huge areas of coral with many colourful fish, such as barracudas, parrot fish and black-tipped sharks."

One of Angus's tasks involved talking to visitors about turtle conservation. "Basically, we explained how they couldn't touch the turtles or take pictures of them at night using a flash as they come up the beach to lay eggs in the sand. We also advised them not to leave their hut lights on at night as this confuses the turtles, who only lay three times per season."

Angus's average day involved turtle monitoring, which took place

from 10pm to 2am or 4am each night. This was organised on a rota basis. "You wait, watching the stars, and look along the entire beach. It's completely quiet as you wait for a turtle to arrive – it's really magical. It takes them three hours to walk up the beach, lay their eggs, make a dummy nest and walk back to the sea. We took loads of measurements and produced information allowing us to spot trends relating to why turtles arrived on some nights and not others."

Cleaning up the beaches helps both the environment and the local people.

> You wait, watching the stars, and look along the entire beach. It's completely quiet as you wait for a turtle to arrive – it's really magical

Monitoring endangered sea turtles is a fantastic way to spend a year out.

For Angus, his trip combined many wonderful experiences. "I had such an amazing time – apart from getting burnt! – and the people I met were so friendly and like-minded."

As well as all the hard work, Angus also managed to make it to Long Island for a night out, enjoying the party side of the area!

You can explore the coral reefs and crystal clear waters off the coast.

India

A gap year here is truly intoxicating, and the incredible diversity of India's people, religion, geography and culture – along with the food! – will leave you breathless

Photo: INDIAN TOURIST BOARD

↘ India

Spend your year out in this awe-inspiring region and you'll experience a real feast for the senses

First made popular in the 60s by backpackers who were drawn to the mysticism of this incredible region, today travellers flock in their droves to experience India's colourful festivals, diverse creeds, ancient temples and eclectic history, all of which are in evidence in every city, town and street corner that you visit.

A whirlwind of colour, noises and smells, a gap year here is intoxicating, and the incredible diversity of India's people, religion, geography and culture – not to mention the food! – will leave you breathless.

The gap year options in India are as varied as the geography. Adrenaline junkies can trek the Himalayas or the tropical rainforests of Kerala, while those who just want to soak in the sights can spend their days touring the many ancient temples and ruins. You can follow the classic Golden Triangle route of Delhi, Agra and Jaipur, or observe wildlife at its wildest.

Of course, you need to be aware that you're also likely to be confronted with dirt, poverty and overcrowding. However, volunteers will find that there are many people and communities who will repay their efforts with unparalleled warmth and kindness. While initially you may feel overwhelmed by the hustle and bustle, you can rest assured that you'll soon uncover a truly absorbing continent.

⬇ TOP 5 DESTINATIONS

Photo: STEVE EVANS / FLICKR.COM

⬇ NEPAL

💰 **VISIT** Kathmandu and see the temples, then trek the Annapurna Circuit, the Himalayas' most famous route.

💰💰 **BIRDWATCH** in Shangri La, go white-water rafting and explore the temples in Bhaktapur Durbar Square.

💰💰💰 **TAKE** a course in meditation, see the mountains from a hot air balloon and organise a pilgrimage trek.

Photo: STEVE EVANS / FLICKR.COM

⬇ PAKISTAN

💰 **SEE** the Swat valley and its Sufi architecture, tour Lahore's museums and follow the Karakoram Highway.

💰💰 **TREK** the Hindukush, Himalaya and Karakoram mountains, enjoy city life in Karachi and view Hunza Valley.

💰💰💰 **TOUR** the Sindh region, ski in Malam Jabba, visit Peshawar and catch a top-level cricket or polo match.

3

↘ INDIA

💰 **HIRE** a rickshaw and visit Jal Mahal, Gaitor and the Amber Fort of Jaipur. You can then ride the Ganges River in the Holy City of Varanasi, spend time at Delhi and see the Taj Mahal, before visiting the romantic city of Udaipur.

💰💰 **TOUR** the golden triangle of Agra, Delhi and Jaipur, go on a tiger safari at the Ranthambore National Park, experience rafting on the Indus, view the Himalayan Valley and enjoy a camel trek across the desert of Thar.

💰💰💰 **TRAVEL** to the luxurious island of Goa, view the Buddhist cave temples at Ajanta, take a tour of the Keralan backwaters, go on safari at one of the 70 national parks and then take the 'Toy Train' to Darjeeling.

⬇ TOP 5 DESTINATIONS

4

> ## ➥ BANGLEDESH

💰 **STOP** off in the historic city of Dhaka, explore the temples of Dhamrai and see the relics at Sonargaon.

💰💰 **GO** birdwatching and tiger spotting in the national parks, or try sailing, swimming or fishing on Kapati Lake.

💰💰💰 **HEAD** to Patenga for the beaches, take a pilgrimage in Sitakund and tour the treasures of North Bengal.

5

> ## ➥ THE HIMALAYAS

💰 **CLIMB** the Druk Path in Bhutan and view the temples and palaces, or choose from one of the many treks.

💰💰 **EXPLORE** Sikkim by mountain bike, tour the eastern monasteries and discover the Himalayas by motorbike.

💰💰💰 **TOUR** the mountains by jeep, then get off the beaten track and take a sunrise hot air balloon excursion.

🛍 Discover Ladakh

Location: India

Duration: 11 days. Price: £350+

Spend ten exhilarating days on your gap year abroad traversing the Himalayas on the way to Ladakh, also known as Little Tibet. Ladakh is set high between two of the world's highest mountain ranges, the Karakoram and the Himalayas, and it shares many ties with Tibet, such as its religion and culture. If you've ever wanted to explore India's mountainous regions then this is the perfect gap year adventure for you.

Starting in Delhi, this expansive journey takes you through some of the world's most breathtaking scenery and to monasteries situated on the roof of the world. You'll have the chance to hike through the mountain passes and camp under the stars, while you can also visit many of Ladakh's beautiful towns, including the spectacular Leh, where you'll get the chance to see traditional nomadic tribes and ancient palaces. As well as learning about the culture and history of the region, you'll be mixing with its people and finding yourself in the true India.

This tour provides one of the most spectacular and unforgettable adventures in the world, particularly if you enjoy camping and being outdoors, and it will be one of the best and most awe-inspiring journeys you're ever likely to take.

Gap Guru, 1st Floor, Bankside House, West Mills, Newbury, RG14 5HP, 0800 032 3350, www.gapguru.com

🛍 See tigers on a safari

Location: India

Duration: 10 days. Price: £350+

Travel to New Delhi, Ranthambore, Bharatpur or Bandhavgarh in search of the elusive tiger. Get your camera out and get ready for the most exciting gap year experience: big cats up close! India today has over 80 national parks and 441 sanctuaries. Each of these parks provides ample opportunity for wildlife viewing, whether it's from camouflaged machans, boats, jeeps or even the back of an elephant.

Gap Guru, 1st Floor, Bankside House, West Mills, Newbury, RG14 5HP, 0800 032 3350, www.gapguru.com

💰 Teach English in Calcutta

Location: Calcutta, India
Duration: 4-12 weeks. Price: £995+

This project is based at a school for disabled children who are taught through creative teaching methods in order to promote self-sufficiency. Learning is through art activities so be prepared to dance, sing, act and draw, as well as teach English! Alternatively, you could work in a school for underprivileged children aged between two and 17, teaching English, history, geography, science and music. With the younger students, you'll be able to lead classes in storytelling, singing and poetry. Full TEFL training is included.
i-to-i UK, 0870 333 2332, www.i-to-i.com

💰 Teach English in Nepal

Location: Nepal
Duration: 4-8 weeks. Price: £799-£1,349

Volunteer in Nepal and you'll discover the country at the roof of the world. Nepal is desperately poor and so volunteers are incredibly appreciated here. There's a variety of projects to choose from, including teaching in schools, monasteries and orphanages, learning Buddhism and working on medical projects. You should consider this programme if you're interested in having a real cultural experience and discovering the true Nepal through work in various local villages.
Responsible Travel, 0870 0052 836, www.responsibletravel.com

💰💰 Teach salsa dancing

Location: New Delhi, India
Duration: 3- 6 months. Price: £1,850+

Do you want to learn how the entertainment industry works in India, and do you want to combine your dance skills with your gap year out? This is a great opportunity for you to earn money as you help to teach Salsa and other forms of dance to the Indian community, while learning about the social behaviours and customs of this fascinating country. You'll be required to assist and instruct classes during the week, and also to participate in a number of fun events.
Gap Guru, 1st Floor, Bankside House, West Mills, Newbury, RG14 5HP, 0800 032 3350, www.gapguru.com

↖ 💰 Teach slum children

Location: Bangalore, India
Duration: from 2 months. Price: £1,400+

Teach English, maths and other subjects, plus activities such as sports, art or music in schools that are run especially for some of Bangalore's poorest children. Coming from local slums and orphanages, ordinarily these children would receive no schooling, so you'll be helping to give them the best education possible, as well as food, clothing, medical attention and some invaluable life skills.

Gap Guru, 1st Floor, Bankside House, West Mills, Newbury, RG14 5HP, 0800 032 3350, www.gapguru.com

↖ 💰💰 Work in publishing

Location: New Delhi, India
Duration: 3-6 months. Price: £1,850+

If you're interested in publishing then this gap year work option provides an unmissable opportunity for you to gain valuable work experience abroad, while supporting a charity organisation at the same time. You'll be working as an editorial assistant at a unique and award-winning non-profit organisation that publishes almost 100 new titles each year, and which works with some of the leading publishing groups.

Gap Guru, 1st Floor, Bankside House, West Mills, Newbury, RG14 5HP, 0800 032 3350, www.gapguru.com

↖ 💰💰 Train in hotel management

Location: Cochin, India
Duration: 4-6 months. Price: £1,200+

This is your opportunity to gain valuable experience during your gap year by working in one of India's top luxury hotels. The chain is located in Cochin and it provides an unparalleled ethos for community development, environmental awareness and the practice of traditional Indian holistic therapies, such as Ayurveda. These hotels are designed to blend into their environment, offer support to the local community and co-exist harmoniously with nature.

Gap Guru, 1st Floor, Bankside House, West Mills, Newbury, RG14 5HP, 0800 032 3350, www.gapguru.com

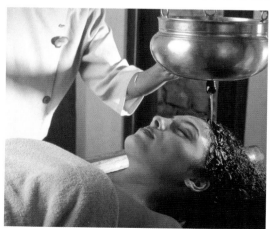

⬇ 💰💰 Practise veterinary medicine

Location: India
Duration: from 1 month. Price: £1,045+

Whether you're a pre-university student considering a career in veterinary medicine, an undergraduate or a graduate, shadowing local vets in practice will give you a real insight into the way they work in developing countries. You may also come into contact with diseases that have been eradicated in the west, and you'll understand the problems that vets and farmers face in developing countries and rural areas.
Teaching & Projects Abroad, Aldsworth Parade, Goring, Sussex, BN12 4TX, 01903 708300, www.projects-abroad.co.uk

⬇ 💰 Work as a research intern

Location: Chennai, India
Duration: 2-4 months. Price: £1,400+

Spend your gap year as a volunteer research intern abroad, conducting research into areas related to finance and development. This will give you a better understanding of socio-economic conditions across India. You'll work and travel with renowned individuals from top global research institutions, investigating the effects of financial management across the country, and you'll aid the planning of public spending.
Gap Guru, 1st Floor, Bankside House, West Mills, Newbury, RG14 5HP, 0800 032 3350, www.gapguru.com

⬇ 💰 Work as a journalist

Location: India
Duration: from 1 month. Price: £1,195+

If you're contemplating a career in journalism then this placement will set you on the right track. On the Print Journalism placements, you not only get an insider's view of how publications are run, but you also get the chance to put together a portfolio. Alternatively, a Radio or TV placement will provide you with an array of tapes and a host of broadcasting or production experience. Whatever placement you choose, you'll gain a valuable insight into the workings of the media in a new setting.
Teaching & Projects Abroad, Aldsworth Parade, Goring, Sussex, BN12 4TX, 01903 708300, www.projects-abroad.co.uk

↘ **CASE STUDY**

Who: Helen Rothwell
Location: India

Helen spent three months teaching underprivileged children in India. Following her experience, she's due to return for a third time and she hopes to get a job working with street kids in Delhi.

Teaching needy kids is a fantastically rewarding way to spend your year out.

Helen's adventure started the day she got on the bus to Manali, where she spent the next three months teaching some amazing children. "I don't think I'll ever get across the atmosphere there as it was unlike anywhere I've ever been before," she recalls. "The views from my window were absolutely out of this world – snow-capped mountains, a river and valleys that stretched as far as you could see."

A typical day in Dar-ul-Fazl started at 6.30am, ready for devotions – a mini church service. "The kids sang songs and then listened to a short sermon. Seventy or so kids singing hosanna at seven in the morning really wakes you up!"

Lessons started at 9.30am. "I taught about five lessons a day with my partner Hannah. Most of the classes had no more than 12 students in them, and we taught spelling, reading, songs and rhymes, games and drawing with children who were between three and 17 years old."

"At first I was absolutely petrified of standing up in front of them, but the kids really wanted to learn and always said 'thank you' after every lesson. It was quite hot during the day so a lot of the time we had our lessons outside in the sun, with the mountains in the background. What a place to teach!"

One of Helen's most memorable times in India was the day it snowed. "We were all really wrapped up, but without modern clothes the children were freezing, so Hannah and I took off our scarves, gloves, hats and fleeces and gave them to the kids. The snow was still falling thick and fast and I was in a classroom in India with a group of amazing kids singing every worship action song we could think of at the top of our voices. It was amazing!"

'

I don't think I could ever explain how amazing and rewarding it was. Being in India really opened my eyes to a lot of issues in the world...

'

"I don't think I could ever explain how amazing and rewarding it was. Being in India really opened my eyes to a lot of issues in the world. It has made me realise how lucky I am and that I really want to make a difference in the world. I know I can't make miracles happen but I know that I can make a small difference to children's lives."

You can explore some of the world's most spectacular scenery in India.

Teaching enables you to discover life in some of the area's remote villages.

Get off the beaten track and you'll discover the beauty of this region.

⤵ 💰💰💰 Live and work in India

Location: India

Duration: 12 weeks. Price: £3,495

This trip is divided into three sections. First there's a cultural orientation, including an introduction to the religions, castes and curries. You then live and work with village communities before trekking to the base camp of Everest. India has absorbed and integrated centuries-worth of foreigners into a strikingly complex society and as the trip progresses, what's likely to have begun as bewilderment will become a genuine appreciation of India's great fusion.

Responsible Travel, 0870 0052 836, www.responsibletravel.com

⤵ 💰💰💰 Learn about Nepal

Location: Nepal

Duration: 6 weeks. Price: £2,895

From the Himalayan peaks of the north, Nepal descends to the sub-tropical Terai plains. The people of the Terai are as unhurried, hospitable and good humoured as their fellow countrymen in the north, the Sherpas. These are the world's natural mountain men: their stamina, mountain knowledge and the support they provide are legendary. Your memories will be shared evenly between the breathtaking mountains and their remarkable people.

Responsible Travel, 0870 0052 836, www.responsibletravel.com

⤵ 💰 Help the community

Location: India

Duration: 4-12 weeks. Price: £995+

India is crowded and, economically, it's very poor. As a result, volunteers are always needed. These volunteer projects are aimed at improving the lives of the disadvantaged people of India. You'll need huge amounts of energy and patience, but you'll receive the warmest welcome into Indian society that it's possible to get, and you'll take home a life-changing experience. You'll be involved in meaningful work alongside local people, from teaching impoverished street children to helping the deaf and physically handicapped.

Responsible Travel, 0870 0052 836, www.responsibletravel.com

⬆ 💰 Work in the Himalayas

Location: Himalayas, India
Duration: 6-10 weeks. Price: £2,110-£3,200

This is a placement for the adventurous, set in the majestic Himalayas. You'll live among the local Almora community, helping to set up a luxury trekking camp while completing community and conservation projects. Almora is set in a stunning location in a verdant mountain valley, deep in the Himalayas, and it's one of the most beautiful places in India. Adventure options include trekking the mountains, fishing, horse riding and going on tiger-spotting safaris.

The Leap, 121 High Street, Marlborough, Wiltshire, SN8 1LZ, 01672 519922, www.theleap.co.uk

⬆ 💰 Become a broadcaster

Location: Dehli, India
Duration: 4-12 weeks. Price: £889

On this gap experience, broadcasting volunteers are fully incorporated into a 24/7 news and talk radio station. You'll get experience of programming, production, recording, research, reporting, copy-writing and even newscasting. You can work your way round different departments, or choose to specialise in just one. In a country of diverse social values, radio encourages harmony and helps to unify communities, and this project educates, informs and encourages such cultural interaction.

i-to-i UK, 0870 333 2332, www.i-to-i.com

⬆ 💰 Be a sports coach

Location: India
Duration: from 1 month. Price: £895+

Talk to anyone who's been to an Indian cricket match and you'll be left in no doubt that this is a nation that's passionate about sport! Embracing this commitment at grass-roots level, on this sport placement you'll work with schools all over the southern provinces. You can help coach enthusiastic children in volleyball – a sport rapidly growing in popularity in India – basketball, athletics and football, as well as the established favourites, such as badminton and cricket.

Teaching & Projects Abroad, Aldsworth Parade, Goring, Sussex, BN12 4TX, 01903 708300, www.projects-abroad.co.uk

Explore the mountains

Location: Himalayas, India
Duration: 6-10 weeks. Price: £2,115-£3,200

On this programme, you'll have the opportunity to get involved in sustainable eco-tourism, working with the community on conservation projects while experiencing India's diverse countryside and habitats. The projects are managed by an in-country team that provides volunteers with an induction and orientation programme, covering issues of safety, responsibilities, projects, health, culture, politics and conservation, so you're fully equipped for your break.

Responsible Travel, 0870 0052 836,
www.responsibletravel.com

Work as a music journalist

Location: Bangalore, India
Duration: 4-12 weeks. Price: £995+

If you love music and are looking for a career in the music or media industry then how does work experience on India's foremost music magazine sound? You could be helping with the day-to-day duties on either the editorial or design side of the magazine, and you'll have the chance to attend some of India's best music events. You'll even have the opportunity to meet some top stars! This is a unique way to kickstart your career, raise awareness of the importance of Indian music, and have a great time doing both.

i-to-i UK, 0870 333 2332, www.i-to-i.com

Help the local community

Location: Himalayas, India
Duration: 1-12 weeks. Price: £927+

Volunteers on these programmes are involved in everything from caring for and teaching children to working towards women's empowerment, assisting local medical professionals, caring for people with disabilities and assisting teachers in special education. Previous volunteers on these projects have said that this experience is the most rewarding when it's coupled with the opportunity to learn about the local culture, customs and community development, and all of these will be incorporated into your placement.

Responsible Travel, 0870 0052 836,
www.responsibletravel.com

↘ CASE STUDY

Who: Lizzi Middleton
Location: India

Lizzi took a gap year in north-west India with the Jamyang Cholin Institute, where she spent her time working in a Buddhist nunnery. The experience was one she believes changed her life and provided the ideal break between A-levels and university.

Lizzi spent her gap year living and working in a Buddhist nunnery.

Lizzi is a firm believer in the saying, "To the world you may be one person but to one person you may be the world," and so after finishing her A-levels, she decided to set off for India.

"I found myself living in a Buddhist nunnery in north-west India for five months, teaching English to the most dedicated, loving, trustworthy and crazy women I've ever met!"

Lizzi reveals that however much thinking, dreaming and planning you do, nothing can prepare you for the experience of actually working in India. "There really was no way I could have imagined that on a sweltering Saturday afternoon, I would be dive-bombing Buddhist nuns in a river!"

Of course, there were downsides to her trip. "For me, the hardest thing was being away from my family for such a long time. However, I found that the best remedy for homesickness was to get out there and to plough my energies into doing what I was in India to do: to help out."

There's so much to experience on a gap year in India that it can be rather overwhelming, and Lizzi agrees that it can be hard to take in what you're doing while you're working there. "It's only when you get home that you realise what you've done, how you've changed and how you feel."

Her experience in India has left a permanent impression. "My gap year is part of who I'm going to be for the rest of my life. Everything that I've learnt about myself, about the world, and about the people in it will help to form my opinions and shape my decisions in the future. Just as I've been able to give something to the world, I'm also able to take a lot from my experience. I now believe you can make a difference and I've learnt that everyone you meet will teach you something new about yourself.

The Indian culture and lifestyle has opened Lizzi's eyes to the world.

Lizzi found the scenery of north-west India stunningly beautiful.

> **My gap year is part of who I'm going to be for the rest of my life. Everything I've learnt will help to shape my decisions in the future**

So does Lizzi have any advice for would-be gappers thinking of heading to India? "My gap year in India opened my eyes to the truth behind the time-honoured phrase 'You only get out what you put in'. You really do – and it's more than worth it."

The main reason why Lizzi took a gap year was to help people.

Europe

'Why not enjoy Parisian chic, tuck into tapas in Spain, frequent the beer cellars of Bavaria or revel in the romance of Rome?'

Photo: ALAMY

➲ Europe

Often overlooked by gappers, Europe offers an incredible wealth of culture and activities

E urope is known as a living museum, but many of us may well forget this. Ease of travel means that we no longer regard Europe as being an exotic destination and it's sorely overlooked by its own residents, despite offering so many diversions.

From the heat of the Spanish coast to the snow of Scandinavia, this continent is as diverse as the weather is variable. You can quaff espresso in one of Europe's continental cafés or get away from it all in peaceful countryside. Why not enjoy Parisian chic, tuck into tapas in Spain, frequent the beer cellars of Bavaria or revel in the romance of Rome? Stray outside the perimeters of Western Europe and you'll discover untamed landscapes and Slavonic cultures that offer a striking alternative to the more well-known countries.

Gappers are spoilt for choice in Europe. The Alps are on hand for skiers, the surfing mecca of Tarifa is only a short hop away, and cyclists can take advantage of the pancake-flat roads of Belgium and Holland. Also, many gappers choose a year in Europe in order to learn a language while enjoying the culture and climate of a new country. So whether you want to lose yourself in the Transylvanian wilds, stay in a Bulgarian monastery or sit back and enjoy a *cerveza* on sunny Las Ramblas, you'll find your ideal location in Europe.

⬃BARCELONA

🔟 **STROLL** along Las Ramblas and indulge in a spot of people watching, head for Barceloneta beach or lose yourself in the Gothic Quarter. Free sights include Parc Güell, the Olympic Stadium and Caixa Forum art museum.

🔟🔟 **BUY** a ticket for the Bus Turistic – it's €22 for a two-day ticket and the bus stops at 44 sights around the city, including the Olympic Stadium, Nou Camp, Miró Museum, Gaudí's Sagara Familia and the hills of Montjuïc.

🔟🔟🔟 **SIP** cava on the roof of the Gaudí's La Pedrera, spend a night out in Sitges, have a meal at the Torre de Sant Sebastiá and enjoy the city-wide views on offer, then enjoy a top show in Barcelona's fabulous theatre.

2

➘**PARIS**

💰 **BROWSE** the Marche aux Puces de Saint-Ouen flea market, enjoy a picnic by the Seine, wander the back streets and alleys, enjoy a coffee in one of the many cafés or climb to the top of the Eiffel Tower for the views.

💰💰 **WATCH** a film in the Oriental La Pagoda, visit the Musée Picasso, Louvre and Musée d'Orsay, take a boat trip along the Seine at night or take a tour to Giverny – the home of Claude Monet – or around Green Paris.

💰💰💰 **SHOP** till you drop along the rue du Faubourg Saint-Honoré or the Champs Élysées, eat out in one of the city's top Michelin-starred restaurants and sample some fine vintages in the numerous trendy wine bars.

3

➥ROME

💰 **WALK** the streets of Rome, stopping to throw a coin in the Trevi fountain, admire the Piazza Navona and climb the Spanish Steps. Marvel at the Vatican in St Peter's square and view the Forum from the Tarpeian Rock.

💰💰 **VISIT** the Vatican museum, home of the Sistine Chapel, sample the chic boutiques on the via Nazionale, eat out in the Centro Storico, tour the affordable Museo Nazionale and stop off to explore the Colosseum.

💰💰💰 **SAMPLE** the Roman nightlife and dance the night away, take a day trip to Viterbo, go shopping in the ultra-chic boutiques around the Spanish Steps and tickle your tastebuds in some of Rome's finest restaurants.

4

⬊ISTANBUL

🛍 **HAGGLE** with traders in the city's bazaars, enjoy fresh fish at one of Kumkapi's 50 restaurants, tread the Ortakoy boardwalk, which is jammed with markets, bars and teahouses, and finish off at the spice bazaar.

🛍🛍 **VISIT** the famous sites of Topkapi Palace and the Blue Mosque, wonder at the spectacular frescoes of the Kariye Museum and cruise the Bosphorus, enjoying the spectacular views of Istanbul from the water.

🛍🛍🛍 **STAY** in Taksim, the city's central business and shopping hub, swig a cocktail at one of the sumptuous bars along the Bosphorus, visit the Church of Aya Sofya and indulge in a massage at the Çinili Hamami baths.

5

↘ DALMATIAN COAST, CROATIA

💰 **EXPLORE** the vibrant city of Split, with its chaotic streets. To get off the beaten track, head for the Zadar archipelago or the town of Skradin in the Krka National Park. Alternatively, try camping out in Mlaska bay.

💰💰 **STAY** in Trogir, one of the coast's finest towns, enjoy the café life of Zadar and visit Dubrovnik during the summer festival. Also, savour the flavour of Vis' locally produced wines and bask in the island's dramatic scenery.

💰💰💰 **TRAVEL** the coastline, from northern Zadar to the Bay of Kotor, visit Havr Town, which is the region's most exclusive centre, and sample the vibrant nightlife, fine restaurants and top resorts of the Makarska Riviera.

1 Spain

🕴 Teach English

On this project, you'll learn how to teach English as a foreign language, and then you can put your skills into action as you enjoy a break in Barcelona, Cadiz, Madrid, Palma de Mallorca, Seville or Valencia.

You'll be organised into groups of five or six. After each teaching practice session, an evaluation will be led by a course tutor. You'll be expected to liaise with other volunteers in order to plan your teaching practice classes.

Spain is very much the mecca of English language teaching. The combination of wonderful people, an agreeable climate and a culture that's very much the missing ingredient in the Anglo Saxon world makes it an irresistible destination. Everywhere you go, it's useful to speak at least a smattering of the local language and this is particularly the case in Spain, so look out for courses combining TEFL with a couple of chill-out weeks of learning Spanish. These also provide you with accommodation and something to do while searching for that first job!
www.cactustefl.com

2 Italy

🕴🕴 Study art history abroad

If you really want to broaden your mind and make firm friends on your year out, look no further than Art History Abroad's fantastic courses that will take you to Italy's most famous hotspots.

The course is six weeks long and includes trips to stunning places like Venice, Siena, Naples and Rome. It's run four times a year and is a once in a lifetime experience that will introduce you to some of the most awe-inspiring art in Italy. It will also give you the ideal preparation for any university degree.

Daily on-site tutorials in small groups will inspire and inform you, while the course will give you exciting knowledge that will last your whole life.
**Price: from £4,950
See page 171, or see the website at www.art historyabroad.com**

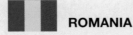

ROMANIA

- **Area:** 238,391 sq km
- **Population:** 22.6 million
- **Capital:** Bucharest
- **People:** Most are Romanian, with some Hungarian and German

- **Languages:** Romanian, although English, French and German are widely spoken
- **Currency:** Leu (plural Lei)
- **Exchange rate:** £1 = 5.12 lei
- **Government:** Parliamentary democracy
- **Religion:** 86.8% are Orthodox Christian

3 Romania

👤 Help orphans

If you're looking to volunteer on a worthwhile project, this could be ideal for you: building an orphanage in Romania. If you want to give these children a home then you should really consider this programme.

Duration: 4 weeks
Price: £999+
This rewarding project is run in collaboration with the Bogdana monastery in Radauti, which is the oldest monument remaining in the whole Bucovina area.
www.realgap.co.uk

A building volunteer should be prepared for physical labour but also a rewarding volunteer experience. The time you spend here as a volunteer will enrich the lives of the local people and provide a brighter future for many underprivileged children. Typical volunteer tasks include:
- Unloading and transporting material
- Laying bricks and concrete and mixing cement
- Painting
- Landscaping
- Fitting electrical cables and other equipment
- Building walls

4 Portugal

👤 Learn to surf

Discover surfing on perfect glassy waves on a coastline that faces both west and south. This experience offers intensive surf development courses to either learn from scratch or improve your surfing skills.

The courses run from April to October and are ideal for groups. Surfing is a way of life in the Lagos area of Portugal, so you'll meet lots of like-minded people while enjoying this fantastic sport.
itime Experience
0845 355 1183
www.itimeexperience.com

5 Germany

👤 Help the community

On this gap placement, not only will you improve your German language skills, but you'll also get to know the country, as well as its fascinating history and culture. Opportunities are spread fairly widely across Germany. You could work in a school with both boarding and day pupils, where you're likely to have supervising duties, as well as the opportunity to assist with the teaching and extra-curricular activities. Caring positions may be in hospitals, in residential homes for the elderly, with young people with disabilities, or with pre-school children. You may be working alongside German volunteers of a similar age too.

In some placements, a full year-long commitment – in effect, full-time from September to June – is preferred. However, six-month breaks can often be arranged. September, January and February are the usual start dates for placements.

Price: £950
www.gap.org.uk

FRANCE

- **Area:** 547,030 sq km
- **Population:** 61.2 million
- **Capital:** Paris
- **People:** French, with North African, Basque, Indochinese and Slavic minorities
- **Languages:** French
- **Currency:** Euro
- **Exchange rate:** £1 = €1.48
- **Government:** Parliamentary democracy
- **Religion:** 90% are Roman Catholic

⤵ 💰 Sail the south of France

Location: St Tropez, France
Duration: 1 week. Price: £329+

Have an adventure, activity and watersports holiday in the exclusive resort of St Tropez in the south of France. Each day you'll enjoy a breakfast of croissants and fresh French coffee on the terrace of your marina apartment as you decide which activities to do. You can choose from water-skiing or wakeboarding, visits to St Tropez, Port Grimaud and St Maxime, or anchoring off a beautiful cove to snorkel and swim in the clear sea.
Element Internet, Kensington Studios, Kensington Street, Brighton, BN1 4AJ, 01273 872242, www.adventuresportsholidays.com

⤵ 💰 Trek Estonia

Location: Estonia
Duration: varies. Price: £780+

On this guided walking trip, you'll travel around Estonia, taking in the sights of Tallinn with a sightseeing tour of the city and Old Town, before stopping in Lahemaa National Park. You'll then continue on to the Russian border before setting off around Estonia's other highlights. Activities include trout fishing, cycling, saunas, a traditional Estonian dinner with folk music, quad biking, roller skating and much more!
Trek Baltics, Heki Tee 16-22, 74001 Haabneeme, Harjumaa, Estonia, 00372 5623 3255, www.trekbaltics.com

⤵ 💰 Explore Tuscany

Location: Tuscany, Italy
Duration: 1 week. Price: £550+

This is a fantastic opportunity to explore one of Europe's finest cultural hotspots and to see the surrounding countryside. You'll be based in the town of Barga in northern Tuscany and from here, the variety of walks will allow you to experience the Apuane Alps, the Alpine meadows of the Orcchiella and the hilltop villages of Garfagna. The walks last from between five to seven hours and are generally of moderate difficulty, taking in mule tracks, mountain paths, country lanes and single-track roads. The holiday includes a free day, when you can relax or visit Pisa, Florence or Lucca.
www.europe-culture-activity-tours.com

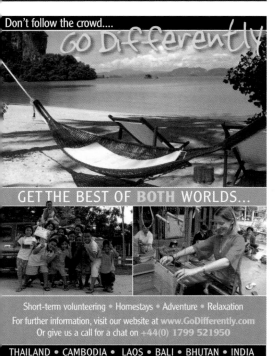
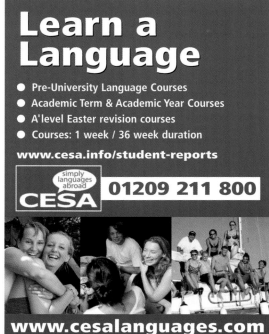

⬇ 💰 Master rock climbing

Location: Costa Blanca, Spain
Duration: From 4 days. Price: £439+

The Costa Blanca is one of Spain's biggest beach and party venues, and for those of you keen to combine these elements with an activity holiday, then this is the ideal gap option! Costa Blanca offers the biggest variety of rock climbing experiences in Spain, plus it's the country's most developed climbing venue. To top it all off, it also boasts the mildest winter climate in Europe, making it a great year-round location!

Costa Blanca has everything from single- and multi-pitch sports climbs and traditional routes to sea cliffs and mountain climbs. With the convenience of cheap flights and great local amenities, this makes Costa Blanca a hugely popular destination for climbers. On this programme, you'll have the opportunity to learn how to climb, or to improve your current climbing ability, in the stunning surroundings of Spain's White Coast.

This holiday will suit people with a range of climbing skills and experience, and it's also ideal for novices and beginners. You'll have six days of guided and instructed climbing for a one-week holiday, and three days for a long weekend, making this the perfect opportunity to enjoy lots of climbing in the presence of trained instructors. The programme is tailored to suit your personal requirements, and so you're sure to increase your confidence and ability.

Rock and Sun, 2 Blaenymorfa, Llanelli, Carms, SA15 2BG, 0871 871 6782, www.rockandsun.com

⬇ 💰 Discover Turkey's culture

Location: Near Bodrum, Turkey
Duration: 1 week. Price: £408+

The Bodrum area boasts numerous historical sites and landscapes of rugged beauty, and you can discover them all on this walking tour. A typical itinerary takes in Gölköy village, a visit to the famous Milas Bazaar, a stop-off at a traditional Turkish bath and a stroll around Bafa Lake and the ancient ruins of Heraklia. There's also the chance to see Bodrum and its numerous historical sites, such as St. Peter's Castle, the Museum of Underwater Archeology, the Myndos Gate and the impressive amphitheatre. Every evening, you'll dine on delicious Turkish cuisine too!

www.europe-culture-activity-tours.com

↘ 💰 Explore hidden Portugal

Location: Portugal
Duration: 1 week. Price: £685

This is a great chance to walk in Portugal's unspoilt country paradise and enjoy the wonderful scenery and exceptional people. You'll pass rare orchids and fields ablaze with poppies, and you'll discover secret coves and deserted beaches as you explore this incredible area. From day hikes along coastal footpaths to exploring ruined castles hidden deep in forests, you'll view a side of Portugal that few tourists ever see.

Serac Outdoor Sports, 37 Lilburn Close, The Pastures, East Boldon, Tyne & Wear, NE36 0TZ, 0191 519 4495, www.seracoutdoorsports.co.uk

↘ 💰 Master the mountains

Location: Glencoe, north-west Scotland
Duration: 1 week. Price: £599+

This winter skills course covers the multitude of disciplines required to take on the harsh environment of mountains in the grip of winter. You'll learn the arts of winter navigation, snow profiles, avalanche awareness, basic winter climbing up to grade 2 or 3, abseiling, snowholing, survival skills and much more. You'll stay in Glencoe, a magical, haunting valley that's home to some of the best winter climbing to be had in Britain.

Serac Outdoor Sports, 37 Lilburn Close, The Pastures, East Boldon, Tyne & Wear, NE36 0TZ, 0191 519 4495, www.seracoutdoorsports.co.uk

↘ 💰 Enjoy winter sports in Lapland

Location: Rauhala, Lapland
Duration: 14 days. Price: £445

Rauhala is situated on the bank of Lake Jeris in Lapland, in the middle of a 100-kilometre mountain chain. On this winter programme, you'll be able to go on ski treks through the Pallas Ounastunturi National Park, enjoy wilderness ski wandering and cross-country skiing, and you can try a multi-activity week with snowmobiles, reindeer and dog sledging, and showshoeing. In autumn, there's a hiking tour accompanied by reindeer, a mountain trekking week and a multi-activity week with canoeing, mountain biking and hiking.

www.europe-culture-activity-tours.com

↘ 💲 Enjoy winter sports in France

Location: Bourg St Maurice, French Alps
Duration: from 1 week. Price: £600+

Go trekking in one of the most beautiful mountain regions in France. A chalet is available for self-catering groups in the summer and is located in the heart of the trekking paths – you can literally walk straight out of your front door into the mountains. There are hundreds of paths to choose from, and they run along mountains and rivers and under waterfalls, enabling you to experience real peace and tranquility. You'll have the opportunity to spot some of the region's rare mountain animals and birds on your break.

You'll find all the extra activities you could want only a five-minute drive away, with 36 tennis courts, a large outdoor pool with diving boards, climbing walls, white-water rapids and the opportunity to canoe, canyon, swim in live waters and go white-water rafting. Golf courses, an adventure park, trekking, walking, motorbiking and cycling are all available on this adventure holiday, and to cap it all, there's the glacier in Tignes – only a 20-minute drive away – for snowboarding and skiing.

In the evenings, there are bars and clubs in both Bourg St Maurice and Les Arcs, with concerts for every taste, from blues to classical, along with street parties, festivals, markets, cinemas and more.

Element Internet, Kensington Studios, Kensington Street, Brighton, BN1 4AJ, 01273 872242, www.adventuresportsholidays.com

↘ 💲 Learn to surf

Location: Portugal and France
Duration: from 4 days. Price: £325+

This is a great chance to travel to and experience some of Europe's premier surfing locations. There's a range of trips to a wide variety of destinations, including the world-famous beaches of Hossegor in south-west France and the endless points of Ericeira in Portugal.

This adventure break offers you a unique opportunity to take your surfing to the next level through dedicated coaching and good practice. If surfing is the sport you really want to master or it's something that you've always wanted try, then this break is exactly what you've been looking for.

Ticket to Ride, 0208 7888 668, www.ttride.co.uk

⬇ **CASE STUDY**

Who: Olivia Dobell
Location: Italy

During her six weeks in Italy, Olivia travelled extensively and thanks to her tireless tutors, discovered not only all about the country's history and culture, but also some great restaurants, bars and clubs – and all while finding time to practise her artistic skills!

The breathtaking façade of the San Marco Basilica in Venice.

Meeting her fellow students at the pre-course supper, Olivia was struck by their diversity. "In some cases, our interest in art seemed our only common point. However, during our six weeks together, I grew very fond of them all. Thanks to our tireless tutors and the organisation from AHA, my six weeks in Italy were some of the best of my life and it seems incredible how much we saw in that time – Venice, Verona, Florence, Sienna, Naples and Rome, with day visits to Padua, Vicenza, Mantua, Pisa, Arezzo, Orvieto, Pompeii and Capri."

Venice was the starting point of Olivia's trip. "Here the tutors led us about the city, revealing beautiful churches and scuolas, as well as the magnificent Basilica of St Mark. We were taught about Gothic painting and about painters such as Bellini, Titian and Tintoretto."

Continuing on to Verona, the group delved deep into the history of the city, and on reaching Florence, everyone felt at ease with airing and debating their opinions. Olivia recalls, "We learnt about the rise of the Medici family and even used role-play to bring the story to life."

While Olivia loved the intensity of Florence, she was relieved to reach serene Siena. "After visiting the wonderful cathedral, we climbed the discarded façade and found a gorgeous view of the Tuscan landscape at sunset and stayed long after the end of our session."

Next came the vibrancy of Naples, where the group were taken deep below the city to explore the ancient aqueduct and theatre by candlelight. They then headed to Rome. "Our first days were spectacular as we walked around the Forum and learnt the colourful history of Rome. Last came our private viewing of the Vatican and the Sistine Chapel, which was an unforgettable experience.

Sunset at the Capitoline Hill in Rome, where Olivia ended her tour.

A view over the campo in Sienna – Olivia loved the serenity of the city.

❛
My six weeks in Italy were some of the best of my life and it seems incredible how much we saw in that time…
❜

"This is just a small part of my time in Italy. Some of my more exceptional memories include playing football in St Mark's Square in Venice at two in the morning, watching the sun rise over the Forum in Rome and swimming off Capri. In a word, it was magical."

The bell tower and Ducal Palace in San Marco Square, Venice.

Learn German

Location: Berlin, Frankfurt or Munich
Duration: 1 week. Price: £242+

This is your opportunity to learn German in one of the country's three most dynamic and exciting cities. Berlin boasts a cosmopolitan atmosphere, multicultural ambience and breathtaking architecture. To the west lies a range of stylish shops, restaurants and theatres, while in the city's east is an unrivalled cultural scene, with trendy bars and nightclubs. The cities of Frankfurt and Munich are equally exciting and culturally rich, making them the ideal places to get to grips with the language, while enjoying the local hospitality.
STA Travel, 0870 1630 026, www.statravel.co.uk

Teach English in Romania

Location: Romania
Duration: 4 weeks. Price: £999

You can provide an important service to Romanian students who need practice reading, writing and speaking in English. Your role will be to get the students to actually apply their knowledge of the language to everyday subjects. You'll also play a vital role in the 'eco-school' project, which is helping to raise community awareness about the necessity of maintaining a healthy natural environment.
Real Gap Experience, First Floor, 1 Meadow Road, Tunbridge Wells, Kent, TN1 2YG , 01892 516164, www.realgap.co.uk

Work as a journalist

Location: Romania
Duration: from 14 days. Price: £1,730+

Working on the English-language publication *Brasov Visitor* gives you the chance to get hands-on journalistic experience, as well as a real insight into life in mountainous Transylvania. One day you might be interviewing a local politician, the next you could be sampling the delights of a new restaurant in town. You'll work alongside experienced Romanian journalists and see how a small publication is run, from writing articles to designing and sending the publication to print.
Teaching & Projects Abroad, Aldsworth Parade, Goring, Sussex, BN12 4TX, 01903 708300, www.projects-abroad.co.uk

⬎ 💰💰💰 Discover the history of art

Location: Italy
Duration: 6 weeks. Price: £4,950+

If you really want to broaden your mind and make firm friends on your year out, look no further than this six-week course that gives you the opportunity to travel to the stunning cultural centres of Venice, Siena, Naples and Rome. Art History Abroad runs this year-out course four times a year and it's an incredible experience that will introduce you to some of the most breathtaking and mind-boggling art in Italy.

Daily on-site tutorials in small groups will inspire and inform you, while the course will give you exciting knowledge for life, and is an excellent way to prepare for the rigours of any university degree.

Time abroad with AHA is never just senseless escapism. Instead, it's a time for excitement, new horizons and a massively worthwhile explosion of your senses. You'll travel throughout Italy, studying on-site the real masterpieces of Italian art, western culture and civilisation as a whole.

Come with an open mind, enthusiasm and curiosity. Over 70 per cent of our students have never studied art or art history before, and they go on to work and study in every discipline. This unbeatable break gives you the opportunity to get an education and a passion for art, Italy, culture and life.

Art History Abroad, 179c New Kings Road, London, SW6 4SW, 020 7731 2231, www.arthistoryabroad.com

⬎ 💰💰💰 Become a skiing instructor

Location: Switzerland and Verbier
Duration: 11 weeks. Price: £6,250

For 11 weeks from December to February, you can experience great skiing in the world-class resort of Verbier, while training to become a BASI instructor. If you're thinking of spending your gap year or career break qualifying and working as a ski instructor, this is the ideal course as it's designed to find you work on qualifying. On completing the training, you'll be employed as an instructor and you'll get two months' paid work experience at a leading Alpine school.

Peak Leaders UK, Mansfield, Strathmiglo, Fife, Scotland, KY14 7QE, 01337 860 079, www.peakleaders.com

Dig up Dracula!

Location: Brasov, Romania
Duration: from 1 month. Price: £1,145+

Based in Brasov, a city which has occupied a strategic location since the 12th century, you'll be working with the History Museum of Brasov to investigate ancient Dacia and the medieval environs of Transylvania. Archaeological sites here have already yielded some remarkable information about the time of Vlad the Impaler, the inspiration for Dracula, and you'll be able to work on digs and help assess sites around Brasov.
Teaching & Projects Abroad, Aldsworth Parade, Goring, Sussex, BN12 4TX, 01903 708300, www.projects-abroad.co.uk

Help protect Butrint

Location: Albania
Duration: 4 weeks. Price: £979

This project is located in Butrint, until recently one of the world's most endangered sites thanks to continued political instability and the threat of coastal development that would encroach on the ruins and artefacts of this ancient settlement. You can help save this historic site by helping with vegetation clearance, project management, rebuilding dykes, environmental auditing and assisting on community projects.
Real Gap Experience, First Floor, 1 Meadow Road, Tunbridge Wells, Kent, TN1 2YG , 01892 516164, www.realgap.co.uk

Conserve the Carpathians

Location: Brasov, Romania
Duration: from 14 days. Price: £1,730+

The pine-clad mountains surrounding the city of Brasov in Transylvania are home to many interesting species of plants and animals, including wild carnations and the lynx – both of which are on the endangered list. You can help to protect the delicate ecosystems of Transylvania's Carpathian Alps by observing and recording the habits of wildlife, helping to maintain mountain paths, erecting signs or assisting with projects that aim to raise the awareness of this area.
Teaching & Projects Abroad, Aldsworth Parade, Goring, Sussex, BN12 4TX, 01903 708300, www.projects-abroad.co.uk

⬇ 💰 Build an orphanage

Location: Romania

Duration: 4 weeks. Price: £999+

If you're looking to volunteer on a worthwhile project, then this is ideal for you: building a children's establishment for orphans in Romania. This placement is run in collaboration with monks from the monastery of Bogdana in Radauti, and the reward for working on this project will be the smiles on the children's faces and the hope you can give them.

The building work can be fairly demanding, which means you should be prepared for physical labour. However, this is a very rewarding volunteer experience as it will mean the world to the children to have a place they could call home. Typical volunteer tasks include:

▪ Unloading building materials, such as bricks, sand, cement and wood tiles
▪ Using wheelbarrows to transport the materials
▪ Laying bricks, mixing cement and laying concrete
▪ Painting
▪ Landscaping
▪ Fitting electrical cables and other equipment
▪ Building walls

If you have special building skills, such as plumbing or carpentry, you'll be more than welcome. However, untrained help is needed too, and you'll pick up a number of handy skills on this placement.

Real Gap Experience, First Floor, 1 Meadow Road, Tunbridge Wells, Kent, TN1 2YG, 01892 516164, www.realgap.co.uk

⬇ 💰 Help the disabled

Location: Romania

Duration: from 6 weeks. Price: £599+

You can help young adults with disabilities. These people have lived their whole life in an orphanage and have been shielded from the outside world. At the age of 18, they were told to leave the orphanage and pretty much fend for themselves. Due to living in an institution, these individuals haven't learnt important life skills, such as how to cook a meal, shop, open a bank account or even use a phone. This project is vital for them, as is your help.

Real Gap Experience, First Floor, 1 Meadow Road, Tunbridge Wells, Kent, TN1 2YG, 01892 516164, www.realgap.co.uk

⬎ 💰 Volunteer in Germany

Location: Germany
Duration: from 6 months. Price: £950

On this gap break, not only will you be able to improve your German language skills, but you'll also get to know the country's fascinating history and culture. Opportunities are spread fairly widely across Germany, in major cities, small towns and the countryside.

You can work in a school, teaching and dealing with extracurricular activities; care for people in hospitals or residential homes for the elderly; or work with young people with disabilities, or with pre-school children.

GAP Activity Projects, 44 Queen's Road, Reading, Berkshire, RG1 4BB, 0118 959 4914, www.gap.org.uk

⬎ 💰 Conserve the Lake District

Location: Lake District, UK
Duration: 1-2 weeks. Price: £464+

Cumbria in the Lake District boasts some of the UK's most stunning scenery, stretching from the endless expanses of Morecambe Bay to lush, undulating countryside, serene glacial lakes, scree-clad peaks, forested slopes and lush pastures. This volunteer programme centres on the philosophy of engaging people in improving their environment through practical action. You'll be part of a group of conservation-minded volunteers from around the world, and on this project, you can make a real difference to this beautiful area.

i-to-i, 0870 333 2332, www.i-to-i.com

⬎ 💰 Master French chalet cookery

Location: La Rosière, France
Duration: 2 weeks. Price: £495+

This is an all-encompassing course designed to teach you everything you need to know about running a successful chalet. You'll learn recipes that are quick and easy, tasty, varied and nutritious. You'll get top tips on menu planning, shopping, managing your budget and portion control, as well as essential health and safety practises for maintaining a clean kitchen and keeping food safe. You'll also discover basic language skills and some tricks of the trade, all of which are designed to save you time so you can get out on the slopes as much as possible!

Snow Crazy, 01342 302910, www.snowcrazy.co.uk

↘ **CASE STUDY**

Who: Steve Howling
Location: France

During a summer holiday with his parents, Steve saw Campsite Couriers at work and decided that as soon as he could, he wanted to spend his summer working on a Canvas Holidays campsite.

The Campsite Couriers relaxing in the beautiful French countryside.

Explaining his desire to spend the summer working on a campsite, Steve explained, "The outdoor lifestyle and the way all of the couriers got on so well together really sold it to me."

Having applied for the position online and attended an interview, it took just three days for Steve to be offered the position of Campsite Courier. He accepted straight away and looked on the internet to find out about the area where he'd been placed – Tours in the beautiful Loire Valley in France.

Before starting his time in Tours, Steve attended a training day in Paris and helped to set up three campsites throughout France. "It's hard work but it's very rewarding as you can see the results of your work every day. Once dropped off at my site, Parc de Fierbois, near to Tours, the main task was to clean all the mobile homes and tents before opening for customers. During this time, I got the opportunity to make friends with the colleagues I would be living and working with during the season."

On the opening morning, Steve recalls that everyone in the team was nervous. "It's hard to imagine showing real families into the accommodation we'd spent the last two weeks cleaning. I'll always remember showing in my first arrivals and getting a

real confidence boast to hear that they were happy with the accommodation. It's also important to visit all of the families regularly. I could never have imagined how much customer contact the job actually entailed."

Steve got one day off every week. "Those days were great as you'd get off-site and discover the local area. We'd often go into Tours, go for cycle rides or walk into the local village. On most working days, there was also normally some time off to enjoy the facilities on the site."

Steve went on numerous bike rides around Tours in his free time.

> **It's hard work but it's very rewarding as you can see the results of your work every day. A summer on a campsite is great fun and I'd recommend you try it!**

During the time he spent in France, Steve made lots of new friends.

Steve found the season great fun. "It was hard saying goodbye to my friends and from the start of September, most nights were spent saying goodbye, which was sad, although we've kept in touch. Still, a summer on a campsite is great fun and I'd recommend you try it!"

You'll get the chance to work with all ages, from kids to pensioners.

South America

It's a land of fiestas, salsa and tequila, and what could be more appealing to a gapper than working their way through this feisty continent?

⬃ South America

From lush rainforests to beaches, thriving cities and ancient civilisations, this region has it all...

Latin America is one of the most colourful and vibrant destinations on the planet. It's a land of fiestas, salsa and tequila, and what could be more appealing to a gapper than working their way through this feisty continent? You'll be able to experience the heady blend of charming cities, stunning tropical landscapes and a myriad of flora and fauna, both above and below sea level.

Running from the expansive beaches of Cancun in Mexico through Belize, Honduras and Costa Rica, down to the lush rainforests of Brazil and Argentina in the south, the region is awash with opportunity. Think towering peaks, verdant vegetation, endless beaches and dynamic cities. Combine this with the remnants of the ancient civilisations of the Incas, Mayans and Aztecs, along with multicultural communities, and you have a truly breathtaking gap year on your hands.

The adventurous can follow the Inca trail, uncover an ancient Mayan city, trek the rainforests or brave the heights of Sugarloaf mountain. Hedonists can party the night away in Rio or Buenos Aires, or spend a summer on the Mexican coast. The volunteering opportunities are endless and range from working with children to building homes and community centres. Whatever floats your boat, this fabulous continent is sure to provide you with some unforgettable experiences.

1

⬎MACHU PICCHU, PERU

💰 **HEAD** to the Guardian's Hut, the Funerary Rock and Intihuatana. From here you have the classic view of Machu Picchu, with the ruins spread out before your feet and the awesome Huayna Picchu in the background.

💰💰 **TREK** the Inca Trail and feel the exhilaration of reaching Machu Picchu at sunrise. Visit the temples, Sacred City and the Sacred Plaza, then climb to the ruins on Huayna Picchu to savour the fabulous views.

💰💰💰 **TOUR** Machu Picchu by helicopter, or combine a tour of the area with an adventure expedition, taking in Cusco and the Inca Trail, along with a spot of rafting. Alternatively, visit during the famous Inti Raymi sun festival.

2

↘**BELIZE**

💰 **LEARN** about the island at Belize Museum, bathe under one of the many waterfalls, witness the sunset from the top of a Mayan temple, island hop by kayak, snorkel the reef and hike under the shady rainforest canopy.

💰💰 **SAMPLE** the nightlife of Caye Caulker, stop off at Belize Zoo, indulge in a spot of shopping in Belize Tourist Village, visit Crooked Tree Wildlife Sanctuary and the Mayan ruins at Caracol, and scuba dive at Glover's Reef.

💰💰💰 **TAKE** a tour of the Mayan temples and cities, learn to scuba dive on the beautiful reef, enjoy a spot of ocean fishing, stay in the 200-acre jungle retreat of Ek' Tun and book a place on one of the adventure tours.

3

↘ RIO DE JANEIRO, BRAZIL

💰 **DANCE** to the samba beat, sunbathe on the beaches, visit the Botanical Gardens and enjoy Tijuca Forest.

💰💰 **TAKE** the train to see the statue of Christ, then take a cable car ride to the top of Sugar Loaf Mountain.

💰💰💰 **PARTY** during the Carnival, go sightseeing by helicopter and watch football at the Maracana stadium.

4

↘ MEXICO CITY

💰 **SEE** the views from the Torre Mayor tower, tour the city on the tourist buses, and visit the Coyoacan district.

💰💰 **EXPLORE** Zona Rosa, visit the Teotihuacan pyramids, and see the sanctuary of the Virgen de Guadalupe.

💰💰💰 **EAT** out in San Angel, go to Xochimilco for a gondola cruise, and take a Frida Kahlo or Aztec tour.

5

↘ THE GALAPAGOS ISLANDS, ECUADOR

💰 **HIKE** the Sierra Negra volcano on Isabela Island, follow the Darwin Trail with its seabird colonies, visit the Charles Darwin Research Station on Santa Cruz, and try to spot some of the unique species in Tagus Cove.

💰💰 **EXPLORE** the underwater sites of Cousin's Rock and Wolf Island, dive with sharks off Darwin Island, visit Dragon Hill for the fabulous wildlife, take a boat tour of the four main islands and pursue your choice of watersport.

💰💰💰 **TAKE** a luxury cruise on the Galapagos Explorer II, enjoy a round of golf, sign up for a whale-watching or diving tour of the islands, be pampered for a day at the spa, tour the volcanic sites or take an archaeological tour.

1 Costa Rica

👀 Conservation

There aren't many places in the world where you can relax on a beach while being watched by inquisitive sloths and howler monkeys, peering out from their jungle canopy hideout!

This small country has it all: beaches, rainforests that spread right down to the edge of the ocean, enchanting people and exotic wildlife, and you can help protect it. Prices start at £1,786 for six weeks. Visit **www.theleap.co.uk**

Your role

Live and work among the community at El Silencio on the Pacific Coast. You'll help run the eco-lodge while assisting with conservation and community projects. Jobs include demonstrating recipes in the kitchens, teaching English to the staff, maintaining the Medicinal Plants garden and assisting with the reforestation project. You can also get involved with teaching volleyball, football, dance and handicraft skills, and you'll be able to look after rescued ocelots, monkeys and exotic birds, as well as reconstructing bridges and trails. To relax, you can enjoy white-water rafting surfing, fishing and snorkelling.

2 South America

👀 Explorer tour

This is an expedition through three immense countries, with an astonishing variety of activities on offer as you explore some of this amazing continent's harder-to-reach highlights. **www.questoverseas.co.uk**

This is the journey of a lifetime, from trekking in the Chilean Lake District, mountain biking and horse riding through ancient forests and kayaking around immense glaciers to dolphin and whale watching, tangoing in Buenos Aires and dancing on the beaches of Rio.

This fun-filled expedition takes you through three countries and lasts for six weeks. It costs £2,495 and this price includes all activities, food and accommodation for the trip. Note that it excludes flight costs and insurance.

BRAZIL

- **Area:** 8.5 million sq km
- **Population:** 182.1 million
- **Capital:** Brasilia
- **People:** Most Brazilians are of European origin, especially Portuguese and Spanish

- **Languages:** Portuguese
- **Currency:** Real
- **Exchange rate:** £1 = BRL4.18
- **Government:** Federal republic
- **Religion:** Mainly Roman Catholic with some Pentecostal and Animist

3 Bolivia
👀 Help wildlife
This is a rare chance to gain hands-on experience of looking after endangered species, such as monkeys, jaguars, pumas and toucans, rescued from illegal traders in the Bolivian Amazon.

You can combine this experience with a three-week language course in Sucre, and an action-packed Andean Explorer Expedition, which takes in the highlights of Peru and Bolivia. See www. questoverseas.com

The Bolivian Amazon rainforest is known for its vast biodiversity, but among these species are many endangered animals. Volunteers are urgently needed to improve the lives of these beautiful creatures and to help combat illegal trade. This sanctuary strives to enhance the animals' quality of life and reintroduce them back into the wild where possible. This is an immensely valuable project that's a world away from anything you've seen before. It costs £4,920, including all activities, food and accommodation, with a £680 donation to the sanctuary.

4 Ecuador
🎵 Teach music
This is the ideal placement for the musically talented – an opportunity to teach music to street kids. A grade 5 knowledge of music is essential, as is an ability to speak Spanish.

The placements cost a flat fee of £900, and food and accommodation are included in the price. Flights and insurance are not included. For details on this rewarding project, see the website.
www.gap.org.uk
See page 192

5 Ecuador
🎵 Teach football
Based at one of four soccer schools (co-ordinated by the National Association of Professional Soccer) in Ecuador's capital city, Quito, this is your chance to help teach and coach young players ranging from between five years old and 18. You'll be helping them both with their soccer and with their English-language skills. Working alongside a professional coach, you'll have the opportunity to assist throughout the coaching sessions and provide basic English lessons for the students. As well as experiencing this incredible culture, you're likely to improve your footy skills too!

This project lasts for between four and 12 weeks, and it costs from £1,095. This includes your accommodation, all meals, full TEFL training, airport pick-up and insurance. For further information, please visit GAP Activity Projects' website at www.gap.org.uk

ARGENTINA

- **Area:** 1.08 million sq miles
- **Population:** 36.2 million
- **Capital:** Buenos Aires
- **People:** Most Argentines are of European origin, especially Spanish and Italian

- **Languages:** Spanish
- **Currency:** Peso
- **Exchange rate:** £1 = ARS5.97
- **Government:** Constitutional republic
- **Religion:** 90% are Roman Catholic, with Protestants, Judaism and Islam

⬇ 💰 Coach sports

Location: Rio de Janeiro or Foz do Iguaçu, Brazil
Duration: 14 days. Price: £1,149+

Brazilians are passionate about sport and the national obsession with football appears to be instilled in children of all ages and classes, who can often be seen having a game of barefoot soccer on the dusty back streets of towns and cities across the country. Thanks to this, Brazil offers a rewarding opportunity for you to pass on your sports skills to kids who will really appreciate it. You can absorb this country's culture by becoming a part of its community, and it's no surprise that most volunteers here choose to extend their stay.

The schools and centres you'll work in are poor but the children are rich in spirit. You'll spend time sharing your skills and building confidence and team morale while working towards improving technique and strategy. What you'll offer through coaching is immeasurable in terms of the children's social skills, team work, self development, confidence, and the positive effects it will have on their English language.

With a little time, energy and patience, your placement will be thoroughly rewarding and enjoyable for both you and the children you'll be working with. You'll no doubt learn a thing or two from your students and fellow coaches, as well as helping to give the children hope and renewed confidence.

Travellers Worldwide, 7 Mulberry Close, Ferring, West Sussex, BN12 5HY, 01903 502595, www.travellersworldwide.com

⬇ 💰 Discover the Galapagos

Location: Galapagos Islands
Duration: from 10 days. Price: £1,150+

This carefully planned multi-activity tour is perfect for all lovers of outdoor adventure and wildlife. We combine activities such as snorkelling, kayaking, horse riding, biking and diving in a unique itinerary that takes in the highlights of the islands, while scuba diving is an optional extra that can be arranged. Whether you're diving with harmless sharks, playful sea lions or giant manta rays, or just enjoying the company of the Giant Galapagos Tortoise, you'll go home with memories that will last a lifetime.

Responsible Travel, 0870 0052 836, www.responsibletravel.com

↘ 💰💰 Master the beautiful game

Location: Brazil
Duration: 4-8 weeks. Price: £1,499-£2,799

Real Sport Experience's International Football Academy in Brazil gives you the chance to take your football skills to the next level or beyond. Training alongside former Brazilian internationals with other hopefuls from all over the world, you can learn about the beautiful game in a country where football is more a way of life than a sport. This experience will leave you with vastly improved skills and some great memories.

Real Gap Experience, First Floor, 1 Meadow Road, Tunbridge Wells, Kent, TN1 2YG, 01892 516164, www.realgap.co.uk

↘ 💰 Develop children's sport

Location: Guatemala
Duration: 4-8 weeks. Price: £499+

Sport is a passion in Guatemala, but all too often it's just for the privileged few, with the poorer communities having limited facilities to teach sports, or no facilities at all. This means children have to play in the street or in unkempt fields. By volunteering on this programme, you'll have the opportunity to help establish and manage a sports training programme in a school, helping kids get more out of the sports they love.

Real Gap Experience, First Floor, 1 Meadow Road, Tunbridge Wells, Kent, TN1 2YG, 01892 516164, www.realgap.co.uk

↘ 💰💰💰 Explore the Inca Empire

Location: Bolivia, Chile, Ecuador and Peru
Duration: 15 weeks. Price: £5,134+

Explore the jungles, deserts and mountains of the Inca Empire, between the northern outpost of Quito and the southern capital, Cusco. Highlights include a travel survival course before departure; three weeks of Spanish tuition and cultural introduction; community development projects in Ecuador and Peru; two high-altitude expedition treks in the Andes; Amazon wildlife and jungle exploration in Bolivia; and adventure activities such as mountain biking, surfing and white-water rafting. A truly wonderful adventure experience.

Responsible Travel, 0870 0052 836, www.responsibletravel.com

⬎ 💰 Become an adventure guide

Location: Malargue, Argentina
Duration: 14 days. Price: £1,149+

This unusual placement is situated in and around the beautiful and popular town of Malargue, which is located in the foothills of the Andes Mountains. You'll be able to gain unique experience working in tourism and, if you're suitably qualified, assisting with adventure guiding. The Hostel Internacional Malargue provides its guests with adventure tours, such as rafting, horse riding, trekking and mountain climbing, and for this project you should love horses and be confident about leading groups. Your work will consist of:

■ Horse feeding and brushing
■ Teaching horse handling skills
■ Guiding tourists on one- to six-hour circuits on horses
■ Taking tourists on mountain-bike rides
■ Leading tourists on treks
■ Taking riding tourist groups on circuits lasting several days, sleeping in mountain camps while accompanied by a local guide and a cowboy (optional)
■ Working at Malargue's natural reserves, assisting guides and helping out as a translator
■ Doing some relevant administration work
■ Possibly marketing the tours
■ If you're participating during winter, you'll also be taking tourists groups to Las Lenas Ski Centre

Travellers Worldwide, 7 Mulberry Close, Ferring, West Sussex, BN12 5HY, 01903 502595, www.travellersworldwide.com

⬎ 💰💰💰 Explore South America

Location: Peru, Ecuador and the Galapagos Islands
Duration: from 20 days. Price: £3,299+

You'll land in the city of the conquistadors and explore Lima, Peru's capital, before flying into the heights of the Andes, where you'll visit the colourful sights of Cusco before trekking to the ancient ruins of Machu Picchu. Then it's on to Ecuador and an eight-day exploration of the pristine Galapagos Islands. You'll sail with an expert naturalist guide and encounter the Giant Galapagos Tortoise, marine iguanas and blue-footed boobies, and you'll have the chance to walk across volcanic lava flows and snorkel among the sea lions too.

Responsible Travel, 01273 600030, www.responsibletravel.com

Start your American adventure

Location: Bolivia
Duration: from 4 weeks. Price: £869+

This is a great way to kick off your time in Latin America, and the most exciting way to learn the language, experience local cultures, make friends and meet travel companions. Highlights include salsa dancing classes, festivals, visits to indigenous Bolivian villages, trekking in the Andes and horse riding. You'll start by getting a basic grounding in Spanish and you'll receive a certificate at the end of your studies.

Real Gap Experience, First Floor, 1 Meadow Road, Tunbridge Wells, Kent, TN1 2YG , 01892 516164, www.realgap.co.uk

Explore South America

Location: Bolivia, Brazil, Paraguay and Peru
Duration: 45 days. Price: £1,570+

This 45-day tour is a cross-continental adventure through South America's most fascinating countries, from Peru and Bolivia to Brazil and Paraguay. You'll get the chance to explore colonial Cuzco, follow the Inca Trail to Machu Picchu, observe the Pantanal's magnificent wildlife and listen to the deafening roar of Iguassu Falls. Follow the Southern Cross with us and experience the best Latin America has to offer in this fascinating and unforgettable journey!

Responsible Travel, 01273 600030, www.responsibletravel.com

Discover the Andes

Location: Peru, Bolivia and Chile
Duration: 9 days. Price: £350

This is your chance to travel from the Andes to the Amazon. The route will take you from snow-capped mountains to pristine white beaches. It will combine vibrant cities and remote, indigenous communities. It will let you experience the magic of the Amazon rainforest, and the exhilaration of sand-boarding, ice climbing and trekking the Inca Trail. You'll even get to swim with the legendary pink river dolphin!

Quest Overseas, The North-West Stables, Borde Hill Estate, Balcombe Road, Haywards Heath, West Sussex, RH16 1XP, 01444 474744, www.questoverseas.com

💰💰💰 Experience South America

Location: Ecuador, Bolivia and Galapagos Islands
Duration: up to 5 months. Price: £5,699+

Spend five months or more on an amazing gap year in Latin America. This programme provides all the structure you need, with a host of activities, including Spanish lessons and volunteer projects with wildlife or disadvantaged street children.

This programme also includes a 39-day tour from Bolivia to Ecuador, and features all of the main highlights of the Andean region, including Machu Picchu, the Amazon, Lake Titicaca and Nazca Lines. There are also plenty of opportunities to do your own thing and explore this incredible region. You'll find these highlights included in the trip:

■ Education at the Bolivia Language School
■ Two to three organised activities per week, such as Bolivian cooking and salsa classes
■ An overland tour from La Paz to Quito
■ Tuition at the Ecuador Language School
■ Your choice of Ecuador volunteer project
■ A stay on the Galapagos Islands and four weeks helping on a Giant Tortoise project

At the end of your time, you'll feel at home in South America and you'll have an excellent grasp of the language. So whether you want to explore the ancient temples or get to know the local people, this is for you!
Real Gap Experience, First Floor, 1 Meadow Road, Tunbridge Wells, Kent, TN1 2YG, 01892 516164, www.realgap.co.uk

💰 Explore Venezuela by car

Location: Venezuela
Duration: 16 days. Price: £590+

This tour takes you on a journey along the western front of Venezuela, beginning in the Caribbean village of Choron on the northern coast and ending in the Llanos plains of the south, making stops in villages, national parks and the Andes mountains along the way. This trip can be tailor-made at a time to suit you, and it can also be adapted to suit your particular interests, budget and requirements as necessary. So forget about stressing over missed flights – on this break, you can just relax and enjoy yourself at your own pace.
Responsible Travel, 0870 0052 836, www.responsibletravel.com

◥ 💰 Teach music to street kids

Location: Ecuador
Duration: 6-12 months. Price: £1,250+

Teach music to the underprivileged children of Ecuador and not only will you get a real feeling of satisfaction as you watch them learn a musical instrument, but you'll also improve their social skills and English language knowledge – although an ability to speak Spanish is essential for this placement. You'll also get to live and work in stunning surroundings. For the musically talented – those of you with knowledge of music to Grade 5 – this could be the ideal placement!
GAP Activity Projects, 44 Queen's Road, Reading, Berkshire, RG1 4BB, 0118 9594914, www.gap.org.uk

◥ 💰 Help street children

Location: Argentina
Duration: 5-8 weeks. Price: £899+

Volunteers are needed to help in all aspects of daily activities, such as preparing meals, helping with homework and joining in the educational and cultural activities. This is an excellent opportunity to contribute directly to the education and social development of street children in Argentina, and it's a very rewarding experience that should be considered by gappers who want to help underprivileged children and communities.
Real Gap Experience, First Floor, 1 Meadow Road, Tunbridge Wells, Kent, TN1 2YG, 01892 516164, www.realgap.co.uk

◥ 💰 Market traditional arts

Location: Buenos Aires, Argentina
Duration: 5-8 weeks. Price: £859+

This is a unique volunteer placement. Although it involves working with people in Argentina, the focus is primarily on the promotion of art, culture and commerce. During the volunteer project, you'll work with an organisation that's responsible for promoting and organising work for local artistic designers. The overall goal is to develop a commercial chain that's active at a local and national level, while also helping to preserve traditional local art and culture.
Real Gap Experience, First Floor, 1 Meadow Road, Tunbridge Wells, Kent, TN1 2YG, 01892 516164, www.realgap.co.uk

⬎ 💰💰 Help Bolivian orphans

Location: Cochabamba, Bolivia
Duration: from 2 weeks. Price: £745+

This delightful town is surrounded by fields and valuable pre-Inca vestiges, and it occupies a fertile green bowl. Founded in 1574, it's also Bolivia's largest market town, which makes it very entertaining and lively! Travellers Worldwide works with many different orphanages in Bolivia – some are for very young kids and babies, while others for older children – and you'll have the opportunity to help needy kids of all ages.
Travellers Worldwide, 7 Mulberry Close, Ferring, West Sussex, BN12 5HY, 01903 502595, www.travellersworldwide.com

⬎ 💰 Learn Spanish or Portuguese

Location: Brazil or Guatemala
Duration: from 2 weeks. Price: £845+

Learn Spanish on a structured course in Guatemala, one of the most beautiful and culturally rich countries in Central America. You'll absorb the language while attending classes, and you'll hear it and speak it while shopping or socialising on a bus or in a restaurant. Alternatively, our Portuguese courses take place in both Rio de Janeiro, near the beach, and Foz do Iguaçu, close to Brazil's borders with Argentina and Paraguay.
Travellers Worldwide, 7 Mulberry Close, Ferring, West Sussex, BN12 5HY, 01903 502595, www.travellersworldwide.com

⬎ 💰 Help favela kids

Location: Rio de Janeiro, Brazil
Duration: 2-4 weeks. Price: £959+

This programme provides an excellent opportunity to do volunteer work in Brazil and help make a difference to the children from the favelas of Rio de Janeiro. The Community Education Centre offers full-time schooling and day care to about 400 children, from three months to 14 years old. The centre relies upon volunteer assistance, and so this rewarding placement will let you meet like-minded people from all over the world on working holidays, gap years and career breaks.
Real Gap Experience, First Floor, 1 Meadow Road, Tunbridge Wells, Kent, TN1 2YG, 01892 516164, www.realgap.co.uk

↘ 💰💰 Learn to play polo

Location: Buenos Aires, Argentina
Duration: 6-10 weeks. Price: £2,265+

On this gap year break, you'll get the chance to play polo at an amazing *estancia* close to Buenos Aires. You'll spend your mornings working alongside the *gauchos* (cowboys) with general stable work, while learning stick-and-balling, 'baby chukkas', and playing in matches. No previous experience of polo is necessary but you must be able to ride pretty well.

There's also plenty of time to sample traditional Argentinian hospitality, whether that's chilling out with the *gauchos* or going to parties in Buenos Aires. Top of the list is a visit to a high-goal tournament, as the Argentinian passion for this sport creates a tense and unforgettable atmosphere.

In addition to all this, you'll help the polo club by lending a hand and socialising with other guests. You'll also have the chance to learn Spanish by working alongside the *gauchos*, as well as enjoying tennis, golf, swimming, walking and cycling, exploring Buenos Aires and watching some of the world's best players competing in tournaments.

This isn't your typical gap year experience, but it's ideal for those who love sports and adventure. Whether you want to discover polo or improve your game, all while learning a new language and experiencing a different culture, this is the gap break for you.

The Leap, 121 High Street, Marlborough, Wiltshire, SN8 1LZ, 01672 519922, www.theleap.co.uk

↘ 💰 Learn to tango

Location: Buenos Aires, Argentina
Duration: from 2 weeks. Price: £795+

During this placement, you'll have lessons with a private tango teacher, who will tailor the programme to your individual level of expertise. In the first week, you'll be taken to see a tango show within the wonderful city of Buenos Aires. For the rest of your placement, you'll attend lessons with one of two private tango teachers. These lessons include three private tango classes per week, one group class per week and one Milonga – an open tango party where all levels mix together.

Travellers Worldwide, 7 Mulberry Close, Ferring, West Sussex, BN12 5HY, 01903 502595, www.travellersworldwide.com

➘ **CASE STUDY**

Who: Niamh Kennedy
Location: Brazil

Niamh's placement was in Recife, a large city in the north east. There she worked in a joint caring/schools placement, living with two very different families, both of whom she grew to love, especially as it meant she had a little sister!

For Niamh, one of the main things she'll always cherish about her trip is the time she spent with her host families. "The love and warmth they showed me is something that will stay with me forever. Nay and Rebecca are two of the most wonderful people that I've had the privilege of meeting."

Niamh worked in two very different centres. The first was in Cultura Inglesa, were she learnt the meaning of the word 'flexible' as the Conversation Club teacher. "My students ranged in age from five to 55. I was involved with the Fun Club for the younger students too. We got them to learn English through arts and crafts and games, which the children loved."

Niamh's second placement was very different. "Here, the kids' football was a bag filled with paper. One thing my placement taught me was the difference in the social situation. I went from teaching children that spent their free time in front of the PlayStation to children who wore the same clothes every day. Projeto Barnabe really gave me the chance to see the two heartbreaking realities of Brazil and the huge social divide."

Niamh taught a bit of English but spent most of her time playing with the children. "This wasn't a formal school, just a place where they could get a warm meal and get away from the favela. Their time was more recreational, but there was also an educational element.

"My time in Recife is one I'll always cherish, and the kindness of the people I met will stay with me forever. I learnt a lot and can now dance *forro* like a local, while my Portuguese is something to be proud of – but it still needs some work! And there's no question that I'll go back to Brazil.

❜
What I found took my breath away. The people and the culture completely engulfed me. You can't just live in Brazil – you have to live Brazil...
❜

"I arrived in Brazil completely unprepared for what I had to deal with. I hadn't truthfully thought of what to expect when I got there, and what I found there really took my breath away: the people and the culture completely engulfed me. You can't just live in Brazil – you have to live Brazil."

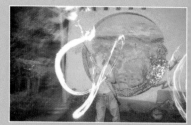
Experience the festivals and fiestas, including the famous Rio carnival.

South America is an unbeatable destination for football fanatics.

From rainforest and mountains to waterfalls, this area has it all.

Brazil's teeming cities are lively and exciting places to explore.

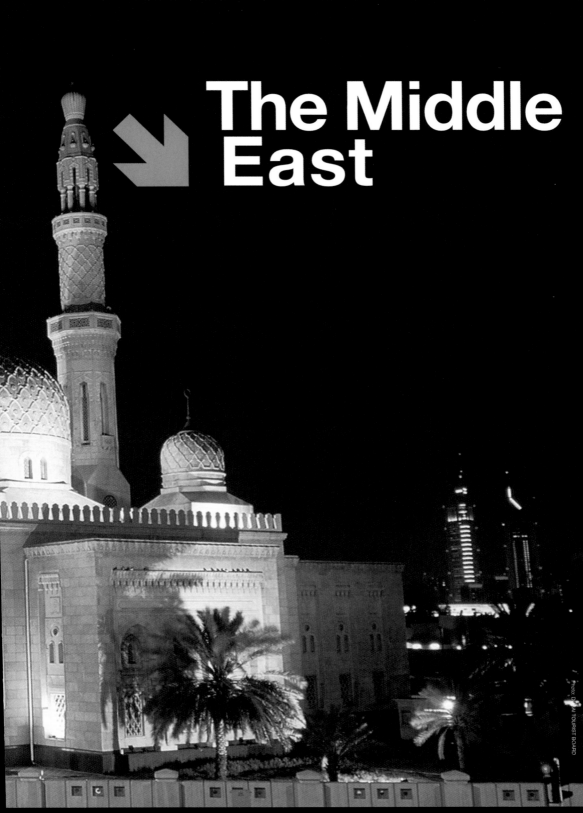

The Middle East

'Despite the fact that this may not be your traditional gap year destination, it could provide the most rewarding experience of your life'

Photo: INDIAN TOURIST BOARD

↘The Middle East

This historic region may be politically turbulent, but it offers a wealth of unique gap opportunities

The mystery and magic of the Middle East has been overshadowed in recent years by political instability and conflict. However, despite these tensions, there are still many intriguing regions that can be visited by the gapper.

Simply put, the Middle East is an area that brings the tales of Arabian nights to life: the air is full of spices, the cities full of antiquities and the bazaars are exotic. The birthplace of the world's greatest civilisations and religions, from the ancient hieroglyphics of Giza to the Syrian city of Damascus and Israel's Jerusalem, everything is interwoven with an air of mystique.

Against this backdrop, you can take a camel trek or climb the spectacular landscapes of Wadi Rum. The Red Sea is a haven for lovers of all things aquatic, while it's even possible to ski on the slopes in Beirut. Alternatively, you could try the overland journey from Istanbul to Cairo, which is truly unforgettable.

History buffs can join an archaeological dig – the region's colourful history means there's always one in progress – while there are numerous opportunities to teach and work with the local community.

Despite the fact that this may not be your traditional gap year destination, it could provide the most rewarding experience of your life, and you'll meet some of the most friendly and charismatic people on earth.

↘ TOP 5 DESTINATIONS

1

↘THE RED SEA

💰 **VISIT** Pharaoh's Island, the Coptic monasteries, the Emerald Mines, Sinai and some of the many temples.

💰💰 **SNORKLE**, play a round of golf or take an inland tour on a quad bike – there's a wealth of activities to try!

💰💰💰 **CRUISE** the Red Sea in style and then stop off at one of the many shoreline spas for a spot of pampering.

2

↘MOUNT SINAI

💰 **CLIMB** the slopes of Mount Sinai and watch the sun rise – there's a wide variety of tours available.

💰💰 **VISIT** the historic Moses Well, the Steps of Mount Moses and the Chapel of the Holy Trinity.

💰💰💰 **RETREAT** to St Catherine's Monastery, which is overshadowed by the towering Mount Sinai.

3

↗ WADI RUM

💰 **LIVE** like Lawrence of Arabia by hiking across Wadi Rum, a vast area of dry riverbeds, mountains, black hills and sand dunes. This beautiful, desolate area is located some 50 kilometres (30 miles) north-east of Aqaba.

💰💰 **STAY** with a genuine Bedouin tribe for a true taste of Middle Eastern life. Many of the tribespeople are thought to be descended from Mohammed, and most still live in the Wadi Rum valley in traditional tents.

💰💰💰 **JUMP** on the back of a camel and go for a trek in the desert. The less adventurous can take a jeep trip! Alternatively, you can experience a hot air balloon trip over Wadi Rum's spectacular Valley of the Moon.

4

↘PETRA

💰 **CLIMB** Petra's mountains to the High Place of Sacrifice, walk through the As-Siq gorge, climb 800 stairs to reach Ad-Deir Monastery, and walk the Street of Façades to the ancient amphitheatre, stopping off at the temples.

💰💰 **VISIT** Petra at night and marvel at the sight of a city lit by candlelight – it's an unforgettable experience. Tour the local market, sample some of the hearty traditional Jordanian cooking and haggle for some local crafts.

💰💰💰 **TOUR** Petra on a donkey or camel and then enjoy a guided tour of the site, accompanied by a local Bedouin. The members of this ancient tribe will be able to reveal all the secrets of this incredible place.

5

↘**CAIRO**

👛 **WANDER** the streets of Cairo, visit the Citadel and tour Coptic Cairo, stopping off at Ben Erza Synagogue, the Hanging Church and Abu Serga Church. Also, don't miss the Giza Pyramids and the world-famous Sphinx.

👛👛 **WATCH** the Giza Light Show, visit the Egyptian Museum, ride a camel around the pyramids, take time out to visit Sakkara Memphis, take the Cairo City tour, cruise down the Nile, and then finish off with a trip to Luxor.

👛👛👛 **CRUISE** down the Nile for four days, get fit on a belly dancing course, and take the Arabian Horse Riding tour so you can view the pyramids from horseback. Finally, take a two-week tour of Luxor, Aswan and Cairo.

1 Middle East

🔥 Overland tour

Spend 35 days travelling from Istanbul to Cairo via Turkey, Syria, Jordan and Egypt, taking in numerous sites of historical interest. See **www.overlandclub.com**
Price: £500

The Bedouin town of Dahab offers opportunities for diving and snorkelling. Inland, you can climb Mount Sinai. A visit to Cairo and the Pyramids marks the end of an unforgettable journey.

This expedition starts in Istanbul and from there you'll travel to Gallipoli and the straits of the Dardanelles. From Gallipoli, you'll follow the Mediterranean coast south to the legendary city of Troy and the magnificent ruins at Ephesus. Then it's on to Cappadocia to visit the spectacular Goreme Valley, before crossing into Syria. In Jordan, you can bathe in the buoyant Dead Sea and visit the rose-red city of Petra, before crossing the plains to reach the spectacular Wadi Rum desert.

2 Egypt

🔥 Epic journey

Visit the pyramids and Sphinx, Aswan and Luxor, cruise the Nile, see the Valley of the Kings and Queens, then tour Sinai, Dahab, Petra and Wadi Rum.

This incredible tour encompasses Egypt's greatest ancient sites. You can sail on a traditional felucca, chill out at the Red Sea resort of Dahab and cross into Jordan to visit Petra, before exploring Wadi Rum.

Duration: 17 days
Cost: £699
This is a fantastic way to see the most spectacular sites in this region, and it's a tour you'll never forget. For further details, see www. overlandclub.com

---

EGYPT

- **Area:** 997,739 sq km
- **Population:** 70.5 million
- **Capital:** Cairo
- **People:** 99% of the population are Eastern Hamitic (Egyptians, Bedouins and Berbers)

- **Languages:** Arabic, English and French
- **Currency:** Egyptian Pounds
- **Exchange rate:** £1 = E£10.24
- **Government:** Semi-presidential republic
- **Religion:** 90% are Muslim (mainly Sunni), and most others are Coptic Christians

3 Egypt
ŏŏŏ Learn to windsurf

The Pro Traineeship leads to qualification as a windsurf instructor and includes a post-qualification period of instructor development.

The course is designed to allow maximum time for developing your skills on the water, making it suitable for beginners and early intermediates who are happy to accept a steep learning curve

The first four weeks of training are based at Club Dahab, a high-performance windsurfing centre on the Red Sea. You'll stay at the beachfront Ganet Sinai Hotel. As a break from windsurfing, you'll be able to enjoy the world-class diving here. Weeks five to ten take place in a Mediterranean base, Club Vass, which is located in Greece.

Duration: 10 weeks. Price: £5,590
www.flyingfishonline.com

4 Israel
ŏ Live and work in a kibbutz

This is a great chance to live and work in a co-operative community while you learn Hebrew.
www.kibbutzprogram center.org
Price: £1,400+

Kibbutz Ulpanim offers five months of studying Hebrew, during which time you'll work on the kibbutz for three days a week to pay for your upkeep. The program also includes a number of trips and seminars, with some enrichment activities too.

5 Sinai desert
ŏ Experience a survival expedition

This break involves a three-week journey through the Sinai with the local Bedouin, combining trekking in the high mountain region, learning about team management and survival, and working on community-based projects for the Bedouin. You'll increase in confidence and gain a deeper understanding of other cultures and peoples, as well as getting an idea of what it means to work and live in a different and difficult environment. **www.responsibletravel.com**

Projects include working on a local garden regeneration within a mountain area. The tasks are chosen in conjunction with the Bedouin and are designed to ensure they meet a very real need.

Price: £1,390+

JORDAN

- **Area:** 89,213 sq km
- **Population:** 5.3 million
- **Capital:** Amman
- **People:** 98% are Arabic

- **Languages:** Arabic and English
- **Currency:** Jordanian Dinar
- **Exchange rate:** £1 = JD1.3
- **Government:** Constitutional monarchy
- **Religion:** 92% are Sunni Muslims

⬇💰 Study yoga in Egypt

Location: Egypt
Duration: from 8 days. Price: £375+

This eight-day yoga holiday is set in Dahab, an oasis on the Red Sea coast. One of Egypt's forgotten treasures, Dahab overlooks the second most extensive reef system in the world. Year-round warm water has led to the development of an ecosystem where clown fish play and elegant rays glide. As well as daily yoga and plenty of time relaxing on the beach, you can enjoy a trip to Mount Sinai, camping with Bedouins in the desert, scuba diving and camel trekking.
Responsible Travel, 0870 0052 836, www.responsibletravel.com

⬇💰 Journey through the desert

Location: Wadi Rum, Jordan
Duration: 10 days. Price: £1,045+

The desert between Wadi Rum and Petra is an awe-inspiring, lunar-like landscape. This is a history-filled region, with battles and revolutions reaching back as far as the Old Testament. The journey starts at Petra, a symbol of success that's still one of the wonders of the world, and finishes in Wadi Rum, scene of the Arab uprising of the 1920s that was championed by Lawrence of Arabia, and it's a trek you'll never forget.
Element Internet, Kensington Studios, Kensington Street, Brighton, BN1 4AJ, 01273 872242, www.adventuresportsholidays.com

⬇💰 Learn to dive in the Red Sea

Location: Red Sea, Egypt
Duration: from 7 days. Price: £355+

This is your chance to learn to dive in the Red Sea! Whatever your ability, you'll find it fascinating, with a number of fish unique to these waters. In addition to the diving, there are plenty of other activities to enjoy, such as windsurfing, camel riding, horse riding and quad bike trips. There's amazing scenery to explore, and there's a lot to be said for chilling out on the private beach and reading a good book under the palm trees! You'll be based a short walk from Dahab's central bay and the Bedouin village of Assalah.
Responsible Travel, 0870 0052 836, www.responsibletravel.com

↘💰 Discover the Middle East

Location: Jordan

Duration: 9 days. Price: £770+

The mountains and deserts of Jordan radiate a wild and desolate beauty all of their own. It's these sun-baked wadis and giant granite crags that Lawrence of Arabia describes in his *Seven Pillars of Wisdom* – the rock-hewn city of Petra, the sandy landscape of Wadi Rum and ancient Jerash. You'll be able to visit them all on this trip, and have time to enjoy the Red Sea too.

Beginning at Jerash, one of the most impressive Roman cities surviving anywhere, you'll travel via Umm Qais and Mount Nebo to Madaba, and then southwards along the legendary King's Highway towards Kerak. Here you can explore the castle of Kerak, which is imposingly sited on a crag overlooking the rocky desert.

Petra is one of the world's archaeological wonders. It's carved from a mountain of multi-coloured sandstone and you'll enjoy two days there: ample time to explore the hidden corners, including the vast monastery and the High Place, with its views of distant Wadi Araba.

Leaving Petra in 4WD vehicles, you'll push deep into the craggy desert and cliffs of Wadi Rum. This is 'Lawrence of Arabia' country, where you'll sleep in a Bedouin-style encampment under a star-filled desert sky. You can explore this majestic landscape by camel, before continuing on to the Red Sea coast, where you can unwind and snorkel over the coral reef.

Responsible Travel, 0870 0052 836, www.responsibletravel.com

↘💰 Enjoy a spa treatment and tour

Location: Jordan

Duration: 8 days. Price: £360+

On this trip you'll visit Jordan's spectacular sites, including Jerash, with its triple-arched gate, huge hippodrome and the only Roman forum surrounded by 63 ionic columns. Next comes Petra, the awesome 'rose-red city'. You'll then travel the King's Highway along Jordan's hilly backbone, before reaching the Dead Sea. There you can enjoy the bizarre sensation of floating on the surface of the buoyant waters and relax with three days of spa treatments and pampering.

Element Internet, Kensington Studios, Kensington Street, Brighton, BN1 4AJ, 01273 872242, www.adventuresportsholidays.com

NEW LIFE. NEW ZEALAND.

More space in every class.

Step on board an Air New Zealand flight and you'll find we've echoed the freedom, relaxation and personal space of New Zealand. With a choice of three new cabins, including one of the world's best lie-flat business seats for a greater sense of comfort and style in every class. And with a baggage allowance of up to 64kgs, plus cabin baggage, you'll be able to pack in a lot more. Fly direct from London to Auckland or Christchurch via Los Angeles, then on to 25 destinations in New Zealand. Visit our website to start your new life in style.

AIR NEW ZEALAND

A STAR ALLIANCE MEMBER

Bringing New Zealand clos

airnewzealand.co.uk/space

Progressively introduced for London flights from November 200

↘ 💰 Go caving in Oman
Location: Majlis al Jinns, Oman
Duration: 7-10 days. Price: £1,189
The descent into Majlis Al Jinns is an experience of a lifetime. Majlis Al Jinns is the second largest chamber in the world and the only way in is via a 180-metre abseil! This isn't an extreme package, though – anyone with an average fitness level can accomplish the descent as the training you'll receive ensures that you're ready to be inspired by the mysterious Majlis. You'll also get a chance to explore magical Oman.
Element Internet, Kensington Studios, Kensington Street, Brighton, BN1 4AJ, 01273 872242, www.adventuresportsholidays.com

↘ 💰 Trek the Spice Trail
Location: Jordan
Duration: 8 days. Price: £809+
On this journey along Jordan's spice trail, you'll see Petra, one of the most magnificent sites in the Middle East, and Wadi Rum, arguably Arabia's finest desert, and you'll have plenty of time to explore them in depth. As well retracing the steps of the ancient Nabateans and hiking through breathtaking siqs and wadis, you can also absorb some of the region's other attractions, from the Dead Sea to the preserved city of Jerash.
Element Internet, Kensington Studios, Kensington Street, Brighton, BN1 4AJ, 01273 872242, www.adventuresportsholidays.com

↘ 💰 Explore the Middle East
Location: Egypt, Jordan and Israel
Duration: 21 days. Price: £1,130
Enjoy this fabulous tour of some of the world's finest treasures. Highlights include the Pyramids of Giza and the Great Sphinx; Memphis and the step pyramid of Sakkara; plus the Egyptian Museum. You'll visit the temples at Karnak and Luxor before travelling to the Red Sea to enjoy some snorkelling in the Blue Hole. You can then climb Moses Mountain, cross into Israel and visit Jerusalem's Via Dolorosa. Next comes Petra and Wadi Rum, before you finish your trip in Cairo.
Element Internet, Kensington Studios, Kensington Street, Brighton, BN1 4AJ, 01273 872242, www.adventuresportsholidays.com

⬇ 💰 Tour Jordan's castles

Location: Jordan
Duration: 8 days. Price: £388+

On this tour, you'll visit Jerash, the city of 1,000 pillars, and view its Roman remains before travelling on to the Ashrafia mosque and King Hussein Sport City. After a sightseeing tour through Amman, you'll visit desert castles built by early Islamic Umayyad Caliphs in the seventh and eighth centuries. Qasr Amra, Qasr Kharaneh and Qasr Azraq are some of the best-preserved examples of Umayyad art and architecture, including castles, baths, mosques, water and agricultural systems, mosaic floors and frescoes.

Many highlights can be found along the King's Highway, one of the oldest trade routes in the world. You'll stop at the Byzantine church of Mount Nebo and then proceed to Madaba, where you'll see a unique map of Palestine. Afterwards, you'll reach the Dead Sea, the lowest spot on earth, where you can enjoy floating in the buoyant waters.

No visit to Jordan is complete without seeing Petra and its awesome treasury, and Wadi Rum, another of nature's wonderlands. Wadi Rum – the land of Lawrence of Arabia – is an unusual desert terrain and here you'll be able to enjoy a camel ride and jeep safari. This is an authentic Middle Eastern experience and one you won't forget in a hurry.

Element Internet, Kensington Studios, Kensington Street, Brighton, BN1 4AJ, 01273 872242, www.adventuresportsholidays.com

⬇ 💰 Enjoy an overland tour

Location: Egypt, Jordan, Syria and Turkey
Duration: 22 days. Price: £690+

This is an exciting adventure through the heart of the Arab world. From the land of the Pharaohs to modern Istanbul, via Jordan and Syria, you'll discover awesome deserts, colourful bazaars, crusader forts, fascinating cultures, beautiful beaches, underground cities and the incredible Dead Sea on this quintessential Middle Eastern adventure. Some of the other highlights include a tour of the incredible city of Cairo, snorkelling in the Red Sea, exploring the lost city of Petra, a Wadi Rum desert safari, and a visit to Cappadocia.

Responsible Travel, 0870 0052 836, www.responsibletravel.com

↘ 💰 Tour the Middle East

Location: Jordan, Lebanon and Syria
Duration: 16 days. Price: £999+

On this trip, you'll visit the atmospheric souk of Aleppo and the ancient city of Damascus; the beautiful hidden mountain monastery of Mar Moussa and the picturesque Qadisha Valley. The more active can swim in the Dead Sea, snorkel in the Red Sea and head into Wadi Rum for a night under the stars. You'll also see the magnificent city of Petra, the ruins of Palmyra, the Roman sites of Baalbek and Jerash, and the cathedral-like caves of Jeita, making this an amazing experience.
Responsible Travel, 0870 0052 836,
www.responsibletravel.com

↘ 💰 Discover Syria and Lebanon

Location: Syria and Lebanon
Duration: 11 days. Price: £745

On this expedition, you'll visit the museum, bazaars and breathtaking Umayyad Mosque in Damascus. Then it's on to Palmyra, the ancient site at Apamea and the acropolis at Baalbek. Krak des Chevaliers, the world's finest Crusader castle, whets the appetite for Saône and the ports of Tartus, Tripoli, Byblos and Sidon, while in Aleppo, you'll explore vaulted bazaars and stay in a historic hotel. You'll see mosaics at Maarat, explore the palace at Beit Eddine and end up in lively Beirut.
Peregrine Adventures, 0844 736 0170,
www.peregrineadventures.com

↘ 💰💰 Explore the western desert

Location: Egypt
Duration: 16 days. Price: £1,800

This is a great expedition for desert lovers, and you'll get to venture where few people have ever been. From Cairo, you'll travel to the oasis towns of Bahariya and Dakhla, before turning to the Gilf Kebir, a huge plateau with dozens of valleys. At Uweinat – a mysterious place made famous by *The English Patient* – you'll discover thousands of rock art images left by ancient nomads. You'll then head north to the Great Sand Sea, and you'll camp out under the stars. The trip ends at Siwa Oasis, before a return to Cairo.
Peregrine Adventures, 0844 736 0170,
www.peregrineadventures.com

⬇ 💰 Become a windsurfing instructor

Location: Dahab, Egypt
Duration: 10 weeks. Price: £1,149+

Egypt is a fantastic place to learn to windsurf. This Pro Traineeship leads to qualification as a windsurfing instructor and includes a post-qualification period of instructor development. You'll spend a huge amount of time developing your skills on the water, making it suitable for beginners and early intermediates who are happy to work hard and learn quickly.

The first four weeks of training are based at Club Dahab, which is a high-performance windsurfing centre located on the Red Sea, and you'll stay at the beachfront Ganet Sinai Hotel.

The programme includes training and assessment for the RYA Windsurfing Intermediate Instructor qualification. The instructor course is included at no extra charge for candidates who are already qualified at Start Windsufi ng Instructor level and have at least 50 hours of teaching experience.

As a break from windsurfing, you'll also find world-class diving here, while quad biking is also available, camels are plentiful and you can play volleyball. If that's not enough for you, Mount Sinai is easily accessible, you can arrange a trip to Cairo and the pyramids, and Mazbat is only ten minutes away by taxi, meaning it's easy to shop, eat out or party – if you can get away from the fantastic Club Dahab bar, that is!

Flying Fish, 25 Union Road, Cowes, Isle of Wight, PO31 7TW, 0871 250 2500, www.flyingfishonline.com

⬇ 💰 Learn survival skills in Sinai

Location: Sinai desert, Egypt
Duration: 3 weeks. Price: £1,390+

This expedition is a journey through Sinai with a local Bedouin, combining trekking in the high mountain region, learning about team management and survival, and working on community-based projects for the Bedouin people. This programme helps to create a deeper understanding of other cultures and peoples, and provides an idea of what it means to work and live in a very different and difficult environment. Projects include such tasks as local garden regeneration within the mountain area, and all meet a very real need.

Responsible Travel, 0870 0052 836,
www.responsibletravel.com

Off the beaten track, but not off ours.

With an international network spanning 83 destinations and an unparalleled service to more than 60 Australian cities, no one covers Australia better. So wherever you want to go to get away from it all we can take you. That's the Spirit. Phone 0845 7747 767 or visit your local travel agent. **The Spirit of Australia.**

qantas.co.uk

QANTAS

◥ 💰 Learn to scuba dive

Location: Red Sea, Egypt
Duration: 8 days. Price: £320+

If you're looking to learn scuba diving, where better than among the coral reefs in the warm and clear waters of the Gulf of Aqaba? Virtually anybody in general good health and fitness can learn to dive, making this course suitable for all, and the dive centre here is the ideal place to learn. It has two large classrooms (plus tables outside for outdoor sessions) and these have all the video and audio facilities, instructional materials and manuals required to teach the various PADI courses that are on offer here.

The PADI Open Water course is taught by experienced and qualified diving instructors, who all have a laid-back attitude and make learning fun. It takes four days, during which time you'll learn the fundamentals of scuba diving, including basic theory, with skill practice in a confined area of the sea and four open-water dives. You'll finish this experience with four recreational dives on sites such as Eel Gardens, The Islands, Coral Gardens or even The Canyon.

Accommodation is on a B&B basis in a hotel on the northern side of Dahab's seafront, about 15 minutes' walk from the dive centre. This new hotel is designed with a Bedouin ambience, offering clean rooms with en-suite bathrooms, balcony and fantastic sea views, making it the perfect base for this break.
Responsible Travel, 0870 0052 836,
www.responsibletravel.com

◥ 💰 Learn Arabic in Cairo

Location: Cairo, Egypt
Duration: 4 weeks. Price: £333+

Home to the famous pyramids, Cairo is one of the world's most ancient and historically significant cities. A vibrant and colourful metropolis, it offers a fascinating combination of Arabic and western culture. You can discover the hidden side of Cairo in the back streets of Khan el-Kalili, with its charming souks, before exploring the new town, with its gleaming shop windows. Weave your way through the chaotic markets and gaze at the palaces and mosques. Learning Arabic in Cairo has a significant advantage as Egyptian colloquial Arabic is the most widely understood dialect in the Middle East.
STA Travel, 0870 1630 026, www.statravel.co.uk

Snorkelling in the Red Sea is an experience kids of all ages will love.

↘ **CASE STUDY**

Who: Jo Wise and family
Location: Egypt

Jo was keen to take a break and wanted to visit the pyramids of Egypt with her young family. A trip with Responsible Travel proved to be the perfect choice...

Jo Wise decided she wanted more from her family holidays than a standard package, or a sterile world of crèches and kiddies' clubs. She wanted her children to get up close and personal with the pyramids and Tutankhamun, and so she chose to book a tour with Responsible Travel. Not only would she get to see both the pyramids and King Tut's gold, but she'd also sail on a felucca, see the Valley of the Kings and swim among the fishes in the Red Sea.

"I'm reborn! It was simply the best experience I've ever had! Of the organised activities, the felucca trip was a real highlight as it was so fantastic seeing my kids playing with the local children on the boat and at the Nubian village. For the kids, the donkey trek and camel rides were favourites.

"Without a doubt, the whole experience was made unforgettable by our tour leader, Hatem. Our group was small – only two families – which meant we were spoilt in terms of attention. Hatem really made us feel like friends rather than clients – so much so that both my eldest son and myself were reduced to tears at the thought of never seeing him again!"

So what would Jo's main recommendations be for anyone else taking a family tour? "Take modest clothing for any females

in your family, eat lots of falafel and fried aubergine, make time for a cheap windsurfing lesson at Hurgada and get a simple book on ancient Egyptian gods for the kids – it makes them much more interested in the temples! Get some small notes (especially €1) for the toilet attendants, and then just sit back, relax and enjoy the ride."

'I have no hesitation in recommending a family tour – it whet's the kids' appetites for experiencing different cultures in a fun and safe environment'

When asked how many stars she'd give her holiday, her response was, "Definitely 5! Not only did taking a responsible travel holiday benefit the local people and minimise the effect on the environment, but we enjoyed it and can't wait to book another trip. I have no hesitation in recommending these family trips to anyone who enjoyed independent travel before children and who wants to whet their kids' appetites for experiencing different cultures in a fun and safe environment."

The guides on the tour provide a personal and friendly service.

The donkey trek proved to be really popular with Jo's kids!

Camel trekking is an unmissable part of any Middle Eastern experience.

⬦ 💰 Live and work in a kibbutz

Location: Israel
Duration: 5 months. Price: £1,400+

The epitome of gap year travel to the Middle East, this is a great opportunity to live and work in a co-operative community while you learn modern Hebrew. Kibbutz Ulpanim offers five months of language study and allows you to work on the kibbutz for three days a week to pay for your upkeep. The program also includes occasional trips, seminars and enrichment activities. This is the ideal way to learn about the Hebrew lifestyle and to integrate into the Jewish community while learning the language and meeting other students.
www.kibbutzprogramcenter.org

⬦ 💰💰 Study and volunteer in Israel

Location: Israel
Duration: 6 months. Price: varies

Sherut Laam enables college graduates to work in their own field of expertise in Israel. After four months of working and learning Hebrew in a kibbutz, you'll work for six months in a non-profit organisation related to your profession. Previous volunteers have done social work, teaching, film editing, photography, archaeology, diving, computing and human rights work. The programme also offers seminars and trips.
Student Affairs Co-ordinator, Jewish Agency, Aliyah Department, 741 High Road, London, N12 0BQ, 0208 3695220, aliyah@jazouk.org

⬦ 💰 Search for the Arabian leopard

Location: Oman
Duration: 2 weeks. Price: £1,190+

On this expedition, you'll conduct a survey of Arabian leopards, as well as its possible prey species, such as feral goats. You'll also survey the mountains for water holes as possible hotspots of leopard movement, and conduct interviews with local people in an effort to establish whether the Arabian leopard survives in the rugged mountains of the Musandam peninsula. Nothing is known about its status and distribution here – while historical accounts tell of a leopard presence in the area, no scientific survey has yet been conducted.
Responsible Travel, 0870 0052 836,
www.responsibletravel.com

⬇ 💰 Protect the Red Sea

Location: Red Sea, Egypt
Duration: from 4 weeks. Price: 1,450+

This is your chance to play your part in the long-term survival of the coral reefs of the Red Sea and the Gulf of Aqaba, which are under increasing pressure from tourism and development. Working alongside the National Parks of Egypt and their volunteer scheme, you'll establish baseline data and identify areas in need of protection, helping to promote eco-awareness and appropriate behaviour in this fragile environment.

The first three weeks of the programme are based in Dahab, where you'll undergo an intensive training programme to develop your technical diving skills. You'll get to your survey site by jeep, boat or camel. Some of the sites are remote so you may have to carry your supplies in with you and camp overnight. Generally, though, you'll return to base to log the information you've collected on the computer.

Depending on the length of your stay, you may also have the opportunity to work with local inhabitants and dive schools in and around Dahab, discussing the issues that face the reef and how individuals can play their part in protecting it. The working week is flexible but in general, it's eight hours a day for five days a week. This is a challenging project, but the more effort you put in, the more you'll get from your experience.
Work and Volunteer, 0800 80 483 80,
www.workandvolunteer.com

⬇ 💰 Teach English to refugees

Location: Lebanon
Duration: varies. Price: £400

Unipal is a charity that sends British volunteers to Lebanon to spend a summer teaching English to the children in Palestinian refugee camps. They welcome applications from anyone who has an interest in working with children, learning more about the Middle East and forming some very special friendships. You'll live and work in refugee camps, running summer projects in UN schools in the mornings and working on community projects, such as adult education, in the afternoons. This is a thoroughly rewarding – and sometimes challenging – experience.
Unipal, info@unipal.org.uk, www.unipal.org.uk

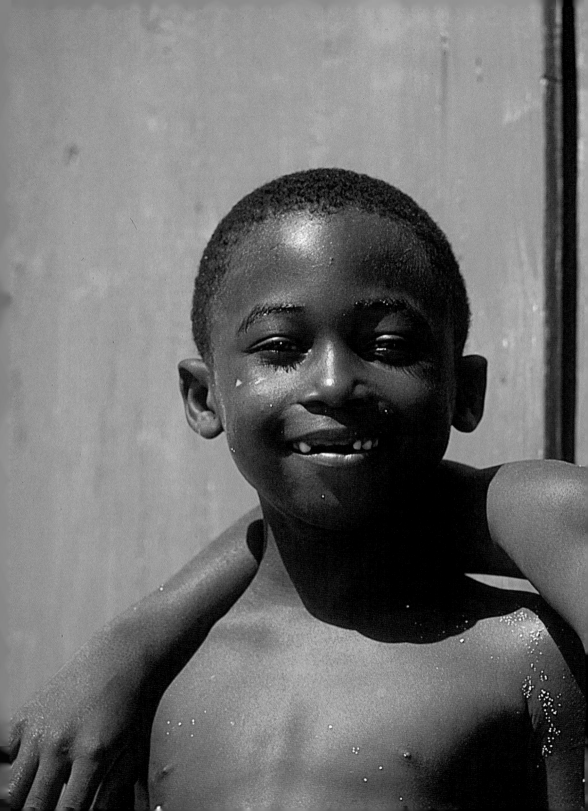

North
America

‘You’ll be bowled over by its natural wonders, from the wilds of the Canadian Rockies and Niagara Falls to the Florida everglades and the amazing volcanic landscape of Hawaii’

↘ North America & the Caribbean

From the bustle of New York to the wilderness of Alaska, this is the place to fulfil your American Dream

Stretching from northern Alaska down to the long, sandy beaches of the Caribbean, the sheer scale of this awesome continent can be hard to grasp. While you may think you know North America, scratch the surface and you'll be surprised at what you find. You can do everything from exploring the vast expanses of the Grand Canyon and the backpacker's paradise of Yellowstone Park to diving in the crystal clear waters of the Caribbean.

America and Canada are ambitious, commercialised countries, where everyone and everything seems big, shiny and new. While the America Dream may be an outdated concept, this remains the place to pursue your wildest fantasies. While you won't find the landscape littered with romantic medieval castles or gothic architecture, you'll still be bowled over by its natural wonders, from the wilds of the Canadian Rockies to the amazing volcanic landscape of Hawaii.

In stark contrast is the relaxing, sun-filled and rum-soaked paradise of the Caribbean. The ultimate island experience, it's a nirvana for the watersports enthusiast. The people of these islands take the meaning of 'chilled out' to new levels, and whether you decide to pursue aquatic, conservation or sporting activities, you'll find that everything you do is played out to the distinctive reggae rhythm.

↘ SAN FRANCISCO

💰 MARVEL at the hi-tech skyscrapers of the financial centre, soak up the Oriental ambience of Chinatown, see the city from the famous cable cars, admire the San Francisco murals and walk across the Golden Gate bridge.

💰💰 EAT out at Fisherman's Wharf, now a centre for Italian fish restaurants, spend the night dancing in Little Italy (aka North Beach), take a tour round Alcatraz Island, rent a boat at Stow Lake and visit the Exploratorium.

💰💰💰 SHOPAHOLICS won't be disappointed by the range of shops, arts lovers can enjoy an evening at the theatre or music hall, you can visit opulent Nob Hill, or take a day trip to San Jose and the famous Silicon Valley.

2

➘ THE CARIBBEAN

💰 **PLAY** cricket on the beach, luxuriate on the golden sands and swim in the crystal clear waters. You can then watch the sun set while enjoying a drink on the beach, before dancing the night away to the relaxed reggae beat.

💰💰 **VISIT** Bermuda Zoo, Aquarium and Natural History Museum, take a tour round the islands by ferry, go fly fishing, scuba diving or snorkelling, see the Bob Marley musuem and YS Falls in Jamaica, and try the local rum.

💰💰💰 **ENJOY** a round of golf on the many Caribbean island courses, and take a helicopter tour over the islands. Alternatively, you can go for a more sedate option and enjoy a relaxing cruise around these beautiful waters.

3

NORTHWEST TERRITORIES, CANADA

VISIT the many historical sites, churches and museums, travel along the Idaa Trail, meet the northern aboriginal people, make traditional arts and crafts and take a day hike, boat trip or road tour around the area.

KAYAK the rivers of this region, go fly or ice fishing, hike or backpack through the territories, stopping off at one of the many wildlife sancturaries, and then indulge in a bit of bird spotting or take a snowmobile ride.

TAKE an aurora vacation, combining it with dogsled rides, ice fishing and caribou viewing, take a dogsled tour through the arctic to spot rare wildlife, or hire a bush plane and tour this awe-inspiring region from the air.

Photo: Kate Dirasio / flickr.com

4

↘CUBA

💰 **WALK** the streets of bohemian Old Havana, wander the Vinales Valley park, luxuriate on Varadero beach, visit the Museum of the Revolution and watch the Castillo de San Carlos de la Cabana fire its cannon at night.

💰💰 **EXPLORE** the many nature reserves, especially the Isla de la Juventud with its Indian cave paintings, diving spots and local wildlife, then see the Revolution Plaza and national museum, and the Capitolio's planetarium.

💰💰💰 **DANCE** at the famous Club Tropicana, stop off at La Bodeguita del Medio for a cigar and tequila, tour the Fabrica de Tobaco Partges cigar factory and round it all off with a game of golf at the 18-hole Varadero club.

5

⬊THE GRAND CANYON

💰 **STAND** and admire the incredible 360-degree views, walk the rim of the Grand Canyon, watch the wildlife, admire the Colorado river and then visit the National Park Museum, as well as the Tusayan ruins and museum.

💰💰 **TAKE** a guided tour by horseback or – if brave – by foot. You can then see the scenery from the river with a white-water rafting experience or take a donkey ride to Cape Royal and watch the sun set over the canyon.

💰💰💰 **FLY** over the canyon and enjoy spectacular views of the Havasu Canyon waterfalls, indulge in a luxury adventure tour, stay overnight at a working ranch and dine out in style while enjoying the spectacular views.

READY TO LEAVE ®

Rucksacks

Sleeping Bags

Guide Books

Torches

Medical Kits

Luggage

Penknives

Tents

Adapters

THE GAP YEAR TRAVEL STORE
WWW.READYTOLEAVE.COM

1 Florida

♦ Help animals

When exotic animals are victims of abuse or neglect, they're offered lifetime care by this sanctuary to prevent them from being put down. You can escape the stress of everyday life and enjoy the healing atmosphere of this rural setting.

Everyone pitches in to perform duties such as sorting and cutting up fruit for the fruit bats and monkeys, feeding the animals and cleaning their enclosures, building improved habitats and maintaining the grounds.
Duration: 4-12 weeks
Price: £970+

Training provided

Full training will be given in all aspects of animal care for this project. The sanctuary looks after a wide variety of animals and will do its best to focus each individual's time on the areas that interest them the most. You'll learn about the issues surrounding exotic animals in captivity and the extent of the commitment required to ensure a lifetime of quality care for them. You'll also be taught to understand the behaviours and methods of communication of each species, as well as their natural history.
See page 244, or visit www.gvi.co.uk

2 Caribbean

♦ Learn to surf

Located close to Caberete on the north coast of the Dominican Republic, this is the ideal course for anyone with a passion for surfing. You'll develop your skills while enjoying the famous Caribbean hospitality.

Anyone with a passion for blue seas and white sandy beaches will not only get the chance to develop and improve their surfing skills, but also learn all there is to know about the surf business in one of the world's premier watersports destinations.
www.i-to-i.com

You'll learn to surf to a high standard, discover how to instruct others, and experience the behind-the-scenes elements of running a successful surf school, from organising lessons and working in the shop to building the boards.
Duration: 4-12 weeks
Price: £795+

USA

- **Area:** 9.6 million sq km
- **Population:** 300 million
- **Capital:** Washington
- **People:** 82% white, 13% black, plus Asian, Amerindian, Alaskan, Hawaiian and others
- **Languages:** English (Spanish also widely spoken)
- **Currency:** US dollar
- **Exchange rate:** £1 = US$1.9
- **Government:** Constitution-based federal republic
- **Religion:** 52% Protestant, 24% Roman Catholic, plus Mormon, Jewish, Muslim and others

3 USA
💰💰 Survival training

This is your chance to leave the modern world behind and experience true survival training as you take on this challenge with one of the US's leading experts in outdoor survival skills.

Training takes place in the awe-inspiring canyons of southern Utah. This region contains 45 state parks, combining heritage and dramatic scenery, and with a host of activities to pursue, it's ideal for outdoor enthusiasts.

This placement enables you to explore the desert washes and mountain trails armed with little more than a knife, a water bottle, a blanket and a poncho. These courses keep in line with GVI's philosophy of conservation and allow you to really get back to nature, where you'll discover an unparalleled experience in survival training. Note that you'll need to be physically fit for this expedition as it will involve hikes of up to 30 miles in a day.
Duration: 14-28 days. Price: £950-£1,850
See page 241 for details, or visit www.gvi.co.uk

4 Florida
💰💰💰 Learn to fly

Take to the clear blue skies of Florida as you progress towards your Joint Aviation Authorities (JAA) Private Pilot Licence.
www.theinternational academy.com

You'll be working with first-class instructors to gain your pilot's licence, and you can opt for a four-week group training course, or a more intensive two-week personalised programme.
Duration: 2-4 weeks
Price: £5,250+
See page 242 for details

5 Canada
💰💰💰 Become a ski instructor

Crystal is a specialist provider of instructor training courses, co-ordinated in partnership with the resident ski and snowboard schools in various world class resorts. These courses provide you with the chance to develop and enhance your technical and teaching skills, while also gaining recognised instructor qualifications. The courses are open to people of various standards, abilities, ages and backgrounds, and they enable you to train and qualify on some of the world's finest slopes, such as Whistler-Blackcomb and Banff/Lake Louise, where you'll be able to gain CSIA, CASI or NZSIA qualifications.

Packages and prices vary from one programme to another. A sample price for a five-week ski or snowboard course in Banff/Lake Louise is £4,390; the 12-week course costs £6,650.
Take a look at www.the internationalacademy. com, or see page 242 for further information

JAMAICA

- **Area:** 10,991 sq km
- **Population:** 2.7 million
- **Capital:** Kingston
- **People:** 91% African, 1.3% East Indian, plus Chinese and others
- **Languages:** English and Patois

- **Currency:** Jamaican dollar
- **Exchange rate:** £1 = JD$120
- **Government:** Constitutional parliamentary democracy
- **Religion:** Anglican, Baptist, Protestant, Roman Catholic, Seventh Day Adventists, Rastafarian and others

GET ACTIVE

💰 Have an Alaskan adventure

Location: Alaska, USA
Duration: 15 days. Price: £1,290

This is a fantastic chance to enjoy two weeks of active adventure in the most pristine wilderness in North America. You'll be able to spot bears, whales and moose as you hike through the world-famous rugged mountain landscapes of Alaska and the Yukon, which is as dramatic and unspoiled a landscape as you'll find anywhere in the world. Activities include rafting on world-class rivers, walking on glaciers and ice climbing.

Gap Adventures, Matrix Studios, 91 Peterborough Road, Fulham, London, SW6 3BU, 0870 999 0144, www.gapadventures.com

💰 Discover Navajo culture

Location: Canyon de Chelly, USA
Duration: 8 days. Price: £730

Hike into Navajo history on this expedition through Canyon de Chelly, one of the best-kept secrets of the US south-west. You'll travel with a Navajo guide through the dramatic red rock spires that inspired creation stories, while your evenings will be filled with traditional song and drum shows, Navajo cooking, and stories passed down for generations, all enjoyed around the campfire.

Gap Adventures, Matrix Studios, 91 Peterborough Road, Fulham, London, SW6 3BU, 0870 999 0144, www.gapadventures.com

💰 Explore Vancouver Island

Location: Vancouver, USA
Duration: 13 days. Price: £950

Discover the highlights of the amazing Vancouver Island on this incredible 13-day adventure. You'll travel through stunning coastal islands to Victoria, learn the subtle skills of sea kayaking around Quadra Island, and go surfing in the beautiful Pacific Rim National Park, near Tofino, where you can hone your skills on the fantastic waves. This is the perfect opportunity to see for yourself why this area has become such a mecca for outdoor sports lovers from around the world.

Gap Adventures, Matrix Studios, 91 Peterborough Road, Fulham, London, SW6 3BU, 0870 999 0144, www.gapadventures.com

⬇ 💰 **Enjoy sports in the Rockies**

Location: Rocky Mountains, Canada
Duration: 14 days. Price: £1,120

This is your chance to enjoy an amazing two-week active adventure in the Canadian Rocky Mountains. You'll be able to raft down class IV rivers, hike to immense glaciers, cycle through remote parks and travel high into the Rocky alpine. The stunning mountain scenery will provide the perfect backdrop to whatever sport you're enjoying.

Your trip starts in Calgary, and you can explore this city before departing for a trip up the Ice fields Parkway. In this beautiful landscape, you'll be able to spot bears, mountain goats, elk and deer. After a stop at Lake Louise and Peyto Lake, you'll go white-water rafting down the Kakwa river.

This is followed by a stay in Mt Revelstoke National Park before two days of thrilling mountain biking adventures with an expert guide. After that, it's on to Roger's Pass in Glacier National Park, and a hike to Kootenay National Park, where you can relax in a wood-fired hot tub. This will be very welcome before a 3,000-metre ascent into the Rockies, where you can try First Nation activities such as drumming circles and a sweat lodge. You'll learn about First Nation culture and even get to sleep in a tepee! Finally, you'll head back to Calgary for a farewell dinner.

Gap Adventures, Matrix Studios, 91 Peterborough Road, Fulham, London, SW6 3BU, 0870 999 0144, www.gapadventures.com

⬇ 💰 **Explore western Canada**

Location: Canada
Duration: 14 days. Price: £1,175

Discover the best of the west! On this fascinating expedition across Canada, you'll begin in the exciting city of Vancouver, where you'll have plenty of time to look around. You'll then head out to ranch country before climbing the Rockies. You'll be able to see postcard-famous Revelstoke, Kootenay, Banff, Jasper and the dramatic Ice fields Parkway, and you can even walk on a living glacier. You'll finish your trip in cowboy Calgary, which is the home of the Stampede.

Gap Adventures, Matrix Studios, 91 Peterborough Road, Fulham, London, SW6 3BU, 0870 999 0144, www.gapadventures.com

⬇ 💰 **Take an Arctic journey**

Location: Greenland, Canada and the USA

Duration: 13 days. Price: £1,485

This is an epic journey that takes in some of this region's most spectacular sights. The southerly route takes you from western Greenland, past Baffin Island, to the least visited and hardest to access area of coast of northern Labrador. Here, the Torngat Mountains greet the Atlantic Ocean with ferocity, making this one of the most breathtaking landscapes in all of Canada.

Guided expeditionary stops and Zodiac cruises along Labrador's coast will allow time for wildlife viewing and photography, as well the chance to uncover the hidden mysteries of Labrador's intriguing history. Investigating the Norse past of the region, you'll visit L'Anse aux Meadows, which is the only authenticated Viking site in the whole of North America.

It's then on to Boyd's Cove, an area that was visited by both Palaeo-Eskimo and Maritime Archaic people 2,100-2,700 years ago. Bonavista Bay's rolling hills and sheltered inlets have supported human existence since the days of the Beothuk and early European settlers, and today it's home to six of Canada's nine species of seal, as well as the peculiar yet curious pilot whale. After that, you can settle into Newfoundland where you can enjoy the company of some of Canada's friendliest folks, who live in perfect harmony with the sea.

Gap Adventures, Matrix Studios, 91 Peterborough Road, Fulham, London, SW6 3BU, 0870 999 0144, www.gapadventures.com

⬇ 💰 **Explore Newfoundland**

Location: Newfoundland

Duration: 12 days. Price: on application

This active adventure enables you to fully explore the remote beauty and rich culture that the island of Newfoundland has to offer. From its craggy highlands and snaking inlets to the beautiful glacial landscapes and world-famous views of the ocean, there's always something to take your breath away. On this trip, you'll have the chance to enjoy biking and sea kayaking against the ever-changing backdrop of stunning and inspiring scenery.

Gap Adventures, Matrix Studios, 91 Peterborough Road, Fulham, London, SW6 3BU, 0870 999 0144, www.gapadventures.com

↘ CASE STUDY

Who: Helen Dunbar
Location: Greenland

Helen spent four unforgettable weeks on an epic adventure in the wilderness of Greenland, where she climbed glaciers and mountains, learnt survival skills and spotted some of the wildlife, such as arctic foxes, hares and whales.

The beautiful scenery in Greenland is sure to take your breath away.

During the first two days of her gap break in Greenland, Helen stayed at a base camp to complete training in the use of firearms, crevasse rescue, walking while roped up and polar bear attack procedure. This might not sound like everyone's idea of a fun gap break, but Helen loved being out in the wilds of the country, learning how to survive on the desolate but beautiful glaciers.

"Camp was established on various nunataks high above Kalkdal valley, giving spectacular views over the ice cap, and sightings of arctic hares. I saw bowhead whales swimming up the fjord one morning, which was an amazing sight.

"While on the ice, I learnt how to stop myself sliding down the snow. This was fun as it involved flinging myself down a steep hill head first, feet first, on my back, on my front, and then sideways! The rocks at the bottom of the slope provided an excellent incentive to stop."

Of course, living in such challenging conditions also had its downsides. "Once we camped for three days on the snow. This proved to be difficult as there was no water supply, and so snow had to be melted every time water was needed."

Living on the glaciers was also not without its dangers. "On our way back to base camp, a member

of my group pulled a ligament in her ankle and couldn't walk. With about 10 kilometres to go, and with only one lunch pack left for food, we made very slow progress. This was the day I learnt invaluable teamwork skills as every member had to work together continuously."

As well as working as a team, Helen also got to spend 24 hours alone in the wilderness. "I used this time for poignant introspection, which you rarely have a chance to do in modern life."

Walking across glaciers gave Helen the chance to enjoy the views.

❝

I had many unforgettable experiences and learnt many new skills. Each day brought new adventures, which I otherwise wouldn't have had the opportunity to experience ❞

Helen found her break was a life-changing experience. "During my four weeks in Greenland, I had so many unforgettable experiences and I learnt so many new skills. Each day brought new adventures, which I otherwise wouldn't have had the opportunity to experience."

If you want to get away from it all, Greenland is the place to go!

Helen poses rather precariously in front of an awe-inspiring landscape.

💰 Explore the west coast

Location: Western USA
Duration: 7 days. Price: £430+

This tour provides you with a quick taste of the best that western USA has to offer. You'll visit the area's two most important national parks, Yosemite and the Grand Canyon, as well as the incomparable city of Las Vegas. You can also explore the beauty and desert splendour of the Colorado River region, all of which is sandwiched between America's loveliest city, San Francisco, and its most unique, Los Angeles.

Real Gap Experience, First Floor, 1 Meadow Road, Tunbridge Wells, Kent, TN1 2YG, 01892 516164, www.realgap.co.uk

💰 Discover the east coast

Location: Eastern USA
Duration: 7 days. Price: £349+

The Freedom Trail offers you the chance to take an unforgettable tour of the highlights of the east coast, where you'll be able to explore everything from historic cities to the Appalachian Mountains. There are quaint towns with friendly locals, modern, dynamic cities and amazing natural wonders, such as the awe-inspiring and world-famous Niagara Falls. On this trip, you can really get a taste of this incredible region.

Real Gap Experience, First Floor, 1 Meadow Road, Tunbridge Wells, Kent, TN1 2YG, 01892 516164, www.realgap.co.uk

💰 Experience the USA

Location: USA
Duration: 35 days. Price: £1,334+

Experience the down-home charm of the Deep South, visit the nation's capital, Washington DC, the canyons of the desert south-west, the beaches and sunshine of Florida and discover the nightlife, national parks and wildlife of the west. On this epic expedition, you'll travel through 17 states, enabling you to get a real taste of the different areas and cultures of North America. You'll take in the most exciting cities and most spectacular scenery on a journey you'll never forget.

Real Gap Experience, First Floor, 1 Meadow Road, Tunbridge Wells, Kent, TN1 2YG, 01892 516164, www.realgap.co.uk

Tour the Pacific Coast

Location: Pacific Coast, USA
Duration: 28 days. Price: £1,127

On this Pacific Coast and national park tour, you can explore the three major mountain ranges of the American west: the Sierra Nevada, Cascades and Rocky Mountains. You'll also have the chance to visit the Yosemite, Yellowstone, Olympic and Redwood national parks, among others. Optional extra activities include everything from mountain biking to riding sand buggies and taking a limo trip through Las Vegas.

Real Gap Experience, First Floor, 1 Meadow Road, Tunbridge Wells, Kent, TN1 2YG, 01892 516164, www.realgap.co.uk

Take a trailblazer tour

Location: Across the US and Canada
Duration: 64 days. Price: £2,415

On this grand 64-day tour, you'll visit 29 US states and two Canadian provinces, with stops in both quaint towns and large cities. You can explore this continent's breathtaking national parks and unspoilt scenery on this once in a lifetime adventure. The trek has been designed to run at a consistent but relaxed pace, with plenty of free days built into the itinerary so you can pursue your personal interests.

Real Gap Experience, First Floor, 1 Meadow Road, Tunbridge Wells, Kent, TN1 2YG, 01892 516164, www.realgap.co.uk

Circumnavigate Newfoundland

Location: Newfoundland
Duration: 10 days. Price: £1,300

What better way to see a place so shaped by the sea than by ship? This is a great opportunity to explore the beautiful islands of Newfoundland and Labrador with a full circumnavigation. The warmth, wit and hospitality of these regions' people, the soul-stirring traditional music and the rough beauty of her shores draw a huge number of visitors each year, but this is the most exciting way to discover the best that Newfoundland and Labrador have to offer.

Gap Adventures, Matrix Studios, 91 Peterborough Road, Fulham, London, SW6 3BU, 0870 999 0144, www.gapadventures.com

💰 Learn to run a surf school

Location: Dominican Republic, Caribbean
Duration: 4-12 weeks. Price: £795+

There are many gap breaks that can teach you how to surf or improve your board skills, but this is a rare opportunity to not only become a better surfer, but also to learn everything you need to know to run a successful surfing business.

You'll be based close to Caberete on the beautiful north coast of the Dominican Republic, where you can enjoy the fantastic waves. This is an area of blue seas and white sandy beaches, making it the ideal place to develop your surfing skills. With the help and advice of the world-class instructors, you'll soon learn to surf to a very high standard.

When you're out of the water, you'll be able to fully integrate into the Caribbean way of life in a welcoming, relaxing and rewarding environment. You can meet the friendly local people and enjoy the reggae beats of this popular and breathtakingly beautiful island.

As well as improving your surfing, you'll also be taught how to effectively instruct others, and you'll even experience the behind-the-scenes elements of running a surf school, where you'll discover everything from organising lessons to working in the shop and building your own boards. This is a comprehensive package for any surf lovers, and if you've ever dreamt of giving up the day job and spending your days surfing in the warm ocean, this really is an unmissable opportunity.
i-to-i, 0870 333 2332, www.i-to-i.com

↘ 💰💰💰 Become a ski instructor

Location: Canada
Duration: 5-12 weeks. Price: £4,395+

This placement gives you the opportunity to develop and enhance your technical and teaching skills while gaining recognised instructor qualifications. People of various standards, abilities, ages and backgrounds can train and qualify in some of the world's best ski resorts, including Whistler Blackcomb and Banff/Lake Louise in Canada, and you can gain recognised CSA, CASI or NZSA qualifications.
Crystal International Academy, King's Place,
12-42 Wood Street, Kingston Upon Thames,
Surrey, KT1 1JY, 0870 060 1381,
www.theinternationalacademy.com

⬇ 💰 Enjoy a survival course

Location: Utah, USA
Duration: 14-28 days. Price: £950+

Leave the modern world behind and experience true survival training. You'll be placed with one of the US's leading experts in outdoor survival skills on this challenging course. Your expedition takes place in the awe-inspiring canyons of southern Utah, where there are 45 state parks, combining heritage and dramatic scenery with a host of outdoor opportunities.

You'll get to explore the desert washes and mountain trails armed with little more than a knife, a water bottle, a blanket and a poncho. You'll need to be physically fit and expect to be pushed physically and mentally on this course: you may be hiking up to 30 miles in a day! As well as improving your fitness, you'll also learn a host of survival skills, such as how to make a fire without matches, desert ecology, campsite selection, trail hygiene, shelter location and construction, water location and purification, nature observation skills and the identification of edible and medicinal plants.

These courses have an emphases on using only renewable, natural resources to help the environment. The course motto is 'know more, carry less', and so you'll discover how traditional cultures lived without modern appliances, and how you can live a less intrusive and more harmonious lifestyle.

Global Vision International, 3 High Street, St Albans, Herts, AL3 4ED, 0870 608 8898, www.gvi.co.uk

⬇ 💰💰💰 Become a flying instructor

Location: Florida, USA
Duration: 2-4 weeks. Price: £5,250+

This is a great way to not only learn how to fly, but also to be trained as a flying instructor. You'll be able to take to the clear blue skies of Florida as you progress towards your Joint Aviation Authorities (JAA) Private Pilot Licence qualification. You'll be working with first-class, experienced instructors on either a four-week group training course, or on a more intensive two-week personalised programme.

Crystal International Academy, King's Place, 12-42 Wood Street, Kingston Upon Thames, Surrey, KT1 1JY, 0870 060 1381, www.theinternationalacademy.com

CASE STUDY

Who: Iain Walters
Location: Caribbean

On his gap year, Iain studied language in Guatemala, worked in the Belize jungle, explored the Yucatan peninsula, visited Ulita Island and Costa Rica, and cycled around Cuba, all on one unforgettable expedition

The volunteers enjoying a late supper on the jungle conservation project.

Iain's varied experiences included feeding rare manatees by hand.

Iain met many fascinating people on his break, such as the local boatmen.

Taking a gap year is a pretty serious decision, as Iain explains. "There are several basic things you should establish: will I do something worthwhile? Can I afford it? Will I be able to go to the university of my choice? The things that universities like to see – and which are a lot of fun! – are travelling to somewhere new, doing charity work, learning a foreign language and doing something related to your course."

With this in mind, Iain decided to join Venture Co on a trip to Central America. "I chose them because they were pretty much all-inclusive, so I knew where I was with my money before I went. They also offered some really amazing experiences, such as cycling around Cuba and climbing the highest peak in Central America, not to mention living in the jungle for a month doing conservation work. A three-week language school was also included and trust me, this is a must for any traveller – talking to the locals makes your trip so much better!"

Iain visited quite a lot of Mayan ruins during the trip, and as a student of History in Edinburgh, he found it really worthwhile doing something related to his course.

As well as learning about history, Iain also learnt a lot about the ups and downs of travelling, and reveals that his main concerns were financial. "The money side was hard – travelling isn't always cheap so make sure you go away knowing how much things are going to cost! It's a good idea to make sure you have a job before you start your gap year so you know how much you can spend."

> My break was incredible. The people I met and the experiences I had were truly unforgettable, and I'd definitely recommend it to anyone

Iain had a fantastic time on this expedition and advises anyone considering a gap year to just go ahead and take the plunge.

"My break was incredible. The people I met and the experiences I had were unforgettable. I'd definitely recommend it to anyone, but just make sure you do something extraordinary with the time. After all, these are the best years of your life!"

During his time away Iain had a chance to discover new cultures.

⬇ 💰 Protect wildlife

Location: Florida, USA
Duration: 4-12 weeks. Price: £970+

When exotic animals are victims of abuse or neglect, this sanctuary takes them in. You'll be sorting and cutting fruit for fruit bats and monkeys, feeding the animals, cleaning enclosures, building habitats and maintaining the grounds. You'll be taught all aspects of animal care, as well as the issues surrounding exotic animals in captivity, the behaviours and communication method of the various species, and their natural history.
Global Vision International, 3 High Street, St Albans, Herts, AL3 4ED, 0870 608 8898, www.gvi.co.uk

⬇ 💰 Help conserve California

Location: California, USA
Duration: 4 weeks. Price: £449

Get out in the fresh air, feel the sun on your skin and do something new and challenging on this short break. You'll travel to California, near San Francisco, to work on a voluntary conservation project. There's a range available, from salmon restoration along the Medocino coast and trail construction throughout national parks in northern California to historical building renovation and a number of revegetation projects.
Real Gap Experience, First Floor, 1 Meadow Road, Tunbridge Wells, Kent, TN1 2YG, 01892 516164, www.realgap.co.uk

⬇ 💰 Work in Canada

Location: Canada
Duration: up to 12 months. Price: £799

With its friendly people, beautiful landscapes and its ski seasons that are among the best in the world, Canada is one of the best places to work abroad, and this is your chance to enjoy a seasonal job in this amazing country. There's a wide range of work available, but you'll normally be placed in a ski resort, where you'll also have time to enjoy the pistes. This programme is open to students aged 18-30 who want to experience life and work in a different and exciting country.
Real Gap Experience, First Floor, 1 Meadow Road, Tunbridge Wells, Kent, TN1 2YG, 01892 516164, www.realgap.co.uk

↘ 💰 Work in the USA

Location: Across USA

Duration: from 2 months. Price: £459+

This USA gap year programme is exclusive to university students who want to work in America during their summer holidays. This country offers incredible opportunities in terms of work and travel, making it a great place to spend your summer break.

You'll be given a visa for a maximum of three months' work and one month's travel, and you'll have the option of taking a pre-arranged job or finding one of your own. Your adventure will begin with a two-day orientation in the breathtaking New York City, before you travel to your job site to begin work.

The self-arranged option allows you to find your own job before you travel. The visa permits you to work in almost any job, except for teaching, health and childcare. You simply have to contact employers and get a written job offer from them, and you'll get lots of helpful advice on how to do this.

If that sounds like too much hassle, you can take a pre-arranged job, selected according to your preferences. These are all casual summer jobs and may have accommodation offers included. They're generally in the fields of kitchen help, maintenance, amusement parks, sales and housekeeping, but they all offer a great opportunity to enjoy life in the USA.

Real Gap Experience, First Floor, 1 Meadow Road, Tunbridge Wells, Kent, TN1 2YG, 01892 516164, www.realgap.co.uk

↘ 💰💰 Help underprivileged kids

Location: Dominican Republic, Caribbean

Duration: 4-8 weeks. Price: £859-£1,799

The recent financial problems in the Dominican Republic have left many families impoverished, with the more vulnerable, such as children and orphans, in need of your help. You should consider this placement if you're interested in helping children through care, education and social development. The Dominican Republic has a great deal to offer in terms of both work and travel, making it a rewarding and enjoyable place to take a gap break.

Real Gap Experience, First Floor, 1 Meadow Road, Tunbridge Wells, Kent, TN1 2YG, 01892 516164, www.realgap.co.uk

⬇ 💰💰 Help protect Tobago's coast

Location: Tobago, Caribbean
Duration: 4-16 weeks. Price: £1,300-£3,400

Tobago's reef system has immense importance for the social and economic stability of the island. This project aims to survey and map the coastal ecosystems to provide data for the sustainable use of coastal, marine and wetland resources. Conservation education and training programmes will also be provided for local communities. If you're interested in helping to conserve this beautiful area, this is the perfect break for you.
Coral Cay Conservation, Ground Floor, 40-42 Osnaburgh Street, London NW1 3ND, 0870 750 0668, www.coralcay.org

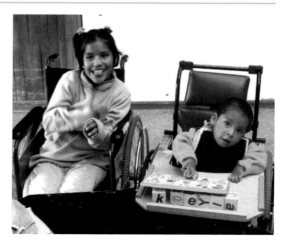

⬇ 💰 Teach underprivileged kids

Location: Santo Domingo, Dominican Republic
Duration: 4-8 weeks. Price: £859-£1,799

This work and travel volunteer project gives you the chance to teach in Latin America in one of the most beautiful tropical islands in the world. Based in Santo Domingo, the capital of the Dominican Republic, you can teach underprivileged children in local schools. This is not only a worthwhile volunteer project, but also a great opportunity to work and travel in the Caribbean, making it a fantastic way to spend your gap year.
Real Gap Experience, First Floor, 1 Meadow Road, Tunbridge Wells, Kent, TN1 2YG, 01892 516164, www.realgap.co.uk

⬇ 💰 Help the disabled

Location: Dominican Republic, Caribbean
Duration: 4-8 weeks. Price: £859-£1,799

This volunteer programme is ideally suited to those who are interested in enjoying a worthwhile and rewarding gap year break. On this project, you'll be helping physically disabled people of all ages, enabling them to live as normal a life as possible. In the Dominican Republic, the concept of volunteering is a relatively new one, and so your help will be gratefully received, and you'll receive an incredibly warm welcome from the friendly local people.
Real Gap Experience, First Floor, 1 Meadow Road, Tunbridge Wells, Kent, TN1 2YG, 01892 516164, www.realgap.co.uk

➤ 💲 Help wildlife in Texas

Location: Texas, USA
Duration: from 1 month. Price: £499+

The main focus of the Texas Wildlife Rescue and Rehabilitation Centre project is to rescue, rehabilitate, and release orphaned, injured and displaced wildlife, and to provide sanctuary with dignity for non-releasable and non-native wild animals.

The project is based near Kendalia, in the heart of Texas hill country, and on this placement, you'll be involved in basic animal care, cleaning cages and feeding, landscaping, data entry, laundry and animal diet preparation. If you have a certain skill, such as mechanics, landscaping, carpentry or maintenance, you'll have the opportunity to work in those fields during your time at the sanctuary. You may have the chance to visit schools or businesses to help educate the public about urban wildlife issues too. If you join the programme for two months or longer, you'll also receiving additional training on admittance guidelines, procedures and emergency arrivals.

You may have the chance to work with animals such as baby squirrels, songbirds and opossums; fawns; armadillos; domestic animals; exotic birds and reptiles; water birds; baby raccoons, skunks and raptors; baby cottontails or jackrabbits; foxes; bats; snakes; primates; and a number of other animals.

Real Gap Experience, First Floor, 1 Meadow Road, Tunbridge Wells, Kent, TN1 2YG, 01892 516164, www.realgap.co.uk

➤ 💲 Build homes in Honduras

Location: Honduras
Duration: 1-24 weeks. Price: £595+

If you get fired up by the prospect of building overseas, head to Honduras! You can help build homes and schools in the poorest parts of the Western Highlands. The native Lenca people live in extreme poverty, often with three families under one roof. However, along with Save the Children, you can help them to make a new start. This is a real hands-on project where you'll help with everything from making sun-dried bricks to painting walls. The best bit is seeing the results of your work as you help families move into their new homes, or watch students attend the first day at a new school.

i-to-i, 0870 333 2332, www.i-to-i.com

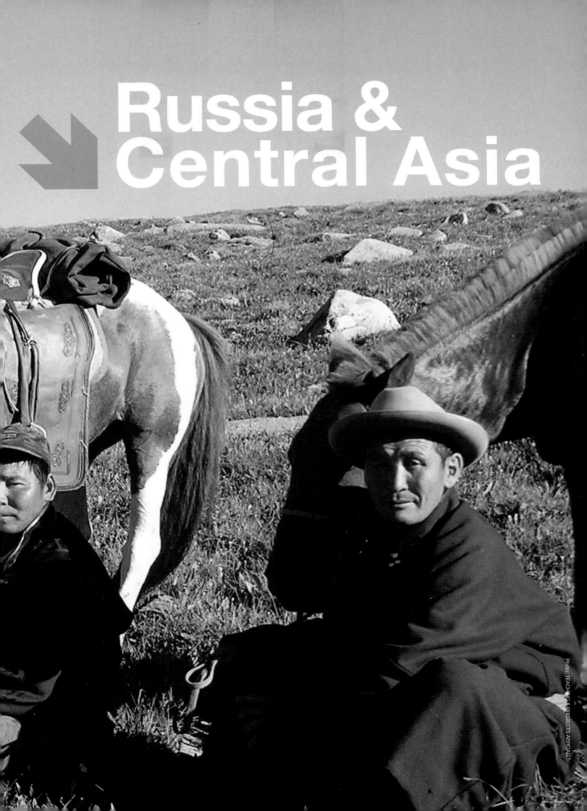

Russia &
Central Asia

This amazing area is larger than Africa and Australasia combined, and so it's no surprise that it offers everything from deserts to frozen steppes and lush valleys

Photo: DIANE/FLICKR.COM

⬊ **Russia**

The vast region of Russia, Central Asia and the Caucasus offers a wealth of top gap experiences

This amazing area is larger than Africa and Australasia combined, and so it's no surprise that it offers everything from oven-like deserts to frozen steppes and lush valleys. Influences here range from Christian to Islamic and Buddhist, and there are fascinating outposts stretching from China to Georgia.

The first attraction is Russia, the world's largest country. Only opened up to the west following the fall of communism in 1989, it has undergone a huge amount of change. When people think of Russia, they conjure up images of Soviet-era concrete tower blocks and grim-faced people struggling through the bleak streets, but nothing could be further from the truth. Instead, think imposing monuments, colourful history and fabulous art, music and architecture. St Petersburg isn't known as the Venice of the North for nothing, while Moscow is an awe-inspiring and fascinating city.

Outside Russia, Mongolia offers you the chance to live the Mongol life on the plains once occupied by Genghis Khan. Travel there via the Trans-Siberian railway and you'll enjoy an unparalleled experience.

The contrasts continue into Ukraine, Belarus, Uzbekistan and Kazakhstan, with their orthodox churches, vast tundra, beautiful lakes and mountains, awe-inspiring vistas and extensive wildlife, all of which few westerners have ever seen.

Photo: BRADY WOOD/FLICKR.COM

⬇ RUSSIA

💰 **STROLL** around St Petersburg, marvelling at the architecture, visit Red Square in Moscow, enjoy a cup of strong Russian tea as you watch the street performers on the Ulitza Arbat, and see St Basil's cathedral at night.

💰💰 **TAKE** a day trip to Nizhny Novgorod and its Kremlin, visit Yaroslav and the Monastery of the Transfiguration of the Saviour, tour Volgograd (previously known as Stalingrad) and trek to the base camp of Mount Beluka.

💰💰💰 **ENJOY** a cultural tour of St Petersburg and Moscow, take a trip on the Trans-Siberian Orient Express, watch the Russian Ballet in Moscow's Bolshoi Theatre and then take a luxury walking tour around Lake Baikal.

2

⬎MONGOLIA

💰 **ENJOY** a night out in the capital, Ulaanbaatar, visit the Tibetan-style lamaseries on the outskirts of the city, spend a few nights in a yurt and live as the Mongolians do, and then take a trip to see the Gobi oasis.

💰💰 **TOUR** the Gobi desert by camel and camp out under the stars, tour some of the abandoned communist cities, and then visit Karakorum, a fascinating archaeological site with an Erdene Zuu temple and monastery.

💰💰💰 **RETRACE** the footsteps of Genghis Khan with a unique cultural tour. Alternatively, you can learn about the Mongolian people and lifestyle on an overland tour, discovering ancient Mongolian history as you travel.

⬇ 💰💰 Dogsled on Lake Baikal

Location: Lake Baikal, Russia
Duration: 9 days. Price: £1,939

Ever dreamt of an adventure holiday in Siberia in the winter? On this trip, you can enjoy the unique and unforgettable experience of a journey across Lake Baikal on dogsleds. You'll love the pristine wilderness, the thrill of being surrounded by abundant wildlife and the majesty of the snow-capped mountains. The clear air and endless ice plane on the surface of Lake Baikal will transport you to a world from a winter fairytale.
Just Go Russia, Boundary House, Boston Road, London, W7 2QE , 0208 434 3496, www.gorussia.co.uk

⬇ 💰 Watch white wales

Location: Solovetsky Islands, Russia
Duration: 7 days. Price: £999

Enjoy the beauty and tranquility of the Solovetsky Islands and watch white whales in their natural habitat. Located in the western part of the White Sea, less than 150 kilometres from the Arctic Circle, the archipelago of the Solovetsky Islands is home to a thriving population of white whales. Here you can witness the diverse ecosystems and abundant floral and fauna of these remote and picturesque islands.
Just Go Russia, Boundary House, Boston Road, London, W7 2QE , 0208 434 3496, www.gorussia.co.uk

⬇ 💰 Enjoy a multi-sport adventure

Location: Lake Baikal, Russia
Duration: 11 days. Price: £1,169

This itinerary gives you a unique chance to experience some of the most popular outdoor activities available on Lake Baikal during the summer. These include hiking, horse riding and rafting, and are suitable for anyone in good physical shape – you don't need to be a proficient raftsman, horse rider or backpacker to enjoy this journey! So if you aren't afraid to hike 20 kilometres a day or take on some challenging rafting, this is a great way to see the beauty of Lake Baikal.
Just go Russia, Boundary House, Boston Road, London, W7 2QE , 0208 434 3496, www.gorussia.co.uk

⬇ 💲 Take the Vodkatrain

Location: Russia to China
Duration: varies. Price: £390+

If you're looking to travel to Russia or Mongolia, there are few better ways than the Trans-Siberian railway. It's also one of the best ways to travel with like-minded people. Vodkatrain enables young travellers aged between 18 and 35 to enjoy Trans-Siberian and Trans-Mongolian railway journeys with no regimented meal or sightseeing times, making it perfect for those seeking flexible and laid-back travel.

Vodkatrain is about experiencing Russia, Mongolia and China at grass roots level, travelling with local people, experiencing the cities with a local leader, and eating out and getting around at local prices.

This experience is a great way for you to see these amazing countries and it offers all the reassurance of organised travel, without the schedules normally associated with tours. You'll travel in a small group, without a tour leader, and on arrival in a city, you'll be allocated a resident guide. They'll show you around, revealing all the local secrets and best places to eat, visit and hang out, and as there's no pressure, you can relax and really get to know the places you visit.

On this expedition, you can choose from the Trans-Mongolian, Trans-Siberian and Moscow to St Petersburg Express.

Vodkatrain, Suite 207B, The Business Village,
3-9 Broomhill Road, London, SW18 4JQ,
020 8877 7650, www.vodkatrain.com

⬇ 💲💲 Watch birds on the Volga

Location: Volga river delta, Russia
Duration: 11 days. Price: £1,559

This tour is specifically designed for those who want a focused birding holiday while enjoying a remote and beautiful part of Russia – the delta of the Volga River. This is the largest delta in Europe and it's unique in that it combines the largest of Europe's rivers with the only sand desert in Europe. Travel dates coincide with the spring and autumn migrations, when most of the breeding birds of the area have either returned or will be returning, ensuring a great spotting experience.

Just Go Russia, Boundary House, Boston
Road, London, W7 2QE, 0208 434 3496,
www.gorussia.co.uk

CASE STUDY

Who: Marcus Lane
Location: Russia

Marcus was 29 years old when he decided to quit his job and set off on an epic overland adventure that would take him across Eastern Europe, Russia and Mongolia, and into the depths of the Orient…

Russia is a land where the traditional coexists side by side with the modern.

After purchasing a one-way bus ticket from London to Poland, Marcus soon realised that good preparation was essential. "I had to ensure that I had all the right visas and that the entry dates were correctly calculated. If you get stuck at the Mongolian border without the correct paperwork, it's a long way back to an embassy in Moscow!"

Marcus travelled by bus and train into Russia, where he stayed with a local resident in his home. "I preferred this to hostels and hotels as it enabled me to experience what life was really like in Russia."

The Trans-Mongolian railway took Marcus to many cities across Russia, but his problem was buying onward tickets at every stop. "Organising train travel locally in Russia is not easy but it's far less expensive than using UK agents, and persistence usually pays off. Locals often helped me out – it's amazing just how friendly and helpful strangers can be, even when you don't speak a word of each others' language."

While on his adventure, Marcus learnt a lot about other cultures. "One tip for Russia is to carry a universal sink plug. You'll never fill a sink or bath otherwise, as plugs are very rare!"

From Russia, he headed to Mongolia, where he noticed cultures and faces changing before his eyes. "Overland travel opens your mind to the subject of anthropology and cultural migration. You miss this if you jump on a plane in London and arrive in Beijing 12 hours later. On land, everything changes much more gradually."

In Mongolia, Marcus found some local students to show him around the area, and he was even invited onto the capital's radio station for an interview.

The Russian people are extremely friendly and always happy to help.

> **Overland travel opens your mind to the subject of anthropology and cultural migration. You miss this if you just jump on a plane from London to Beijing**

Relics of Russia's communist past can be found all over the country.

While on this expedition, Marcus dreamt up the idea of a board game based on his experiences, and he's now had it professionally produced. Called 'Can You Make It As A Backpacker?' it's a hilarious way to plan a safe trip, discover places to go and the pitfalls you really should avoid. It's available now from www.canyoumakeit.co.uk.

This region boasts some awesome and beautiful architecture.

Help Moldovan orphans

Location: Moldova
Duration: from four weeks. Price: £995+

Although not as well publicised as the fate of orphans in Romania, children in Moldova suffer from many of the same problems. You can help in a number of orphanages in and around Chisinau, working with a range of age groups. Whether you're keeping young babies entertained, helping with homework or teaching English to older kids, your help with be really appreciated, and you'll find the work rewarding.
Teaching & Projects Abroad, Aldsworth Parade, Goring, Sussex, BN12 4TX, 01903 708300, www.teaching-abroad.co.uk

Learn Russian

Location: Moldova
Duration: from 4 weeks. Price: £895+

Spread over one month, you'll receive 60 hours of one-to-one tuition tailored to suit your ability. During your placement, you'll live with a local Russian-speaking family, which will give you plenty of opportunity to practise your conversation skills. After the month's language study, you can choose to spend time on a teaching, care or journalism placement, so you can put your new-found language skills into practice.
Teaching & Projects Abroad, Aldsworth Parade, Goring, Sussex, BN12 4TX, 01903 708300, www.teaching-abroad.co.uk

Work as a journalist

Location: Moldova
Duration: from 4 weeks. Price: £1,095+

This project gives you worthwhile practical experience in a newspaper office in Chisinau. You'll start off by shadowing a local journalist, where you'll see how news articles are put together. You'll then spend time researching your own stories and features, as well as conducting interviews. The editor will be keen to hear your ideas and your placement supervisor will be on hand to offer help and advice, though inspiration should come easily in such a different culture.
Teaching & Projects Abroad, Aldsworth Parade, Goring, Sussex, BN12 4TX, 01903 708300, www.teaching-abroad.co.uk

⬇ 💰 Teach English in Moldova

Location: Moldova

Duration: from 4 weeks. Price: £995+

Moldovans are increasingly aware of the importance of learning English in order to help them trade with the west. As such, the number of language schools around Chisinau is growing rapidly, and many of them have taken the best English teachers away from the local schools. Most of these schools were constructed in the Soviet era and appear similar to those of the former Soviet empire. Facilities are basic, with the main resources being a blackboard and a piece of chalk, although increasingly they have computers, as well as video recorders.

On this placement, you'll be working in a secondary school where students start to learn English at the age of ten. Your main focus will be to teach conversational English. Moldovan students are really keen to find out about life outside their country as most haven't had the opportunity to travel, and you'll find yourself a popular addition to the local teaching staff. If you have other skills, you could also put them into practice – maybe you want to coach the football team or help in the music department.

Over the summer holidays, there are lots of opportunities to work at orphanages and disabled centres, or at a centre for African children.

Teaching & Projects Abroad, Aldsworth Parade, Goring, Sussex, BN12 4TX, 01903 708300, www.teaching-abroad.co.uk

⬇ 💰 Work in a Chisinau hospital

Location: Moldova

Duration: from 4 weeks. Price: £1,195+

These medical projects in Moldova are based in the capital, Chisinau, where you'll work at the university hospital. You'll be placed with local English-speaking doctors, and you'll have the opportunity to work in the trauma department, with the possibility of helping in surgery, as well as in the oncology department. Whether you're a potential doctor, nurse or physiotherapist, you'll find that a warm welcome awaits you from the medical community in Chisinau.

Teaching & Projects Abroad, Aldsworth Parade, Goring, Sussex, BN12 4TX, 01903 708300, www.teaching-abroad.co.uk

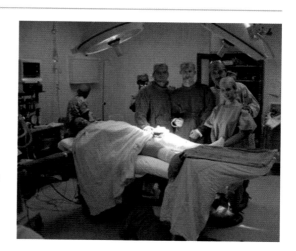

GET EDUCATED

💰 Teach English in Russia

Location: Novgorod or St Petersburg, Russia
Duration: from 1 month. Price: £900+

Have the experience of a lifetime by studying for a
TEFL qualification in Russia. Your time will be spent
working in Novgorod or St Petersburg, teaching
English in local secondary schools. Volunteers will
be expected to help with the preparation of teaching
materials, dictation, and helping out with marking and
drama performances. This is an excellent opportunity
for anyone wishing to learn the Russian language and
discover more about this country's fascinating culture.
**GAP Activity Projects, 44 Queen's Road, Reading,
Berkshire, RG1 4BB, 0118 9594914, www.gap.org.uk**

💰💰💰 Cultural studies course

Location: St Petersburg, Russia
Duration: 6 weeks. Price: £4,850

Are you interested in Russian language and history?
If so, this course offers you a fantastic opportunity,
as you'll be able to study subjects such as history,
architecture, art, literature, philosophy, design,
conservation, ballet, opera, music, contemporary
culture and politics – and you can enjoy troika rides
too! St Petersburg's extraordinary history and vibrant
contemporary life are revealed on this placement
through an inspiring and informative series of lectures,
guided tours, workshops and volunteer schemes.
St Petersburg Studies, www.petersburgstudies.com

💰 Art, culture and history course

Location: Belarus
Duration: 2 weeks. Price: £135+

The project gives you a chance to deal with living
history. There's an ancient Slavonic settlement in a
picturesque setting on the banks of the river Beresina,
and on this placement, you'll be able to help out with
archeological excavations and prospecting in the area.
You'll also have ample opportunity to study the history,
traditions and culture of Belarus, as well exploring
the local surroundings, and the archaeological and
architectural monuments of this region.
**International Voluntary Service, 7 Upper
Bow, Edinburgh, EH1 2JN, 0131 2266 722,
www.ivs-gb.org.uk**

Study medicine in Mongolia

Location: Mongolia
Duration: from 4 weeks. Price: £1,095+

Based in the capital, Ulaanbaatar, you'll be working in busy central hospitals or specialised clinics dealing with paediatrics, maternity or trauma patients. The doctors are keen for you to achieve as much as possible during your placement, and so you'll be working in a number of different departments. There's also a number of private complementary medicine clinics where you'll be able to broaden your medical experience.

Teaching & Projects Abroad, Aldsworth Parade, Goring, Sussex, BN12 4TX, 01903 708300, www.teaching-abroad.co.uk

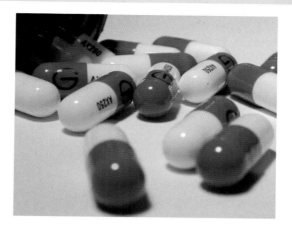

Teach English in Mongolia

Location: Mongolia
Duration: from 4 weeks. Price: £995+

You can help local teachers with the English conversation parts of their lessons. Although language is the aim, many of these lessons will also offer opportunities for cultural exchange. You'll mainly be working with kids aged between 13 and 17, which means they'll be keen to talk about football, current affairs and pop music! With 35 students in a class, you can be sure that there'll be plenty of lively discussion.

Teaching & Projects Abroad, Aldsworth Parade, Goring, Sussex, BN12 4TX, 01903 708300, www.teaching-abroad.co.uk

Practise veterinary medicine

Location: Mongolia
Duration: from 4 weeks. Price: £1,195+

On this fascinating placement, you'll be working at the AMAR Pet Hospital in Ulaanbaatar. This clinic treats all kinds of pets and animals, including everything from dogs and cats to turtles, birds, small mammals and race horses. You'll be working alongside the local veterinary staff and you'll have the opportunity to assist them with basic treatments. You can also observe surgery and gain experience of diseases and ailments that aren't often seen in the west.

Teaching & Projects Abroad, Aldsworth Parade, Goring, Sussex, BN12 4TX, 01903 708300, www.teaching-abroad.co.uk

⬇ 💰 Live with nomads

Location: Mongolia
Duration: from 4 weeks. Price: £1,495+

Get away from it all by living with a local nomadic family. Living in a tent, your daily life may include riding horses, caring for livestock, helping to produce dairy products and teaching English. This is a brilliant way to learn more about this ancient way of life and how it's being affected by modern-day Mongolia. You'll even get the chance to camp in the Gobi Desert, where you can look for dinosaur fossils with a local expert.

Teaching & Projects Abroad, Aldsworth Parade, Goring, Sussex, BN12 4TX, 01903 708300, www.teaching-abroad.co.uk

⬇ 💰💰💰 Help local children

Location: St Petersburg, Russia
Duration: 4 months. Price: £2,799+

There's a choice of volunteer projects available in St Petersburg, where you can help children and adults in deprived areas of the community. You can choose from working in a local children's hospital, helping street children at a drop-in centre, teaching at a local youth club or helping neglected and abused teenage girls at a local shelter. Whatever you choose to do, you'll find the experience incredibly rewarding.

Real Gap Experience, First Floor, 1 Meadow Road, Tunbridge Wells, Kent, TN1 2YG, 01892 516164, www.realgap.co.uk

⬇ 💰 Care for underprivileged kids

Location: Mongolia
Duration: from 4 weeks. Price: £1,095+

There are around 20 orphanages in Ulaanbaatar, the capital of Mongolia, where these placements are based. You can work in either a large orphanage or in a smaller care centre, and you'll be dealing with children who range in age from babies to teenage street kids. Many of these placements are in very poor areas, usually in the middle of tented 'Ger districts', where you can get involved by playing with the children, as well as offering practical help and friendship.

Teaching & Projects Abroad, Aldsworth Parade, Goring, Sussex, BN12 4TX, 01903 708300, www.projects-abroad.co.uk

⬎ 💰 Help Ukrainian orphans

Location: Ukraine

Duration: 4 weeks. Price: £699

This is a great opportunity for you to make an impact in the lives of Ukrainian orphans. Many of these children come from abusive and violent backgrounds, with parents who were drug addicts or alcoholics, and many of them were abandoned. The stories are tragic, and it's a sad fact that many orphans take their own lives or feel so desperate that they turn to prostitution or crime. With your help, they can be encouraged to gain life and employment skills so they can feel accepted and a valuable part of the society.

There are different activities you can get involved with as a volunteer in the Ukraine. You can help to teach English, play with the children, or arrange extra classes such as dance, music, drama and sports. Help is also needed in communicating the importance of protecting the environment. Meanwhile, in the summer, the children stay in summer camps and so other activities can be carried out in the orphanages, such as caring for the disabled children there.

This is your opportunity to brighten the lives of underprivileged young children in Ukraine. Your help will be greatly appreciated and you can show these kids the care that most of them have lacked in their lives so far, making this a really rewarding experience. **Real Gap Experience, First Floor, 1 Meadow Road, Tunbridge Wells, Kent, TN1 2YG, 01892 516164, www.realgap.co.uk**

⬎ 💰 Work in Mongolia

Location: Mongolia

Duration: from 4 weeks. Price: £1,095+

Since Mongolia's democratic revolution in 1990, the country's capital has become one of the fastest-growing cities in central Asia. In Ulaanbaatar, there are two placements you can enjoy in business administration and management, and in a wide range of manufacturing and service companies, including those in the growing tourism industry. The possibilities are almost limitless, but whatever you end up doing, you'll get a fascinating insight into a small-scale but burgeoning business environment.
Responsible Travel, 0870 0052 836, www.responsibletravel.com

⬇ 💲 Work as a journalist

Location: Ulaanbaatar, Mongolia
Duration: from 4 weeks, Price: £1,095+

If you want to gain experience on a top newspaper, this is the placement for you. On the *Ulaanbaatar Post* or *Mongol Times*, you'll initially work alongside local journalists, seeing what they do and where they go on a day-to-day basis. Once you're feeling confident, you may find that you can write your own regular English column in the newspaper. Alternatively, your work might be translated into Mongolian.

Being one of the only English-speaking journalists in the city has its advantages. One volunteer recently interviewed the American ambassador and – to the envy of other newspapers – secured an interview with a famous English-speaking Mongolian pop star!

You can also try a journalism placement in radio or television, and volunteers have recently found themselves presenting shows on both. On FM103.6, one volunteer recently fronted a chat show that went out live to residents of Ulaanbaatar and the surrounding region. On the publicly funded Mongolian National Television, another volunteer was the anchor on the English news, which was broadcast to the entire nation.

You'll have plenty of cuttings and tapes to bring home, meaning a journalism placement in Mongolia really adds something extra to your portfolio or CV.
Teaching & Projects Abroad, Aldsworth Parade, Goring, Sussex, BN12 4TX, 01903 708300, www.projects-abroad.co.uk

⬇ 💲 Help the community

Location: Russia
Duration: 1-12 weeks. Price: £927+

This is a fantastic opportunity to step inside a culture that has been hidden behind the Iron Curtain for 70 years. You can take part in a volunteer or intern programme in Yaroslavl, located north-east of Moscow on Russia's 'golden ring' of historic towns. You'll be caring for infants and children, teaching children, assisting teachers, caring for the elderly, and caring for people with disabilities. This is a great way to make a difference in people's lives while experiencing a new culture and country at the same time.
Responsible Travel, 0870 0052 836, www.responsibletravel.com

⬐ **CASE STUDY**

Who: Rosie Akester
Location: Mongolia

Rosie Akester was studying veterinary medicine at Cambridge when she decided to visit Mongolia. She loved the experience so much that so plans to return to the steppes for a longer trip soon…

Horses play an enormously important role in everyday nomadic life.

Mongolia: for years the words had conjured up a certain magic in Rosie's mind – images of the wide open steppe, vast expanses of desert, and camels, yaks, snow leopards, wild horses, nomads and Genghis Khan. "Months later, as I looked out of the window of the Aeroflot plane, I caught my first glimpse of the steppe and it was as wild and empty as I'd hoped."

It was a stark contrast to arrive in Ulaanbaatar, the capital city. "Less than a century ago, the city was just a horde of white tents surrounding a central Buddhist temple. Today, Ulaanbaatar – known to locals as 'UB' – swarms with people, cars, concrete, dust and litter."

Rosie's time would be spent outside the capital with the nomads, experiencing the lifestyle of a herding community first hand, as well as visiting the famous Przewalski's horses.

First of all, though, she had to master the tricky art of communication. "Day one was challenging: I couldn't introduce myself, read a menu or write my address. On day two, things started to improve as I began my intensive tuition, and the vets brought in their English dictionaries. Soon even the local kids had joined in the mass effort to teach me what seemed like the entire Mongolian language!"

Food vocabulary was high on Rosie's list of priorities to learn. "It's not surprising, considering that the choices might include fermented mares' milk, marmot, yak, and salty tea with lamb dumplings floating in it!"

Just some of the local nomad kids who made Rosie feel so welcome.

> **I was lucky enough to experience life in a country of extremes and contrasts, where the only constant was the unquestioning hospitality of the people**

The desolate Mongolian steppe, which is home to the nomad people.

Despite the culinary challenges, Rosie loved her time in the country. "Mongolia left me with more questions than answers, but also with an incredible array of memories and ideas. I was lucky enough to experience life for a short time in a country of extremes and contrasts, where the only constant was the unquestioning hospitality of the people I met.

"Now I look forward to returning one day, this time for a longer stay so I can discover more of the secrets of this huge, forgotten country."

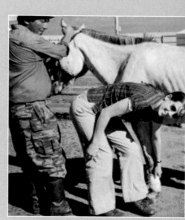

Rosie helped keep the tribe's horses fit and healthy on her placement.

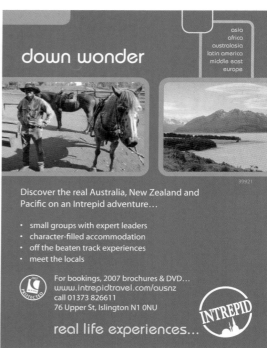

The
essentials

Plan your ultimate year out with our
guide to safety, kit, money and more

↘ WHAT IS A GAP YEAR?

It's estimated that over 500,000 people a year in the UK are taking a gap year. This is usually a break of between three and 24 months, taken from education, work or in retirement. It used to be about 18- and 19-year-olds, but not any more!

WHO TAKES A GAP YEAR?

In general, three groups of people are likely to take a year out:

18- TO 25-YEAR-OLDS

Each year, around 220,000 young people aged 18 to 25 take a gap year and spend about £3,000-£4,000 each. They include:

■ Students who defer a university place, with 15 months between school and university.
■ Those with four months between school and going to university.
■ Graduates who have finished university, before starting a career.

■ Those taking a gap during university holidays.
■ Students taking a year out as part of a course.

Advantages

■ A gap year improves your self-confidence and all-round personal skills.
■ You can apply for uni knowing your grades.
■ You'll be more focused and committed to study.
■ You can change your course to your advantage.
■ Experts believe that you're less likely to drop out of university.

■ Employers look favourably on applications from those who've taken a gap year – if it wasn't just spent travelling.
■ You might not get another chance!

Disadvantages

■ Your friends will have moved on and you'll be a year behind them.
■ You might not go to university afterwards.
■ Your study skills might have diminished.
■ You could be at risk of injury or illness.

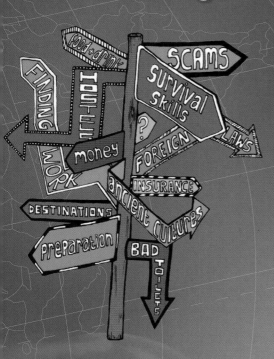

⬆️ HEALTH & SAFETY

The most important thing to remember about getting ready to embark on a successful and enjoyable time away is preparation. If things get left to the last minute, there may be items that you forget or just can't get hold of. This is especially true when it comes to matters of health.

THINGS TO DO BEFORE YOU GO

INSURANCE

Good insurance is imperative. Ensure that it will cover you for all of the countries that you're going to and all the activities that you're likely to undertake. It sounds obvious, but many insurance policies may not cover you in areas that the UK government advises against travelling to, due to civil unrest or suchlike. Also, dangerous sports such as bungee jumping or off-piste skiing will require a good policy.

HEALTH CHECKS

Although you may feel fit and healthy and ready to take on anything, it's still a good idea to get a check-up with your local GP, and have a dental check as well. There's nothing worse than having a tooth explode on a plane because you had a loose filling!

If you have any pre-existing conditions, make sure that they're well managed and that you're aware of how to handle any increase in symptoms, or how your condition may change if you get ill with something else while you're away. For example, if you're a diabetic, how often

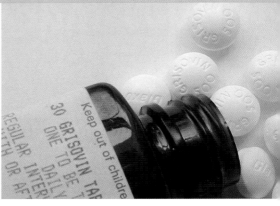

should you check your blood glucose level and what's the best way to get yourself rehydrated?

If your condition needs drug maintenance, you should always split your medication while flying: half in the hold and half in the cabin with you, just in case either gets stolen or lost. If you're travelling for an extended period, your GP may be a little reticent to allow the entire amount on the NHS, so be prepared to pay for

a private prescription and make sure that you know what countries your medicine is available in, and what it's called, since brand names are often different abroad.

Finally, ask your GP to provide you with a covering letter explaining the nature of your illness and the medications that you use. This may smooth difficult passages through customs or help you in an emergency.

BLOOD GROUP

Knowing this could be handy in an emergency. Your GP may have the information, or you could become a blood donor. Do this well in advance of your travels, though, since some vaccinations mean you can't donate.

MEDICAL KIT

A good medical kit can make all the difference when travelling a little off the beaten track as it gives you a degree of

Item	Use
Assorted plasters	General first aid
Steristrip	Wound closure
Non-adherent dressings	Cuts and grazes
Wound dressing	Heavily bleeding wounds in an emergency
Antiseptic wipes or wash	Wound cleaning
Antiseptic paint	Wound cleaning
Paracetamol and/or Ibuprofen	Pain relief
Rehydration sachets	Dehydration
Loperamide capsules or tablets	Travellers' diarrhoea
Antihistamine tablets	Allergies and insect bites
Hydrocortisone cream	Skin allergies and insect bites
Iodine tincture	Water purification
Sterile pack	HIV prevention

self-sufficiency, as well as peace of mind. It's also worth noting that if you do become ill while travelling abroad, you have insurance, so take advantage of the medical services available to you. Don't become ill, not get treatment and later need to be hospitalised or repatriated because you didn't seek medical attention quickly enough!

Your medical kit should be able to cover the most common problems, such as first aid for cuts, grazes and minor injuries, plus medication to manage and treat travellers' diarrhoea and insect bites. You should also have a method of water purification (see later) and if travelling to developing countries, carry a sterile pack: in other words, have needles and syringes with you.

It isn't unusual for steel and glass needles and syringes to be used as they're more cost effective, but they need to be thoroughly disinfected between patients, otherwise the risk of hepatitis B and HIV are high. Remember that sharp items like this can't be taken on board aircraft in hand luggage, but they should be kept with you at all other times.

Those travelling a little further off the beaten track should also take antibiotics. These will be available on prescription only and therefore need to be discussed with either your doctor or your specialist travel health advisor prior to departure.

See the box on the previous page for basic suggested kit contents.

VACCINATIONS

Any vaccination schedule can take up to eight weeks to complete so good planning is vital.

Tetanus: This is present in soil worldwide and it can cause severe illness or death if it's present in even a small cut or wound. A vaccination is recommended every ten years.

Diptheria: Spread by exhaled water droplets, this is a disease that's most commonly caught when spending lots of time with local people. It's potentially fatal if left untreated and so a vaccination is recommended every ten years.

Polio: This virus is passed through contaminated water and the disease can be

fatal. Revaccination is recommended every ten years if you're travelling to a country with known polio cases.

Hepatitis A: This is a virus that affects the liver and it's usually contracted through contaminated food or water. It's most common in developing countries and vaccination is strongly recommended. An initial shot will provide cover for up to a couple of years, while revaccination will protect you for up to 25 years.

Typhoid: Also passed through food and water,

this disease is usually found in areas off the beaten track, in regions with poor sanitation, or where food hygiene is lacking. Vaccinations cover you for three years.

Yellow fever: Only present in sub-Saharan Africa and parts of South America, this is again a potentially fatal virus. The vaccine is highly effective and will provide ten years of protection. You'll also need an approved certificate as some countries will refuse you entry unless you can prove immunity.

Rabies: A course of three injections over a three-week period will provide you with cover for up to two or three years. The rabies virus is invariably fatal and correct treatment following exposure isn't always easy to find, and is sometimes impossible.

Hepatitis B: This is another disease that affects the liver and some long-term complications of the infection can prove fatal. Spread by unprotected sex, blood transfusions and blood-to-blood contact, a course of vaccinations over a month will offer protection to long-term travellers and those at higher risk, such as teachers who may be required to give first aid, or people who stand a chance of being injured, perhaps by working on a charity building project.

Japanese B encephalitis: Not really a disease of Japan any more, this is present throughout Asia and can kill or leave an affected individual with long-term mental or physical disabilities. The disease is rare, so possible

vaccination needs to be discussed with a travel health advisor.

Meningitis: This is most common in west and central Africa during the dry season. However, a single injection will provide five years of cover against four different types of meningitis. It's worth noting that the injection given to individuals going to university in the UK is totally different and will only protect against one type of meningitis.

Malaria: This is also likely to be a major consideration, so discuss your itinerary with your travel health advisor to see what type of vaccination you'll need. There are many options available to the traveller and when you consider the fact that there are at least 300 million cases of malaria worldwide every year, you'll realise that this is a disease that can't be taken lightly.

⬎ RED TAPE

Whether you're travelling, volunteering or working on your year out, you'll need to have your paperwork in order. Trying to find your way through the red tape can sometimes seem a bit dull but it's absolutely crucial to get it sorted out before you leave. You don't want your experience of a lifetime to be cut short because you didn't get the right visas or permits!

PASSPORT

You obviously need a passport to travel, but it's worth knowing that some countries won't let you in unless it's got at least six months or a year left on it. Also, certain stamps in your passport can cause problems if you're trying to enter another country, particularly in the Middle East, with countries such as Israel.

If you think this might be a problem for your particular destination, you can always apply for a second passport. Visit www.passport.gov.uk for more information.

VISAS

Visas vary according to where you're going and what you're doing. You may find you have to get your visa in the UK, while sometimes you can get it abroad from a neighbouring country. Alternatively, you may be able to get a visa when you enter a country

The cost of visas varies according to where you get them. Just make sure you get them as far in advance as you can in case of delays.

Be aware that visa requirements can change frequently, so if you're travelling around, it's a good idea to sign up for email alerts from the Foreign Office. You can do this at the official website, which you'll find at www.fco.gov.uk/travel.

WORK PERMITS

If you're under 31, you can get a working holiday visa for Australia or New Zealand that lets you do temporary work there for up to a year (up to two years in Australia, under certain circumstances).

If you're under 35, you can get a working visa for Canada or the USA, but you have to apply through an agency. In the USA, this is generally aimed at those working in a summer camp. The US also has other work

permit schemes for people up to the ages of 38 and 40, depending on the visa and type of work you intend to do.

In Japan, you can get a working holiday visa for up to a year, but you must be under 25.

In the EU, you don't need to have a work permit, but you do need to apply for a residency permit if you're staying for longer than three months. You may also have to open a local bank account too.

If you want to work in other countries, you can often go through an agency that will sort out your visa or permit for you. Organisations who arrange volunteer placements can also advise you on what visa you'll need, and they'll usually arrange it for you as well.

Going it alone is much harder, but you may be able to apply for a business visa rather than a work permit if you aren't going to be working in a certain country for long.

Of course, there are restrictions, and if you work illegally in a

country, you're likely to be deported if found out.

INSURANCE

Travel insurance is vital, no matter where you're going or what you're doing. Make sure it covers you for all the activities you're planning, as some policies have a supplement for 'adventure sports, such as scuba diving and wakeboarding. Also, be aware that if

you visit a country or area which the Foreign Office advises travellers to avoid, your insurance will almost certainly be invalid. To keep up to date with developments, sign up to email alerts from the Foreign Office.

TAX

Unless you leave your job at the end of the tax year (5th April), you'll probably be able to get a rebate. Get form P50 from your tax office or the HM Customs & Revenue website. Use R38(SA) if you do self-assessment tax returns.

Don't forget council tax and road tax too. For council tax, you can usually just telephone the council to tell them you're moving out. For road tax,

TOP TIP

Photograph or scan your passport, ticket and any other important documents. Leave a paper copy at home and email a digital copy to yourself. If you lose anything, your copies will make it much easier to get a replacement.

you'll need to get form V14 from the DVLA (www.dvla.gov.uk) or the post office. You can use the Money Owed sheet to keep track of any applicable tax refunds.

If you aren't earning money (more than £4,895 in 2005/6) during your career break, tell your bank or building society. They'll give you a form to fill in, which means you won't have to pay tax on any interest your money might earn.

FURTHER INFORMATION

If you're confused about what you need, try the following handy sources of information:
■ A guidebook for your destination – it will usually have visa details.

■ The embassy for your destination.
■ A 'work abroad' or volunteer agency.

USEFUL WEBSITES

There are many online resources that can help you cut through the red tape and make your year out as easy and painless as possible. Our selection here has links to all of the relevant organisations, embassies and agencies that you're likely to need, along with helpful hints and advice.
■ www.fco.gov.uk
■ www.passport.gov.uk
■ www.thecareerbreak site.com
■ www.questoverseas. co.uk
■ www.realgap.com
■ www.i-to-i.com

↘ WHAT TO DO ABOUT YOUR JOB

It may seem obvious, but when you're planning a career break, the first thing you need to think about is your career. Many people worry that a career break will adversely affect their work opportunities, but this is no longer the case. In fact, many people who have been on career breaks report that it has actually improved their career prospects in the long term, as well as their chances of promotion.

When it comes to deciding what to do about your job, you really have four basic choices:

■ Quit. This is an option if you're planning to change jobs, move into a different career or set up your own business. Quitting your job means you have to think about how you're going to get back into work before you go away, in order to minimise your time out of the workforce.

■ Take an unpaid sabbatical. Sabbatical programmes are becoming more and more popular, especially among larger corporations. Even if your company doesn't have an official sabbatical policy, it's still worth asking. Put the business case to your employer and show them how your career break can be useful to the company. For instance, explain what you'll learn during your break that will make you a better employee.

■ Take a paid sabbatical. This option is quite rare, especially outside academic employers, and you usually have to put in many years of service before you qualify.

■ Take holiday time. If your career break is only a few weeks, you may be able to save up holiday

skills and invaluable experience during your time out that you can then bring to your job.

GETTING BACK INTO WORK

If you make a graceful and well-planned exit from your career, it will be a whole lot easier when you come back! If you're going into something new, you'll need even more time to plan.

Tell your clients, colleagues, suppliers and friends what you're doing and when you expect to be back – a global email will be fine for this You can also invite your work partners to join your email list for updates, or to look at your travel blog, if you have one. This will

time, or even buy an extra couple of weeks from your employer. This is a particularly popular option among the over-45s.

Whether you intend to return to your old job or you're expecting to start a new one, make the most of your career break. Emphasise the fact that you've gained useful

remind them when you're about to come back, and a gentle hint from you might prompt them to consider you for a job, or at least recommend you to someone else. Before you set out on your break, make sure you update your CV. You might even want to put that you're on a career break at the top so people understand where you are and what you're

doing. Email a copy of your CV to yourself so it'll be available wherever you are in the world, should you need to send it on. You can take it on CD or disc as well, although don't rely on these as it's easy to lose things when travelling.

FURTHER INFORMATION

For advice visit www. thecareerbreaksite.com.

⬊ CULTURE SHOCK

Going to live in a new country can be like trying to walk on your hands: you're exhausted, totally disorientated, and you can't figure out why you're even doing it, although it seemed such a good idea before. It can be tempting to say, "Enough! I want to be back where everyone walks on their feet!" and run home. But hang on in there and you might end up with some circus skills.

Enough of the extended metaphor. The proper name for the feeling, which can range from mild confusion about your new environment to blind panic, is 'culture shock'. And it is a shock. Nobody goes abroad expecting to hate it: what kind of motivation is that for stuffing all your possessions into a bag that seems the size of a child's sock? It's just that it can be hard to discover you've just paid a small fortune in airfares only to arrive in a new country and want nothing more than to go home.

The first few days in a new place are often exciting, but as a little time passes and it no longer feels like a fortnight's holiday, the very things that seemed novel – such as people saying 'yes' when what they actually mean is 'no' – can make you long for the comforts of home.

Many people choose to go abroad for a few months because it's a challenge. The funny thing about challenges, though, is that they aren't easy. However, you can overcome them, and there are lots of ways to help yourself do that.

PREPARATION

First of all, be prepared. You can never know in advance just what a foreign place will be like and it's a good idea to go without too many expectations. However, you can find out as much as possible before you go so not everything is a total surprise. What will the weather be like when you arrive? What are the local customs? Will there be other foreigners or will you be a novelty?

When choosing where to go, think about exactly what you want from the experience – to grow as a person, learn a language or make a difference to people's lives? Hang on to that list – you're going to need it later.

Also think about what's most important to you in terms of living conditions, and be honest with yourself. Yes, you want to save the world, but while you're doing it, will you be unhappy in a place that doesn't have any running water? If you're a vegetarian, is Argentina, the land of steak, a good choice of destination?

Before you go, pack a few treats, whether it's a jar of Marmite or a CD that always cheers you up. If you want to put your teddy in the bottom of the bag then go for it – we promise we won't tell!

ON ARRIVAL

If you stay in your room, rocking back and forth, or spend the whole time on the phone to your mum, you're unlikely to have much fun, so when you first arrive, explore and keep busy. You may not

know the language but if you can pick up even a few words, along with some essential miming skills, everything will be a little bit easier.

Everyone has culture shock to a greater or lesser degree, and most people still end up having an amazing time. Persevere and you really can overcome it. Bring out that little list of aims again and remind yourself why you're doing what you're doing. The feeling you get when it finally clicks into place and you

really feel like you're part of your neighbourhood is just amazing.

CASE STUDY

Georgina Adams, 19, initially found settling into her volunteer placement in Ghana more challenging than anticipated. However, she's glad she hung on in there, as she reveals.

"I did have a wonderful time in Ghana in the end! There were lots of ups and downs, as is to be expected, but when I left, I was so incredibly different – happy, hippy, confident… I don't think the people who saw me at the start could quite believe I was the same person! It was kind of fun surprising people like that, although I must admit that I surprised myself too!"

There are other ways to ease the transition. If you want to volunteer, consider going through an organisation such as Teaching and Projects Abroad – this way, you'll be given advice about things such as local customs, dress and transport, and it's from staff who actually live in the country and can help you with any problems.

This also gives you a community of other volunteers who can show you the ropes, who

understand what you're going through, who you can travel and socialise with, and who you can complain to when things are just too weird. This can help to negate the feelings of isolation that come with culture shock.

LIVE THE CLICHÉ

There are many clichés about travelling – you have to keep an open mind and a sense of humour, expect the unexpected, remember that another culture is different, not inferior – but they're clichés because they ring true.

You'll have an amazing time if you explore your new home, from the landscape to the national psyche; have an ability to laugh when things go wrong; and

most importantly, have optimism that everything will turn out fine. Plus there's always that teddy you sneaked in…

FURTHER INFORMATION

For more information about making the most of your gap year and coping with the culture shock of living overseas, visit www. projects-abroad.co.uk.

⬇KEEPING IN TOUCH

With the huge growth of international travel and global communications, we're forging a worldwide community where keeping in touch with friends and family on the other side of the world is as simple as contacting your mate up the road.

However, we shouldn't forget that one of the joys of travelling is to have new and different experiences, and part of this comes from being removed from your everyday life. Spending each day in an internet café or chatting with your mate back home about what happened in *Eastenders*

last night won't do this! We recommend that travellers remember to send an email to say they've arrived safely, as well as regular – weekly or fortnightly – updates to family and friends. Just remember to avoid wasting too much of your time in cyberspace!

Before the internet exploded onto the scene and new technologies were discovered, the most popular method of keeping in touch while overseas was with postcards and letters. These either took forever to arrive, so were old news by the time they reached the recipient, or were left at the bottom of the weary traveller's bag

until they arrived home. How many of you still return home with cards you forgot to post?

Still, everyone loves to receive a letter and while you're abroad, you shouldn't forget this

method of keeping in touch. Today, though, the options available to travellers wanting to keep family and friends informed are immense and much more practical. The internet offers a host of options and you'll find online cafés on every street corner of all the major towns and cities. Indeed, you can find web points in the most remote locations you can think of – there's even one on the slopes of Everest!

INCREDIBLE INTERNET

The internet provides the cheapest, fastest and most reliable way of keeping in touch, so it's essential to open an email account that's accessible from anywhere, such as Yahoo or Hotmail. You can opt to use programs such

nails or peel an apple. Don't forget to put it in your main baggage when you're travelling through airports though!

L is for Light. Whether you're camping or travelling in a developing country, you'll always find that you need a torch somewhere down the line. It's often sensible to carry one good head torch and then a cheaper hand-held one as a back-up. You'll find that torches with LED bulbs last for a decent amount of time, although you must still remember to take enough batteries, or be confident you can buy them where you're going.

M is for Money Belt. Personal security should be high on your agenda when travelling and a money belt is a useful way of keeping your essential documentation and some of your money secure. Just be careful not to expose it when you're out shopping – it should always be kept hidden.

N is for Net. If you're travelling to a destination where you'll encounter mosquitoes, a net is essential. Preventing bites is not only a good idea for

CHECKLIST

Address book	Personal preference
Aftersun cream or spray	May be essential
Antihistamine tablets or cream	Essential
Antiseptic cream or wipes	Essential
Baby wipes	Good idea
Backpack	Essential
Bank details	Good idea
Batteries	Personal preference
Bicycle lock	Personal preference
Blister pads	May be essential
Boots	Essential
Bumbag	Personal preference
Camera	Personal preference
Camping equipment	May be essential
Chargers	May be essential
Cigarettes	Personal preference
Condoms	Essential
Contact cards	Personal preference
Contact details	Essential
Credit cards	Essential
Day sack	Essential
Dental floss	Essential
Diarrhoea treatment	Essential
Discount cards	Good idea
Diving qualifications / log book	May be essential
Dressings, tape and bandages	Personal preference
Driving licence	May be essential
Drugs	Do not take!
E111 document	May be essential
Earplugs	Personal preference
Emergency details	Essential
Everything wash ? Shower gel	Essential
Expensive jewellery	Do not take!
Flannel	Essential
Gaffer tape	Good idea
Glasses / contact lenses	May be essential
Guide book	Essential
Hairbrush / comb / bands	Essential
Hat	Essential
Headscarf	May be essential
Insect repellent	May be essential
Insurance policy	Essential
Itinerary	Essential
Jeans	Do not take!
Jewellery	Personal preference
Job reference letter	Personal preference
Key contact details	Essential
Local currency	Essential
Long-sleeved shirts	Essential
Make-up	Personal preference
Malaria tablets	May be essential
Medication for recurring ailments	Good idea
Mobile phone	Personal preference
Money belt	Essential
Mosquito net	May be essential
Multivitamins	Good idea
Music / MP3 player / CDs	Personal preference

PACKING TIPS

- **Lay everything out**

- **Take away half the clothes.**

- **If you can, double the money.**

- **Ask for a second opinion.**

- **If you're travelling with a friend, agree on who will take what – there's no point in doubling up on items like penknives and alarm clocks.**

- **If you're travelling with a friend, you can also 'cross-pack' by splitting your clothes between both bags in case one gets lost.**

- **Separate items for your day sack, such as documents and your kit for flights. Check that the size of your day sack conforms to the new hand luggage regulations.**

- **Ensure that all items forbidden in hand luggage are in your main rucksack.**

- **Use clear plastic bags to separate items.**

- **Put your toiletries in a waterproof washbag in case they leak.**

- **Roll clothes rather than folding – you get more room and they end up less creased.**

- **Write your name and address inside and outside your bag in the case tag comes off.**

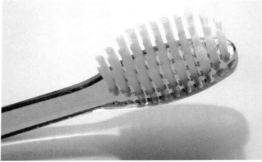

from expensive filters to iodine tincture. You can buy bottled water in most destinations, but it's important to check the 'best before' dates and seals, and have a thought for the effect the plastic waste is going to have on the local environment.

It's always good to take some method of purifying, even if it's just as a back-up. It's also a good idea to carry a couple of good water bottles – you should have the capacity to carry at least two litres of water with you.

Q is for Quiet. It may sound silly but getting a good night's sleep each evening will make your trip so much better! Carrying a pair of earplugs with you might just come in handy when you're staying in a loud city or sharing a tent with someone who snores!

R is for Rucksack. The type of bag you carry can vary depending on the type of travelling

you're doing. If trekking, a top-loading rucksack will probably be appropriate. If not, a travel sack is usually the better option. A travel sack gives easier access to your belongings so you won't have to unpack and repack your bag each day.

S is for Sandals. If you're just moving from hostel to hostel then a pair of flip flops for the shower will probably do, but if you plan on doing any water-based adventure activities or you're camping then a proper pair of sandals is really useful.

T is for Towel. Unless you want a very wet and smelly towel in your rucksack, it's wise to get your hands on a travel towel. These are compact, quick-drying and highly absorbent.

U is for UV: protection from the sun. You aren't going to have much fun if you get burnt, so

avoiding nasty diseases, but you'll also be more comfortable if you aren't covered in bites from a night out in the open!

O is for Oral Hygiene: never forget your fold-up toothbrush and toothpaste because you don't want to end up with toothache overseas. Also have a dental check-up before you leave.

P is for Purification. There are numerous cleaners available, and these mean you'll be able to drink a safe supply of water. They range

buy some sunscreen before you go. Always take a higher factor than you think you need and re-apply it regularly.

V is for Vaccinations. Although the chance of getting any of the diseases you immunise against is statistically very slim, if you do happen to catch one, it can often be fatal. Get a good head start on vaccinations before your departure date. Depending on where you're going, it can take up to two months to get all your jabs.

W is for Waterproofs: jackets, trousers, lightweight packaways or Gore-tex? There are many options, including the possibility of using a versatile poncho. Your destination, time of year and activities you want to do will help you decide what's appropriate.

X is for X-rated. Male or female, don't leave home without some condoms! You never

know what you may end up doing, so be prepared.

Y is for Your Personnel Documents. You won't be going far without these so ensure you store them in a waterproof pouch, keep photocopies of all your essential paperwork and store them separately to your originals. You might want to carry some spare passport photos as well.

Z is for Zzzzzzz… Sleeping is a key aspect of any trip, so having the right kit – sleeping bag, sleeping bag liner, sleeping mat and pillow – is absolutely essential. As these come in numerous forms, having a bit of knowledge about where and when you're going will assist you when buying them.

FURTHER INFORMATION

- http://upl.codeq.info/
- www.nomadtravel.co.uk
- Kate Nelson, Career Break Coach, 07812 021438.

Nail brush	Good idea
Nail scissors / file / clippers	Personal preference
Nightwear	Essential
Notebook and pen	Personal preference
Padlock	Essential
Painkillers	Essential
Passport photos	Essential
Passport	Essential
Penknife / multi-tool	Essential
Phone card	Good idea
Phrasebook	Personal preference
Plasters	Essential
Plastic bags	Good idea
Playing cards / backgammon	Personal preference
Prescription medicine	May be essential
Radio	Personal preference
Razors / shaving cream	Personal preference
Rehydration powder	Essential
Rollmat	May be essential
Safety pins	Good idea
Sandals / flip flops	Essential
Sarong	Good idea
Security alarm	Personal preference
Sentimental items	Do not take!
Sewing kit	Personal preference
Shampoo	Essential
Sheet sleeping bag	Essential
Smarter clothes	Essential
Soap	Essential
Socks	Essential
Spongebag	Essential
Sterile needles	May be essential
Sting relief spray or cream	Essential
Sunscreen	Essential
Sunglasses	Essential
Swimwear	Essential
Tampons / sanitary towels	Essential
Throat sweets	Personal preference
Tickets	Essential
Toilet paper	Personal preference
Toothbrush and toothpaste	Essential
Torch	Essential
Towel	Essential
Travel adaptors	May be essential
Travel alarm clock	Essential
Travel pillow	Personal preference
Travel sickness remedies	May be essential
Travel washing line and pegs	May be essential
Travellers cheque card	Personal preference
Travellers cheques	Essential
T-shirts	Essential
Umbrella	Personal preference
USB memory stick	Good idea
Vaccination certificate	Essential
Visas	May be essential
Water bottle	Personal preference
Water purification tablets	May be essential
Waterproof clothing	May be essential
Whistle	Personal preference

⬇ CHARITY OPTIONS

Have you ever wanted to hike the Great Wall of China, trek to the Everest base camp, mush a dogsled team in the Arctic or climb Kilimanjaro, all while raising money for a good cause? Well, by joining one of Across The Divide's expeditions, you can do just that!

Across The Divide has been running charity and corporate challenges since 1996. Its staffing ratios are the highest of any provider for this type of trip, so adventure comes with the highest standards of safety.

The events it runs are often life-changing experiences: you can visit amazing parts of the world, learn about different cultures and share the spirit of adventure with like-minded people. As Sorcha, who took part in a Sahara desert trek, says, "You'll be very glad you did it and your life will be all the richer for having done it. In one word – unforgettable!"

Across The Divide has something to suit everybody, from overseas challenges ranging from seven to 22 days to raising funds for any charity on an 'Open Challenges' package, or weekend sponsored walks in the UK. All of the charity events are graded in terms of difficulty, so you can pick the one that best suits you.

Across The Divide's charity challenges are unique in that all of its fundraising events are organised as mini-expeditions, with all the

safety and personnel back-up that this entails. The experience of the Across The Divide teams stretches across over 400 charity challenges, in over 35 different countries, and with £25 million already raised for good causes.

TEAM SPIRIT

If you take up an Across The Divide challenge, you won't be travelling alone and so it won't take you long to make some new friends. Your group will have experienced guides, an expedition leader and a doctor to help you along the way. There will always be a guide at the back of the group too, making sure that no one will be walking alone.

OPEN EVENTS

Across The Divide offers a wide range of open challenges every year, from dog sledding in Norway to trekking in the Sahara. These open events are a particularly good way of supporting smaller charitable organisations, as well as enabling you to enjoy a life-changing adventure.

PROJECTS

As well as the selection of projects on the opposite page, Across The Divide also offers everything from treks through the Buddhist kingdom of Ladakh to hiking in Peru, land of the Incas, and dog sledding in the wilds of northern Europe.

FURTHER INFORMATION

For details on these and other events, visit Across The Divide's website at www.acrossthedivide.com.

↘ Run the Taj Mahal marathon

Location: India

The Taj Mahal marathon will be run in September 2007 for the first time. Starting from the sleepy village of Niyamat Pur, the route follows a good tarmac road through beautiful rural countryside and villages, before joining the main highway to Agra. The highway runs through fertile fields dotted with eucalyptus trees and mango groves, with small bazaars and hamlets lining the side of the road. A picture perfect view of the Taj Mahal unfolds over the final kilometres and you'll pass through the heritage garden of the Taj Mehtab Bagh (Moon Garden) on the banks of the Yamuna River, with direct views of the Taj Mahal.

↘ Help to build a school

Location: Namibia

Namibia is one of the few places on earth where the natural environment rules supreme, and it's a country where you can experience a real sense of freedom. On this placement, you'll help to refurbish a local kindergarten by building walls, fixing windows and doors, tiling, installing bathrooms, cleaning, plastering, painting, sanding, replacing flooring, improving the garden and building play areas. This unforgettable programme takes place below the stunning 1,784-metre Spitzkoppe ('Pointed Hill'). This is a beautiful setting, and you'll have ample opportunity to explore, climb, abseil, or discover the ancient bushman art.

↘ Climb Mount Kilimanjaro

Location: Africa

One of the most magnificent sights in Africa, Kilimanjaro's snow-capped peak climbs 5,000 metres over the surrounding plains. This is the highest free-standing mountain in the world and it's made up of three huge volcanoes, all of which have been lying dormant for centuries. On this adventure, you'll take an expedition to the remote north-eastern side of the mountain, where you'll follow the Rongai Trail. This retains a true sense of wilderness, ensuring a memorable and awe-inspiring journey.

Across The Divide, Jubilee House, Fore Street, Thorncombe, Near Chard, Somerset, TA20 4PP, 01460 30456, www.acrossthedivide.com

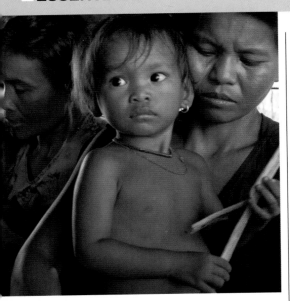

ACTIONAID'S CAMBODIA CHALLENGE

ActionAid has offered amazing challenge treks all over the world for several years. Each incorporates a visit to one of its projects, giving trekkers the chance to see the life-changing work that their sponsorship makes possible. Many cite these first-hand experiences as the highlight of their trip.

With its new Cambodia Challenge, ActionAid has gone one step further, giving you the opportunity to get directly involved. You'll be working with a local community, building the village centre they so desperately need.

Despite being a beautiful country, packed with cultural and historical treasures, Cambodia's people face many problems. The country has the highest percentage of people living with HIV in Asia, and nearly five million of its people live on less than 65p a day. Over 95 per cent of women in rural areas have no access to medical care and over 180,000 children of primary school age are not enrolled in school.

Working with the village, ActionAid and the local people have identified the building of a village community centre as being crucial to solving many of their immediate and long-term problems. It will provide:

■ An invaluable space for children to safely play and take part in literacy and education programmes.

■ Health facilities and counselling services, which are especially beneficial to women.
■ Refuge in times of extreme need for landless families, disabled people, and those with HIV/AIDS.

No previous building experience is necessary, although enthusiasm and energy are essential. Typical activities could include digging, mixing concrete, moving and laying bricks, erecting doorways and windows, plastering and painting.

You'll spend your days working closely with the local community and there'll be plenty of time to really understand the way they live, their fight for a better future and their open desire to make new friends.

In the evenings, there will be a special blend of local music, dance, food and drink to enjoy.

After helping out, you'll have time to explore Siem Reap and the magnificent Temples of Angkor, a UNESCO World Heritage site. This jungle location is brimming with temples, colourful pagodas, havens of tranquility and bustling markets.

If you want to truly experience Cambodia and help its people, while enjoying its beauty and hospitality, this is the challenge for you!

FURTHER INFORMATION

Call ActionAid on 01460 238 047 or visit www.actionaid.org.uk/adventures, quoting reference GAPAD, for more details on this or any other projects. These include treks along the Great Wall of China, through the Brazilian rainforest, Kenya's Rift Valley, the Himalayas and the Inca Trail in Peru.

↘ TILLY'S TOURS

Tilly's Tours is a new ground tour operator in Gambia that works closely with local people, businesses and charities to promote sustainable, responsible tourism in the country, as well as actively promoting the welfare of local communities through employment and a range of other opportunities.

Tilly's Tours aims to provide a unique cultural experience with as much time spent travelling among local people as possible. Life-enhancing travel is not about seeing a place, but experiencing a place, its people, its cultures and ways of life.

To truly experience the spirit of Gambian culture, and fully immerse yourself in its very essence, you need to travel beyond the coastal resort areas and visit the remote villages and historical towns, both in the heart of this captivating country and in its southern region.

Tourism is a vital part of Gambia's economy and the primary area for employment growth within the country's previously disadvantaged communities. By booking through Tilly's, you're contributing to the rebuilding and rebalancing of the country's economy.

RESPONSIBLE TOURISM

Tilly's Tours aims to keep as much money in this beautiful country as possible, as well as employing as many local people as possible. It has recently joined up with two British charities who are based in Gambia and actively work to promote the wellbeing of Gambian people and their communities. Through the Working Holidays and Gap Adventure programs, a proportion of your money is paid directly to the charity involved, which benefits the semi-remote villages in which each charity is based. The money pays for schools, salaries for teachers and more.

CHIMPANZEE PROJECT

Volunteer to help on the chimpanzee rehabilitation project and you can rest assured that your money directly funds the ongoing maintenance of the chimps' environment and the Baboon Islands National Park. Tilly's makes a minimal profit from these placements: the priority is to promote tourism that benefits the local people, their communities and wildlife.

By travelling with Tilly's Tours, you help to support projects such as this, and help local people in their efforts to alleviate themselves from poverty. You also help to conserve the environment and endangered species, and have a great time while you're doing it.

Responsible tourism offers a real alternative to mass packaged holidays, especially when there's a travel ethos that involves close co-operation with the local communities.

FURTHER INFORMATION

■ Tilly's Tours, 369 Kingston Road, Epsom, Surrey, KT19 0BS
■ 0208 873 3148
■ admin@tillystours.com
■ www.tillystours.com

⬎ USEFUL CONTACTS

COOKERY COURSES

Tante Marie Cookery School
Carlton Rd
Woking
Surrey
GU21 4HF
01483 726957
www.tantemarie.co.uk

CAREER COACHING

thecareerbreaksite.com
SugarCat Publishing
32 School Lane
Manchester
M20 6RG
0161 4488846
info@thecareerbreaksite.com
www.thecareerbreaksite.com

Want More Coaching Ltd
Hergest Ridge
Bishopstone
Wiltshire
SN6 8PP
01793 791390
www.careercoach.co.uk

FINANCE

1st Contact Group
Castlewood House
77/91 New Oxford Street
London
WC1A 1DG
020 7759 5424
www.1stcontact.co.uk

DIVING SCHOOLS

Absolute Scuba
308 Protaras Avenue
Protaras 5296
Cyprus
00357 2383 3121
00357 9986 6859
enquiries@absolutescuba.co.uk
www.absolutescuba.co.uk

Dive Australia
0061 7 4946 1067
www.scubacentre.com.au

Key Dives
Mile Marker 79.2
79851 Overseas Highway
Islamorada
Florida Keys
33036
001 305 664 2211
www.keydives.com

GAP YEAR ORGANISATIONS

2 Way Development
Unit 4
25a Vyner Street
Bethnal Green
London
E2 9DG
020 8980 9074
www.2way.org.uk

Acacia Adventure Holidays
23A Craven Terrace
London
W2 3QH
020 7706 4700
www.acacia-africa.com

Across The Divide
Jubilee House
Fore Street
Thorncombe
Somerset
TA20 4PP
01460 30456
www.acrossthedivide.com

Africa & Asia Venture
10 Market Place
Devizes
Wiltshire
SN10 1HT
01380 729 009
www.aventure.co.uk

African Conservation Experience
PO Box 206
Faversham
Kent
ME13 8WZ
0870 241 5816
www.conservationafrica.net

African Safari Roots
01736 367635
www.africansafariroots.com

Sponsored by VentureCo Worldwide
Savvy Traveller Courses: £235
01926 411 122
www.ventureco-worldwide.com

AFS UK
Leeming House
Vicar Lane
Leeds
LS2 7JF
0113 2426136
www.afs.org

Art History Abroad
179c New Kings Road
London
SW6 4SW
020 7731 2231
www.arthistoryabroad.com

Blue Ventures Expeditions
52 Avenue Road
London
N6 5DR
0208 341 9819
www.blueventures.org

BSES Expeditions
1 Kensington Gore
London
SW7 2AR
www.bses.org.uk
020 7591 3141

BUNAC
16 Bowling Green Lane
London
EC1R 0QH
0202 7251 3472
www.bunac.org

Camps International Limited
Unit 1
Kingfisher Park

Headlands Business Park
Blashford
Ringwood
BH24 3NX
0870 2401 843
www.campsinternational.com

Contiki
020 8290 6422
www.contiki.com

Coral Cay Conservation
Ground Floor
40-42 Osnaburgh Street
London
NW1 3ND
0870 750 0668
www.coralcay.org

Crystal International Academy
King's Place
12-42 Wood Street
Kingston Upon Thames
Surrey
KT1 1JY
0870 060 1381
www.theinternationalacademy.com

Element Internet
Kensington Studios
Kensington Street
Brighton
BN1 4AJ
01273 872242
www.adventuresports
holidays.com

Exodus Travel Ltd
Grange Mills

Weir Road
London
SW12 0NE
020 8772 3721
www.exodus.co.uk

Explore
55 Victoria Rd
Farnborough
GU14 7PA
01252 379496
www.explore.co.uk

Flying Fish
25 Union Rd
Cowes
Isle of Wight
PO31 7TW
0871 250 2500
www.flyingfishonline.com

Footprint Adventures
5 Malham Drive
Lincoln
LN6 0XD
01522 804929
www.footprint-adventures.co.uk

Frontier
50-55 Rivington Street
London
EC2A 3QP
020 7613 2422
www.frontier.ac.uk

GAP Activity Projects
44 Queen's Road
Reading
Berkshire

Sponsored by VentureCo Worldwide
Savvy Traveller Courses: £235
01926 411 122
www.ventureco-worldwide.com

'Getting away to the most beautiful locations in the world is easier than ever, and you can do it in an environmentally friendly and ethical way. Find out more on page 318...'

RG1 4BB
0118 9594914
volunteer@gap.org.uk
www.gap.org.uk

Gap Adventures
Matrix Studios
91 Peterborough Road
Fulham
London
SW6 3BU
0870 999 0144
www.gapadventures.com

Gap Guru
1st Floor
Bankside House
West Mills
Newbury
RG14 5HP
0800 032 3350
www.gapguru.com

Global Vision International
3 High Street
St Albans
Herts
AL3 4ED
0870 608 8898
info@gvi.co.uk
www.gvi.co.uk

Go Differently Ltd
19 West Road
Saffron Walden
Essex
CB11 3DS
01749 521950
www.godifferently.com

Greenforce
11-15 Betterton Street
London
WC2H 9BP
020 7470 8888
www.greenforce.org

Green Tortoise Adventure Travel
494 Broadway
San Francisco
CA 94133
USA
001 415 956 7500
tortoise@greentortoisecom
www.greentortoise.com

i-to-i
0870 333 2332
www.i-to-i.com

International Voluntary Service
7 Upper Bow
Edinburgh
EH1 2JN
0131 2266 722
www.ivs-gb.org.uk

Itime Experience Ltd
105 Ladbroke Grove
London
W11 1PG
0207 193 8315
www.itimeexperience.com

Just Go Russia
Boundary House
Boston Road
London
W7 2QE

0208 434 3496
www.gorussia.co.uk

Kiwi Experience
195-197 Parnell Road
Auckland
New Zealand
0064 9 366 9830
www.kiwiexperience.com

The Leap Overseas Ltd
121 High Street
Marlborough
Wiltshire
SN8 1LZ
01672 519922
www.theleap.co.uk

Mondo Challenge
Malsor House
Gayton Road
Milton Malsor
Northampton
NN7 3AB
01604 858 225
www.mondochallenge.org

Outreach International
Bartletts Farm
Hayes Road
Compton Dundon
Somerset
TA11 6PF
01458 274 957
www.outreachinternational.co.uk

Project Trust
Hebridean Centre
Isle of Coll

Sponsored by VentureCo Worldwide
Savvy Traveller Courses: £235
01926 411 122
www.ventureco-worldwide.com

'On a gap year, you can help some of the world's most impoverished and needy people, conserve the environment and learn new skills. See page 310 for gap companies...'

Argyll
PA78 6TE
01879 230444
www.projecttrust.org.uk

Quest Overseas
The North-West Stables
Borde Hill Estate
Balcombe Road
Haywards Heath
West Sussex
RH16 1XP
01444 474744
www.questoverseas.com

Real Gap Experience
45 High Street
Tunbridge Wells
TN1 1XL
01892 516164
www.realgap.co.uk

Responsible Travel
0870 0052 836
www.responsibletravel.com

Rodney Fox Shark Experience
0061 8 8363 1788
www.rodneyfox.com.au

STA Travel
08701 630 026
www.statravel.co.uk

Suntrek Tours
Sun Plaza
77 West Third Street
Santa Rosa CA
California

08700 276101
www.suntrek.com

Teaching and Projects abroad
Aldsworth Parade
Goring
Sussex
BN12 4TX
01903 708300
www.projects-abroad.co.uk

Ticket To Ride
263 Putney Bridge Road
London
SW15 2PU
0208 7888 668
www.ttride.co.uk

Tilly's Tours Gambia
369 Kingston Road
Epsom
Surrey
KT19 0BS
0208 873 3148
www.tillystours.com

VentureCo Worldwide
The Ironyard
64-66 The Market Place
Warwick
CV34 4SD
01926 411122
www.ventureco-worldwide.com

Vodkatrain
Suite 207B
The Business Village
3-9 Broomhill Road
London

SW18 4JQ
United Kingdom
020 8877 7650
www.vodkatrain.com

World Expeditions
3 Northfields Prospect
Putney Bridge Road
London
SW18 1PE
020 8870 2600
www.worldexpeditions.co.uk

Year Out Group
Queensfield
28 Kings Rd
Easterton
Wiltshire
SN10 4PX
01380 816696
www.yearoutgroup.org

GOVERNMENT ADVICE

Foreign & Commonwealth Office
0845 850 2829
www.fco.gov.uk/travel

HEALTH AND SAFETY

Objective Travel Safety
Bragborough Lodge Farm
Braunton
Daventry
NN11 7HA
01788 899 029
www.objectivegapsafety.com

Sponsored by VentureCo Worldwide
Savvy Traveller Courses: £235
01926 411 122
www.ventureco-worldwide.com

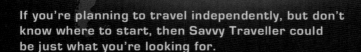

**Travel Health
Information Services**
20 Oaklands Way
Hildenborough
Kent
TN11 9DA
mail@travelhealth.co.uk
www.travelhealth.co.uk

KIT AND EQUIPMENT

Blacks
0800 66 54 10
www.blacks.co.uk

Millets
0800 389 5861
www.millets.co.uk

Nomad Travel
0845 260 00 44
www.nomadtravel.co.uk

Ready To Leave Ltd
Unit 5
Metherell Industrial Estate
Brixham
Devon
TQ5 9QL
0870 8504367
www.readytoleave.com

LANGUAGE COURSES

CESA Languages Abroad
CESA House
Pennance Rd
Lanner
Cornwall
TR16 5TQ
01209 211800
info@cesalanguages.com
www.cesalanguages.com

Cactus Language
0845 130 4775
www.cactuslanguage.com

Language Courses Abroad
67 Ashby Road
Loughborough
Leicestershire
LE11 3AA
01509 211612
info@languagesabroad.co.uk
www.languagesabroad.co.uk

RESPONSIBLE TOURISM

Carbon Footprint
7 Barron Place
Basingstoke
Hampshire
RG24 9JS
07941 732823
info@carbonfootprint.com
www.carbonfootprint.com

Climate Care
112 Magdalen Road
Oxford
OX4 1RQ
United Kingdom
01865 207 000
mail@climatecare.org
www.climatecare.co.uk

**International Centre for
Responsible Tourism**
Department of Earth and
Environmental Sciences
School of Science
University of Greenwich
Medway University Campus
Pembroke
Chatham Maritime
Kent
ME4 4TB
www.icrtourism.org

Sustainable Travel International
2060 Floral Drive
Boulder
Colorado
80304
001 720.273.2975
info@sustainabletravel.com
www.sustainabletravel.com

Tourism Concern
Stapleton House
277-281 Holloway Road
London
N7 8HN
020 7133 3330
info@tourismconcern.org.uk
www.tourismconcern.org.uk

TEFL TRAINING

ITC
26 Cockerton Green
Darlington
County Durham
DL3 9EU

**Sponsored by VentureCo Worldwide
Savvy Traveller Courses: £235
01926 411 122
www.ventureco-worldwide.com**

" There are plenty of
volunteer opportunities
that allow you to work
with children and help
give them a better life.
See page 310 for gap
year organisations "

08456 445464
info@tefl.co.uk
www.tefl.co.uk

INTESOL
Highbury House
12 Victoria Park
Bristol
BS16 2HJ
0845 644 0584
www.intesolinternational.com

TEFL Training
Friends Close
Stonesfield
Witney
Oxon
OX29 8PH
United Kingdom
01993 891121
www.tefltraining.co.uk

TRAVEL ADVICE

gapadvice.org
12 Hutchings Rd
Beaconsfield
Bucks
HP9 2BB
01494 673448
www.gapadvice.org

gapadvice.org
Independent advice on gap years, for people of all ages

Foreign & Commonwealth Office
www.gogapyear.com
020 7008 1500

TRAVEL GAMES

Can You Make It
9 Spinnals Grove
Southwick
Brighton
BN42 4DU
01273 749513
www.canyoumakeit.co.uk

Wildcard Games
22 Downend Road
Horfield
Bristol
BS7 9PF
www.wildcardgames.com

TRAVEL AND TRANSPORT

British Airways
Waterside
PO Box 365
Harmondsworth
UB7 0GB
0870 850 9 850
www.britishairways.com

easyJet
London Luton Airport
Bedfordshire
LU2 9LS
0871 244 2366
www.easyjet.com

Inter Rail
www.interrailnet.com

Jet2
Leeds Bradford International Airport
Leeds
LS19 7TU
0906 302 0660
www.jet2.com

Qantas
24/F Jardine House
One Connaught Place
Central
Hong Kong
00852 2822 9000
www.quantas.com

Ryanair
0871 246 0000
www.ryanair.com

TACA Airlines
Flighthouse
Fernhill Road
Horley
Surrey
RH6 9SY
United Kingdom
0845 838 7940
www.tacaairlines.co.uk

Travellers Auto Barn
0061 2 9360 1500
www.travellers-autobarn.com

Virgin Blue
0061 7 3295 2296
www.virginblue.com.au

Sponsored by VentureCo Worldwide
Savvy Traveller Courses: £235
01926 411 122
www.ventureco-worldwide.com

If you want to experience a whole new world on your gap break, there's no better way than to go diving. For schools all around the world, see page 310 now...

INDEX TO ADS / CREDITS

ACKNOWLEDGEMENTS

Many thanks to the following organisations who have provided images and editorial for this guide:

Art History Abroad Lucie Baird / Aleid Ford

Aurora Expeditions David Mannix

Blue Ventures Richard Nimmo

BSES Expeditions Jenny Palfrey

BUNAC Nicola Rawlins

Camps International Hannah Davies

Career Break Coach Kate Nelson

Challenges Worldwide Helen Tirebuck

Collins Bartholomew Elizabeth Donald

Coral Cay Laura Timms

Ethical Volunteering Kate Simpson

Flying Fish Andrew Lorant

Foreign & Commonwealth Office Steve Jewitt-Fleet

Gap Guru Emily Davies, Indigo PR

Gap Years for Grown Ups Rachael Wood

gap.org.uk Jo Ash

gapadvice.org Phil Murray

Gapyear.com Tom Griffiths

Global Adventures Damian Wade

i-to-i Jo Little

Mondo Challenge Naomi Chamberlin

Nomad Travel Katherine Tory

Quest Overseas Tom Setter

Real Gap Experience Rick Lyne

Responsible Travel Katie Fewings

St Petersburg Studies Alexandra Chaldecott

STA Travel Lesley Davidson / Anna Perkins

Teaching & Projects Abroad Laura Tovey

The Career Break Site Rachel Morgan-Trimmer

The International Academy Alan Bates

The Leap Guy Whitehead

Ticket to Ride Emily Davies / Will Hayler

Travellers Worldwide Letitia Hardy

VentureCo Mark Davison

INDEX TO ADVERTISERS